Avocations

Avocations

ON POETS AND POETRY

Sam Hamill

RED HEN PRESS | Los Angeles, California

Book design by Mark E. Cull
Cover picture: *Strong Enough*,
artwork by Rom LAMMAR from Luxembourg.

ISBN-10: 1-59709-086-7
ISBN-13: 978-1-59709-086-5
Library of Congress Catalog Card Number: 2006936790

Earlier versions of these essays and reviews appeared in *Academy of
American Poets, American Poetry Review, The Georgia Review, Mid-
American Review, Onthebus, Poetry East, Seneca Review, Complete
Poems of Kenneth Rexroth* (Copper Canyon Press, 2004), *Haiku: This
Other World* (Arcade Publishing, 1998), *Narrow Road to the Interior
& Other Writings* (Shambala, 2000), *Spring of My Life & Selected
Haiku* (Shambala, 1997), *Toward the Distant Islands: New & Selected
Poems of Hayden Carruth* (Copper Canyon Press, 2006)

The City of Los Angeles Department of Cultural Affairs,
Los Angeles County Arts Commission
and the National Endowment for the Arts
partially support Red Hen Press.

Published by Red Hen Press
First Edition

To Gray Foster & Eron Hamill
And to Esteban Moore, Paul Nelson and Courtney Hudak

"Love the earth and sun and the animals, despise riches, give alms to everyone that asks, stand up for the stupid and crazy, devote your income and labor to others, hate tyrants, argue not concerning God, have patience and indulgence toward the people, take off your hat to nothing known or unknown, or to any man or number of men—go freely with powerful uneducated persons, and with the young, and with the mothers or families—re-examine all you have been told in school or church or in any book, and dismiss whatever insults your own soul; and your very flesh shall be a great poem, and have the richest fluency, not only in its words, but in the silent lines of its lips and face, and between the lashes of your eyes, and in every motion and joint of your body."

—Walt Whitman,
Preface to 1855 edition, *Leaves of Grass*

"out of key with his time
He strove to resuscitate the dead art
Of poetry; to maintain 'the sublime'
In the old sense."

—Ezra Pound,
Hugh Selwyn Mauberly

Contents

Preface

These essays, introductions and reviews were written mostly in the 1990s, the earliest dating from the first War on Iraq in 1991, and are an extension of the work begun with *A Poet's Work* (Carnegie-Mellon University Press), published in 1988.

Four decades of assaying poetry and its fundamental traditions and practices have shaped my life. Because I believe that poetry can be a path to enlightenment, from my daily Zen practice and daily engagement with poetry, an ethos and an aesthetic emerge. They are not two things, but one—the expression of practice, of being. But I have *never* believed that poetry is *the* path to enlightenment, Buddhist or otherwise. If my engagement with poetry has been thorough—study, writing, editing, translating, printing, publishing, teaching, critical writing, advocacy—that has not been a circumstance of accident. I sought; I seek; I practice.

"Poetry," my old friend Hayden Carruth likes to say, "is nothing special; it's ordinary, like music." Any respectable bricklayer understands that real bricklaying is a path to enlightenment. The grandfather of Zen, Hui Neng, was an illiterate woodcutter who tore up the sutras. Every musician, every bricklayer, knows the importance of practice.

My vows to poetry are almost religious vows. "This is the path I will follow to the end." It is a path, not a destination, an avocation much more than a vocation.

Years ago in Japan, I heard a story about a brilliant young shakuhachi student who wanted to learn at the feet of a great old master. Granted an interview with the Master, he was told, "Play C," and the student blew a resonant C. The Master said, "Pretty good. You work hard on that and come back next year." There are many "pretty good" poets in the world, but mastery is something else. And there are many, many poetry bodhisattvas.

I have always believed that poetry is a very large house. I have never believed that it was my fate or right to become Keeper of the Keys to that mansion. No one holds all the keys. Plenty of room for Beethoven *and* Lady

Day; plenty of room for John Coltrane *and* John Prine; for Hank and for Bird. Every door requires a key. Every door is an opening and a closure. The view from every window and balcony is unique.

And yet nothing is self-originating, neither poetry nor democracy, neither self nor other. We have roots and grow branches. I remain a novice, a servant with many masters. I know in which room I sleep and dream, and I know at whose table I eat. I know what road brought me even as I realize, as Takamura Kōtarō wrote, "No road leads the way; the road follows behind."

Poetry, like Buddhist practice, has no fixed religious belief, and yet, like Buddhist practice, it approaches religious empiricism in its thusness. Kenneth Rexroth wrote, "True illumination is habitude. We are unware that we live in the light of lights because it casts no shadow. When we become aware of it we know it as birds know air and fish know water." For Rexroth, the poem was a sacramental act arising naturally from the rich interior life interacting with the exterior world.

Begun as we began bombing the Middle East, these articles of avocation go to press as we remain at war in the Middle East fifteen years later. While I have grown increasingly pessimistic about the government of our United States, I have grown increasingly convinced that poetry is an essential part of the solution. Since founding Poets Against War in 2003, I have traveled the world and met hundreds of poets and find that we are almost universal in agreement that violence is *not* a solution to anything and that poetry is a path to enlightenment.

When my fellow poets claim, as Mark Strand wrote in a review of Pablo Neruda's poetry, "Political poetry has no legs," or when I am asked, "Why can't you just leave the politics out of it?" by obviously illiterate "media personalities," I want to scream. Our poetry—*American poetry*— grew out of Walt Whitman and Emily Dickinson, Ezra Pound and William Carlos Williams, Muriel Rukeyser and Langston Hughes. Our earlier poets and our traditionalists are a branch of Romanticism, and one needn't read deeply to discover the devout revolutionary tradition in Keats or Shelley.

There is no major poetic tradition in the world that is apolitical. Even the "Buddhist nature poetry" of Asia carries various arguments or affirmations of this or that sect, and often rejects "the world of red dust" in favor of "the world of dew." It's almost impossible to write an apolitical poem. One's politics, Su Tung-p'o declares, should arise naturally—like mushrooms growing from manure.

Pound writes, "More poets fail from lack of character than from lack of talent." Albert Camus drew a very clear line between those "who accept the consequences of being murderers themselves or the accomplices of murderers, and those who refuse to do so with all their force and being."

There are presently more than thirteen thousand members of Poets Against War.

Poets—all conscious people—choose the conditions by which their lives are conducted. Some are seduced by the materialist monoculture; some revolt and become revolutionaries; most live somewhere between the extremes. And, sadly, many simply live unconscious lives, lives without avocations, without imagination, with little passion and little love, lives without poetry.

To resist oppression, to resist tyranny, to resist justifying murder, to practice compassion toward the oppressed is not merely a duty, but a calling, another avocation. But perhaps not for everyone. In the mansion of poetry, I live among those who are engaged activists at various levels and draw from traditions as old as the Chinese *Poetry Classic* and the *Greek Anthology.* Poetry demands, as Rilke said before a bust of Apollo, that we change our lives. Our own history and science make the same demand. *Viva la revolución!* It begins with a few clear words; it is born in choosing the power of the word over the power of bloodshed.

Poetry is (and has always been), for me at least, part of an eternal conversation in which there is a search for the real, a search for the authentic, a belief in justice taken only at substantial personal risk. Buddhist practice and poetic practice are not two things. I follow my avocations, having staked everything—my life's work—on the formidable gamble—to use Camus' words again—that words (poems) are more powerful than munitions.

Sam Hamill
Kage-an, autumn, 2006

Avocations

Against the Tide: 1990-91

In the case of heroes, it is not so much their procedures on the page which are influential as the composite image which has been projected of their conduct. That image, congruent with the reality, features a poet tested by dangerous times. What is demanded is not any great public act of confrontation or submission, but rather a certain self-censorship, an agreement to forge, in the bad sense, the uncreated conscience of a race. Their resistance to this pressure is not initially or intentionally political, but there is of course a spin-off, a ripple effect, to their deviant artistic conduct. It is the refusal by this rearguard minority which exposes to the majority the abjectness of their collapse, as they flee for security into whatever self-deceptions the party line requires of them. And it is because they effect this exposure that the poets become endangered: people are never grateful for being reminded of their moral cowardice.

—Seamus Heaney

A government is, first of all, a government of words. The British Parliamentary Act of 1774 decreed the abolition of any town meeting without prior written consent from a royal Governor, and its passage was in part a response to a Massachusetts Bay Colony law requiring an annual town meeting. Other weekly or monthly town meetings had been conducted among "freemen" eligible to vote since the birth of the Colonies. It was not simply the cry of "No taxation without representation!" that gave birth to the American Revolution, but also, perhaps equally, Britain's attempt to censor our newspapers and our political discourse.

Were it not for continued support for a stupid, brutal war in El Salvador and U.S.-backed terrorism in Nicaragua, were it not for memories of Grenada and Panama, were it not for memories of U.S.-backed terrorism under the Marcos tyranny in the Philippines, and were it not for the astronomical national debt built under Reagan and Bush, 1990 might have been remembered as the year the First Amendment came under its greatest attack since the McCarthy Era.

From the racist, homophobic diatribes of Sen. Jesse Helms to the utterly irrational homophobic rantings of Rep. William Dannemeyer ("Militant homosexuals pose the most vicious attack on traditional family values that our society has seen in the history of our Republic."), the elected officials of this nation attacked the National Endowment for the Arts with a daily barrage of accusations, lies, and deliberate misrepresentation. Motions were made in Congress to abolish the NEA. A "clean art oath" dubbed the "Helms Amendment" was inserted into agreements signed between the NEA and grant recipients, only to be declared unconstitutional by the courts. Fellowships were stripped from controversial performance artists like Karen Finley, and just about everyone held passionate opinions on Robert Mapplethorpe's photographs, with or without seeing them. The controversy played out slowly, day by day, exploited at every possible turn by mass media in a kind of surreal *danse macabre*. Until George Bush began drawing lines in the sands of Saudi Arabia, Kuwait, and Iraq. Arts council budgets across the nation are now being slashed, many by as much as 80 per cent.

On St. Valentine's Day, 1989, the Ayatollah Khomeini, supreme ruler of an Iran then engaged in a bitter war with our "ally," Iraq, pronounced an irrevocable death sentence on Salman Rushdie, author of *The Satanic Verses,* a death sentence with a $3 million bounty that struck at the heart of every writer in the world. In October, 1990, the trade journal *Publishers Weekly* editorialized against publication of a paperbound *Satanic Verses.* In November, Rushdie emerged from hiding with the public announcement that there would be no paper edition. Even from his grave, the Ayatollah had the book suppressed.

Over the past few years, the First Amendment has also come under attack from self-declared "feminists" like Andrea Dworkin who advocate censorship of anything they define as pornography, including magazines like *Playboy.* "In the male system, women are sex; sex is the whore," Dworkin wrote in her 1981 book, *Pornography: Men Possessing Women.* Only war could prevent a little savage laughter over the delectable thought of Andrea Dworkin in bed— as it were—with Jesse Helms and Bill Dannemeyer. In 1984, the Feminist Anti-Censorship Taskforce was founded in New York and Madison specifically to oppose Dworkin's censorious litigation. Most of my feminist friends are not censors, quite the contrary

Public school boards spent the year waging war against *Catch 22, Catcher in the Rye, The Diary of Anne Frank, The Adventures of Huckleberry Finn, Of*

Mice and Men, Understanding AIDS, even *Romeo and Juliet,* and hundreds of other books. *Being Born,* a book about birth, was banned from Washington state public school libraries for using the word "penis" *once.*

A record seller in Alexander, Alabama was arrested last year for selling a copy of a 2 Live Crew record and fined $3000. 2 Live Crew itself was found to be not guilty of committing obscenities in Florida. The media explored and exploited the abundant violent misogyny of Rap music and stand-up "comics" like Andrew Dice Clay. And American poets began to read poetry written by Chinese dissidents after the massacre at Tiananmen.

Although the 100,000th AIDS victim died, his passing was barely noted because of a major troop build-up in the Persian Gulf. Twice as many Americans have died from AIDS as died in Viet Nam, but there will be no marble memorial in Washington, D.C. As 1990 dragged to a close under the cloud of war, Bush declared Saddam Hussein "worse than Hitler," and Congress delayed debate on a war that appeared inevitable.

And now it is February, 1991, and American warplanes are engaged in sortees, *one every minute,* dropping hundreds of thousands of *tons* of bombs on Kuwait and Iraq, a half million Americans entrenched in the sands waiting for a call to Ground War.

•

"All of contemporary culture," Stanley Kunitz has written, "threatens poetry. A primary attribute of the great art of the West is that it persists in opposing the solitary conscience to the overwhelming power of the modern superstate. The poetic imagination lives by its contradictions and disdains any form of oppression, including the oppression of the mind by a single idea."

Robert Duncan has written: "The work of Denise Levertov or Robert Creeley or Larry Eigner belongs not to my appreciations but to my immediate concerns in living. That I might 'like' or 'dislike' a poem of Zukofsky's or Charles Olson's means nothing where I turn to their work as evidence of the real. . . I must study thru, deepen my experience, search out the challenge and salvation of the work."

But what is "salvation of the work," and how does one articulate the solitary conscience that inhabits the middle ground where experience and imagination cross-pollinate? It certainly cannot be found in any idealized "poetic" way of life. When I think of the "Lady" who appears in Robert Creeley's poems, I know that she is tragic in part *because* she is unattainable, and unattainable because she is, like Dante's Beatrice, an idealized form inspired by a human, transient, model. Creeley's self-parody in "The Door," for instance, arises out of the comi-tragic tension between concrete experience and abstract desire. "I grow older, not wiser," the speaker says. In *Pieces,* the Lady even becomes "opaque" as though "painted on a board," is a "reflection," almost a palimpsest upon which Romantic longing may imprint its testament. "What truth is it," Creeley asks, "that makes men so miserable?" His ability to stand naked to experience, naked to the world, is revealed in some of the most endearing poetry of our age.

Olga Broumas sends a small poem—"thankful"—in the midst of the bombing:

> Shortest light
> of the year I greet you
> unfamiliar to the yield of this
> large inhibition the wind
> soughs equally through
> tupelo and lung the sculpt
> of a greater nakedness
> in the bones.

I watch the television reports of the bombing and burning of thousands— mostly civilians—on a highway outside Kuwait City, and an American pilot says, "It was target practice, it was shooting ducks in a barrel."

"What is truth," said Pilate, and washed his hands.

A woman in America is beaten senseless every sixteen seconds. Somewhere between 4,000 and 24,000 women are beaten to death in the U.S. of A. every year. Nearly every woman in this country will be sexually assaulted at least once in her lifetime. One in three will be raped. This is a condition of war. And the money that could be spent in support of nonviolent advocacy and programs to rehabilitate victim and violator alike is being spent on bombing missions; money to provide shelters for battered women and children is being spent on bombing missions. Five million homeless wander the roads and alleys, sleep on benches or behind garbage cans, many in need of mental health care or alcohol rehabilitation programs, but the money to pay for those programs is being spent on bombing missions.

One quarter of American high school students fail to graduate, and half those who do graduate are functionally illiterate. A Japanese graduating high school senior has the equivalent for four more years of education than his or her counterpart in the U.S. But money to rehabilitate American education, to make it competitive, is being spent on bombing missions.

And we turn to poesy for evidence of the real? Muriel Rukeyser wrote, "What would happen if one woman told the/ truth about her life?/ The world would split open." I turn again to Olga Broumas's poem for its sanity.

Robert Duncan, at a poetry reading, maybe thirty years ago, explained softly to the audience that it was not "his" audience, that a poem exists only as a point of entry, beyond any "meaning" gleaned from semi-public approval or disapproval. There is no such thing as a "first-rate" poet any more than there is a first-rate priest, he said, because whoever enacts the sacrament in the name of God is ordained. Neither poet nor priest would usurp such an honor for personal gratification.

The poetry of Creeley, Levertov, Duncan, Rukeyser, Carruth, Kunitz, Olga Broumas— this is work that addresses *my* immediate concerns with living. I am, in general, not much interested in poetry that does not reveal— for *me, myself*— immediate concerns with living, a feeling that is intensified when I consider the life of the imagination and the consequences of a solitary conscience standing in direct opposition to the modern global superstate.

Aristotle founded his ethics on the idea of *arete politike,* a term that translates into "social virtue." From the name of Ares, god of war, Aristotle connotes both "valor" and "virtue." Socrates thought of *arete* as "courage," and defined courage simply as knowledge. Heraclitus warns us,*"Ethos anthropou daimon,"* one's ethics is one's fate. One of the first poems of social protest, Hesiod's *Works and Days* attacks the ethics of aristocratic landholders who served as judges to settle tenant farmers' disputes. He also tells us how evil and labor came into the world. His complaint, like his misogyny, is timeless.

From Sappho to Tzu Yeh, from Catullus to Chaucer, we find poets standing in solitary opposition to the censor and to the warlords. Three hundred years ago, Bashō walked over a hill and saw a broad plain where a great battle had taken place. The experience was brought into sharp focus by Bashō's remembrance of a famous quatrain by the T'ang dynasty poet Tu Fu during the An Lu-shan Rebellion:

> The whole country devastated,
> only mountains and rivers remain.
> In springtime, in the ruined capital,
> the grass is always green.

Bashō wrote: "Summer grasses—/ all that remains of great soldiers'/ imperial dreams." And then he packed up his gear and went off to visit the estate of another patron.

There are also plenty of poets who glorified war, plenty who were religious fanatics, and plenty who were bigots. That heritage stretches from the Hebrew Bible and ancient Greek and Chinese *Poetry Classic* through Ezra Pound, balanced in part by an equally long heritage of meditative, socially engaged poetry of humane values.

How does one go about the difficult business of integrating moral necessity with imaginative invention, how can we simultaneously mourn and celebrate? The poetic imagination thrives on contradiction, anomaly, and enigma. How does one integrate moral invention with imaginative necessity? When I read Czeslaw Milosz on "the poetry of witness," I think yes, a poet *is* a witness. Then I read the beautiful solitary poems of John Haines, poems of radiant inner and outer witness from a world very far removed from centers of literary power politics. The witness of John Haines may be vastly different from the witness of Czeslaw Milosz, but we may turn to each in our search for the challenge, for evidence of the real, for the fundamental concerns of living.

The fundamental teaching of Buddhism is the idea of co-dependent origination, the theory that nothing is entirely self-originating. This is as true of abstract ideas as it is of the gene pool. Every poet develops a personal literary heritage, an imaginative parallel to one's immediate cultural heritage. We cannot stand apart from our environment, and we cannot stand apart from our politics. Nor is there any reason why a poet should *want* to.

Ethos anthropou daimon. My first allegiance is to my *real* community, certainly not to a flag or to a loyalty oath, but to my Muse. My national allegiance is to a *constitution,* not to its public hirelings. I serve as an apprentice priest in the temple of poesy—one way to write *poetry* in Chinese or Japanese is to combine the character for *temple* with the character for *word*—a temple offering sanctuary to those who reject jingoism, the rhetoric of vilification, national and personal violence. The character for *word* is composed of a mouth, open, with sound waves emerging; the character for *temple* is a hand cradling a seedling. Poetry plants its seeds.

In times of war, even my allegiance to my Muse demands opposition to war. I do not suddenly cease being a Conscientious Objector, nor am I permitted the luxury of closing my eyes to the politics of social terrorism practiced daily against women, homosexuals, minority races or religions, and against the incarcerated of this country. We lock up four times as many African Americans per capita as South Africa, and our own inner-city ghettos are every bit as bleak. They don't cease to exist just because we are bombing or just because I happen to write a little poesy about a posy. Being a poet is not, for me at least, a part-time job. It is a calling and I must listen . . .

But *my* temple may not be *your* temple. "If you move from what is to what may be," Odysseas Elytis writes, "you pass over a bridge which takes you from Hell to Paradise. And the strangest thing: a Paradise made of precisely the same material of which Hell is made. It is only the perception of the order of the materials that differs."

What, then, of the "responsibility to society" of the writer? The Thought Patrol is quick to remind us whenever it moves to abridge the First Amendment that "with freedom comes responsibility," presumably a responsibility not to offend the delicate sensibilities of those who would patrol our thoughts. In plain earthy American English, that's bullshit. The work of the writer is to "study thru," to deepen the experience, to open the field of action, and to be as "open" or naked, vulnerable, as one can be to the truth of experience. That a reference to my naked anus should offend Jesse Helms, is not *my* problem.

"War," Heraclitus tells us, "is universal; justice is strife." The Zen master, having struggled for decades to be free, finally gives up, and becomes free. *Ars imitatur naturam in sua actio.* We ourselves are "nature in action." The perfect poem is effortless, like the perfect life. Which of course doesn't exist, even for a Jesus of Nazareth or a Sakyamuni. We are *naturam in sua actio,* interconnected, interdependent, fallible, and inevitably perishable, out of ash into ash.

At the very height of World War II, when thousands of people were dying every day, Matisse was inspired to make paper cut-outs—simple, almost child-like little flowers that, in the very midst of all that death, seemed to offer a little hope and love and innocence to the world. At the same time, we discover the poems of the Holocaust or of the Spanish Resistance; we find Morris Graves painting world-weary birds in glinting shafts of moonlight; we hear Duke Ellington's "A-Train" or Billie Holiday's blues. Even in the face of the most demonic suppression, there is beauty and hope. In the face of terror, we come face-to-face with our own ability or inability to locate and articulate sacramental love.

An ancient Zen master asked, "What is it in the heart? The sound of a pine breeze."

At one time Japanese Zen master Sengai stressed the importance of being *buji,* completely free of self-awareness. "When working, work; when resting, rest." As a writer—whether in poetry, essay, or translation—this is a powerful lesson. Those who rush to the anti-war poem often sound disturbingly like those who rally for war. Anger is not of itself a useless emotion, but it must be disciplined. Sengai's comically huge, erect cock provides Jesse Helms with plenty of food for thought. One's heart is as much in one's humor as in one's pathos.

The poem or essay is a gift, one that is transformed as it passes through my hands; I do not grasp it. I pretty much follow the path defined by Lu Chi in his *Art of Writing,* which I translated—*went to school on.* "When studying the work of the Masters,/ I watch the working of their minds." Watching, one becomes "at one with" what is watched. My "responsibilities as a writer" are defined by principles of Zen and feminism, although I find the latter term inadequate and the former misunderstood. Even "humanism" is too anthropomorphic. Fundamentally, I suppose, I speak here of compassion—compassion expressed even in Sengai's lewd erection as it pokes fun at all of us.

The poem is itself a gift to and from the poet. In my own practice, the poetry is a natural articulation of heightened awareness expressed as a condition of music, its melody improvised in the making of it—like certain kinds of jazz or blues. In the unfolding of the song, I discover my own "interplay" with this or that poet, so that the result is not—as often as not—purely my own composition. Beginning the song, the poet gives up the self in the process of *becoming the song.* Gratitude and generosity are the by-products of compassion. The poet's work is, in part, to "give life" to words. The poet is a magician, a musician, simultaneously pregnant with meaning, and a midwife.

We have all known people whose stinginess of spirit wrings all the life out of words. We see our "leaders" twist and deliberately distort language, we hear them buy and sell lies, and buy and sell death every day. Dante put the corrupters of language in the Seventh Circle of Hell. But Hell is no more acceptable a solution than Paradise. Each of these is projected from within. Shining from within *that* within, within the anger and within the lust, within the selfishness and the unbounded generosity, there is radiant awe, the *ah!* of gratitude, the *ah!* of cognition.

A young man walked with Zen master Ikkyū, and as they passed a shop, Ikkyū said, "Wow! Did you see that beautiful woman?" A few moments later, the young man said, "I thought Zen transcended fleshly desire." Ikkyū nodded.

"But you were lusting after that woman!" the young man cried. Ikkyū smiled. "Are you still thinking about *her?*" So much for Hell, and so much for Paradise.

An ancient Chinese curse runs, "May you live in interesting times!" But what times have not been interesting? Human suffering remains unchanged except in scale. Asked what he might choose if allowed but one thing, Thales replied, "I would choose hope, because they have hope who have nothing else." Hearing this, his accusers tried him, found him guilty of corrupting morals, and threw him overboard at sea.

In a very beautiful fragment that has often been incompletely translated, Sappho writes,

> He is a god, a man beside you,
> enthralled by your talk, by your laughter.
> Watching makes my heart best fast
> because, seeing little, I imagine much.
> You put a fire in my cheeks.
> Speech won't come. My ears ring.
> Blind to all others, I sweat and I stammer.
> I am a trembling thing, like grass,
> an inch from dying.
>
> So poor I've nothing to lose,
> I must gamble . . .

Most translators have seen her "inch from dying" as a natural closure and let the poem end there, seemingly complete. In translating the poem I "restored" the line because I believe it makes a better "complete" poem despite advertising its fragmentary nature with the ellipsis. Only when she is "an inch from dying" can she fully surrender and begin to offer her naked emotional truth. It's a better "finishing line" because it opens out into the possible, because it is a transcending, a "giving up" of all that she might "have to lose."

"What does not change is the will to change," Olson quotes Heraclitus. *Ars poeticae?* After the classics from Plato and Aristotle to Confucius and Lu Chi, dip into Gary Snyder's "What You Need to Know to Be a Poet," Rexroth's "Letter to William Carlos Williams," and enter the enormously invigorating world of feminist literature that stretches from Sappho to Olga Broumas, from the Tzu Yeh songs to Carolyn Kizer's contemporary versions of them. The "responsibilities" of the poet remain unchanged. Authentic transformation, change, is possible only for those willing to "give up" and "gamble," those willing to let go. To fully appreciate life, one faces death equally. Poetry changes lives one life at a time, one poem at a time.

Twenty-five or more years ago, Gary Snyder wrote, "As a poet, I hold the most archaic values on earth." As we have learned from innumerable wars, moral superiority won't save us from ourselves. Yet we persist in using moral persuasion to justify our every act. Snyder addresses a system of values that is profoundly simple, far more inclusive than exclusive, and essentially respectful and non-violent. Maxine Kumin and Wendell Berry also return us to those values of hearth and home, neighborly values extending across nations and eco-systems.

Nevertheless, public schools indoctrinate our children with the lessons of the great war-makers from Caesar and Genghis Khan to Patton and Schwarzkopf, and we "entertain" them with lessons in the "successful" use of violence day in and day out. Our children know something about a hundred war-makers for every peacemaker they can name. Therefore, our language evolves into a language embracing an ever-evolving vocabulary of violence. As we become more accustomed to the vocabulary of violence, we ourselves gradually become more violent, first in speech and later in deed. Rationally, we understand Gandhi when he says, "An eye for an eye leaves the whole world blind," and yet we favor death penalties.

"Murder," Albert Camus noted, "becomes legitimized."

The archaic values of which Snyder speaks are the simplest of human values—those of daily moment-by-moment awareness of what one is actually *doing* and its consequence. The idea is that life itself is fundamentally sacramental.

Four months have passed since I wrote the opening sentence. The "victory" parades and television specials welcome home "our heroes" with yellow ribbons and hosannahs. Kuwait will continue to burn for two more years and tens of thousands of Kurds starve in filth in exile in the mountains of Iraq and Turkey. Across the world, 35 other wars continue almost without notice in the American press. But what would that same press say about a KGB director running the USSR? Former CIA Director George Bush, like all his predecessors in the White House, does what he can to manipulate and manage the news. In the *polis,* changes are small and come very slowly.

As the public learns about Richard Nixon's attempts to sustain the Viet Nam War until he could work it for an election victory over Hubert Humphrey, the news is met with a shrug; no one is surprised. When the public learns that William Casey met with the Ayatollah's thugs to ensure that American hostages in Iran would not be released until after Reagan's election victory over Jimmy Carter, no one is surprised. Casey became

Reagan's CIA Director, one of the primary engineers of "Iran-Contra" conspiracies and illegal arms dealing. The American public responds by electing Bush, who, like Reagan, claims to "know nothing." In the White House with the president, Billy Graham "blesses" Bush's war against Iraq. "God is on our side."

The names change, but the suffering does not. The exiled Dalai Lama reminds his White House audience in April, 1991, "It is important to remember to laugh at yourself in daily life." His remark reminds me somehow of Matisse's paper flowers. I think of Sappho's humor in exile, of Creeley's self-effacing nakedness.

The daily news shames me and I gag on it, choke on it like seawater, and I struggle for breath to cry out. I turn in grief and anger to ancient Japanese poems of solitude and interior exile, of gentle love and humor.

Two hundred years ago, the Zen monk Ryōkan inscribed on a kite, "Above heaven/ big winds." During the war in Iraq, I translated Bashō's *Oku-no-hosomichi, Narrow Road to the Interior,* in part as a response to the war, not to escape the daily realities of fire-bombings and oil spills, but to gain a broader, truer perspective. A Conscientious Objector all my adult life, facing war, I turn again to the teaching of the peacemakers, Ryōkan and Bashō, for their companionship, their vision, and for their courage and humor. In the words of Robert Duncan, "To deepen the experience, to search out the challenge." To reaffirm the absolute necessity of living at peace. Nothing else stands in true opposition to war. Nothing else. One must *embody* peace. A poet must embody a language, embody the poem, *become* the instrument of the poem— become the instrument of peace.

Miraculously—not through any act of sheer will, but through profound inter-connectedness—we have the great teachings of the peacemakers. And we have the poems of Kenneth Rexroth, Denise Levertov, Hayden Carruth, and a hundred, a thousand others, in many languages and traditions, whose poetry leads the way toward peace. They give me hope and courage even as I swim against the tide.

World News Today

At a time when mass media serves as a grand equalizer, flattening all events into 30 column inches of type or ninety seconds on the airwaves, literature, and especially poetry, is removed to the cultural margins. But even amongst the literati, the translator remains least visible. Gary Snyder has called poetry "high quality information," a useful concept. The "news" or high quality information brought by those messengers from other languages and cultures is of an almost infinitely superior quality to that of our major media. "Poetry is news," Ezra Pound said, "that *stays* news."

In the autumn of 1989, the National Endowment for the Humanities sponsored a Gallup poll which revealed, among other things, that 78 percent of all colleges and universities graduate students with no courses in western (or eastern) civilization; 77 percent have no foreign language requirement; 45 percent require no American or English literature; and 38 percent require no history. In short, our institutions of "higher learning" are no more than glorified trade schools whose single-minded purpose is to train people for placement in the "labor market" of the Technocracy. When college-educated adults have no background in literature, philosophy, or history, our future is grim indeed.

Responding to the Gallup poll, Dr. J. Robert Wills, academic provost at Pacific Lutheran University said, "Higher education in the 80s ought to prepare students for the 21st century and not just reinforce the 19th." His comments were underscored by representatives of colleges and universities throughout the northwest in a story carried by the Seattle *Post-Intelligencer*. These "educated" men believe, presumably, that Shakespeare prepares us only for life in the 16th and 17th centuries.

Over the past year or so, I have accumulated a number of books of poetry in translation, each written by a 20th century poet, but for Lao Tzu's ancient Chinese *Tao Te Ching*. There is much to be learned from these books. The "news" of these poets is news of the human condition, changed and changing and unchanged since the dawn of time. Moral and political struggles compete with transcendent vision. Poetry remains the highest quality information of the world community, and it is written by men and women who have learned from the past the necessity of speaking, of clarifying one's vision and experience and passing on whatever revelation results. Our poets know—perhaps better than anyone else—that unless we are connected to Heraclitus, we cannot cross his river; that unless we sail with Odysseus, we shall sail our own wine-dark seas alone, and suffer our trials and tribulations without benefit of counsel.

At a glance, the following books may appear awfully diverse, but these poets all share a common struggle, each having to confront a life at war, personal trials, sexism, racism, poverty, prison, exile—in short, all the horrors of this bloody century. And if our educated public reads no poetry, for whom is the translator's art refined? The translator becomes invisible perfecting an art appreciated only by a nearly invisible secret readership. And our own culture grows, as it has always grown, fed by shards of other languages and cultures.

Steven F. White's translations of poems by the Nicaraguan poet, Gioconda Belli (*From Eve's Rib,* Curbstone Press, 1989 9.95 paper), capture her social-political passions and her intense, steamy eroticism:

> I want to taste
> your salty, strong flesh,
> start with your arms as splendid
> as the branches of a ceiba tree,
> then your chest like a cave
> in a dream I've dreamt,
> chest-cave where my head lies hidden,
> searching for tenderness,
> that chest sounding like drums
> and life's never-ending flow./ . . .

Gioconda Belli graduated high school in Spain, studied advertising in Philadelphia, and worked in Nicaragua as an account executive until she made a commitment to the political struggle to overthrow the Somoza dictatorship. From 1975 to 1978, she was forced to live in exile in Costa Rica, returning after the Sandinista victory of 1979. She presently lives in Managua. Her poems link feminist eroticism with social convictions, and her sense of lyrical structure—an almost incantatory delivery—recalls Pablo Neruda and Federico Garcia-Lorca more than Rubén Darío. In "Patria Libre: July 19, 1979," she writes:

Strange to feel this sun again
and to see the jubilation of streets swarming with people,
the red and black flags everywhere
and a new face of the city awakening
to the smoke of burning tires
and the high lines of barricades.

She finds tremendous joy and pathos in the transformed city, and the shadows of the dead everywhere she looks. As the faces of people pour past her, she longs for "enough arms to embrace each one,/ to tell them I love them,/ for blood has joined us with its painful link,/ and we are together in this learning to speak again,/ to walk again./ . . ." But in the conclusion, she invites us all to embrace the dead, "let our dead be with us," as we work to "draw light from the ashes,/ cement, houses, bread from the ashes;/ . . ."

But how could she foretell Reagan's paid counter-revolutionaries; how could she foretell Bush's continuation of Reagan's policies? As the U.S. poured in hundreds of millions of dollars, Nicaraguan efforts to build homes and hospitals took a back seat to mere survival. Belli's poems return us to the real and permanent news of human suffering and human joy. Her lessons in eroticism and her deeply engaged social conscience and her feminism, her historical perspective and her personal, passionate imagination have marked her poems with the indelible handprint of originality.

A journeyman translator, Steven F. White translated Lorca's *Poet in New York* (Farrar, Straus, Giroux, 1988) with Greg Simon, with remarkable dexterity. He has also published *Poets of Nicaragua, Poets of Chile,* and *The Birth of the Sun: Selected Poems of Pablo Antonio Cuadra,* all with Unicorn Press, which also published White's own poems, *Burning the Old Year,* and *For the Unborn.*

If Gioconda Belli has brought a decidedly feminist voice to the Sandinista literary conversation, she must certainly owe a little something to her Mexican elder sister, Rosario Castellanos, whose *Selected Poems* have been translated by Magda Bogin (Graywolf Press, 1988). Rosario Castellanos published her first book of poems in 1948, and until her death in 1974, wrote innumerable articles, essays, stories, novels, and eight books of poetry.

In her introduction to this selected poems, Cecilia Vicuña says, "She wrote nakedly, openly, about her circumstances and her limitations, and this heroism earned her the misunderstanding and mockery of a primarily masculine literary world." Castellanos responded by intensifying her search for "hard truth" and by indentifying more and more deeply with Indian culture and causes, until she gave up her own inherited land to those who worked it, and went to work for the Indian Institute of Chiapas. Her vision combines elements of Indian and Christian mythology and echoes ancient Nahuatl poetry.

Palm Tree

Lady of the winds,
heron of the plains,
when you sway
your waist sings.

Gesture of prayer
or prelude of wings,
you are the cup into which the skies
pour one by one.

From the dark land of men
I've come kneeling to admire you.
Tall, naked, alone.
A poem.

Hers is an imagination richly detailed by close observation, and, in her way, as formal and refined as Elizabeth Bishop. Her philosophical twists often produce zen-like flashes of brilliance, as in "Nocturne"

Time is too long for life;
for knowledge not enough.

What have we come for, night, heart of night?

All we can do is dream, or die,
dream that we do not die
and, at times, for a moment, wake.

But her best poems are longer, several pages each, poems like "Wailing Wall," and "Return," which, in Magda Bogin's capable hands, become bouyant, limpid, and yet retain much of their sonority, her English versions often eschewing an obvious Latinate possibility for a cleaner, leaner sound, as when he translates *y no puede morir/ en su cuerpo remoto, inexplorado* as "and she cannot die/ in her remote, uncharted body." The easy translation would have fallen back on the literal-sounding "unexplored," whereas "uncharted" carries a grander and more precise implication. These versions, while staying close to literal translation, carry few of the blemishes usually associated with translation: no inversions, no false noises, no prose paraphrases, and best of all, no translator's additions to the text.

Bogin's *Selected Poems of Rosario Castellanos* should be read side by side with the translations of Julian Palley, *Meditation on the Threshold* (Bilingual Press/ Editorial Bilingüe, 1988). Palley's Introduction, "Rosario Castellanos: Eros and Ethos," is an exemplary assessment of the poet's work, and Palley's translations, if not quite as polished as those of Bogin, are not to be slighted. There are enough poems translated by each to provide useful comparison, yet enough differences to make the two volumes mutually complementary.

In Magda Bogin's translations of the twentieth century Catalan poet, Salvador Espriu (*Selected Poems,* Norton, 1989, $15.95 cloth), she again demonstrates conspicuous skills. Espriu, who should be far better known than he is, is a member of the "Generation of '36," writers who were just beginning their careers at the outbreak of the Spanish Civil War. Eschewing the violence of war and exile as alternatives, Espriu became an exile in his own country, a poet writing in a forbidden language in an attempt to preserve the mythopoeia of his culture.

Obsessed with death—both the death he saw everywhere during the war and the burden of cultural death he felt weighing upon his shoulders—his poems are often cryptic, expressing the poet's enormous sense of grief, solitude, and impotence. Only during the 1950s, when the Franco regime eased up on the outright persecution—genocide, really—of all things Catalan, did Espriu taste popular success. He published *La pell de brau (The Bull's Skin)* in 1960, and the poems were met with enthusiasm, Espriu being praised for his clarity and accessibility.

While Magda Bogin has translated several of the poems from *La pell de brau,* we are fortunate to also have Burton Raffel's translation (Marlboro Press, 1987) of the whole book. It is very much a book, and the poem is really one poem in a sequence of 54 parts. In this poem, Espriu wrestles with and overcomes the dark angels of failure, emptiness, and isolation. He comes to embrace a new ethics in which we learn to accept, almost fatalistically, our suffering, because it is only through our suffering that we achieve transcendence. Here is the first part in the original:

El brau, en l'arena de Sepharad,
envestia l'estesa pell
i en fa, enlairant-la, bandera.
Contra el vent, aquesta pell
do toro, del brau cobert de sang,
és ja parrac espesseit per l'or
del sol, per sempre lliurat al martiri
del temps, oracio nostra
i blamsfemia nostra.
Alhora víctima, botxí,
odi, amor, lament i rialla,
sota la closa eternitat del cel.

Burton Raffel presents it thus:

A bull, in a ring in Sfarad,
charges at an unfolded hide
and slowly lifting it high sees it fluttering like a flag—
Yet waving in the wind, this bull-
hide, from a blood-drenched bull,
is only a rag backed hard by the gold
sun, forever surrendered to the martyrdom
of time, our prayer
and also our blasphemy:
victim and executioner, both at once,
and hatred and love, and tears and bitter laughter,
here under the silent, closed eternity of heaven.

The bull's skin reflects the shape of the Iberian peninsula. The conflict is linguistic and cultural, the Catalan with its roots in the Carolingian Empire versus the more dominant Castilian, the "official" language of the Franco dictatorship. Only in 1948 were Catalonian writers permitted to publish in their native tongue. And, of course, the second-to-last line carries a very heavy echo of Catullus's *odi et amo*, "I hate and I love," the resonance delivering Espriu's love/hate of Spain, and indeed of the torn emotions of all the people. Bogin presents the same poem:

The bull, in the arena of Sepharad,
attacked the time-stretched skin,
unfurling it into a flag.

Against the wind, this bull's skin
slick with blood, rag
already thick with the sun's
gold, pledged forever to the martyrdom
of time, our prayer
and our blasphemy.
Now victim, hangman,
hate, love, laughter and lament
beneath the sky's eternal clasp.

The two translations are remarkably discreet. I dislike Bogin's inversion of gold/sun, *"l'or/ del sol."* In Raffel's line, this waving flag/bull-hide/Iberian peninsula "is only a rag backed hard by the gold" (line-break pause weighted with meaning) "sun." Another problem arises with the phrase, *"per sempre lliurat al martiri,"* which Bogin translates "Pledged forever to the martyrdom," and which Raffel translates, "forever surrendered to the martyrdom." To pledge and to surrender are decidedly different undertakings. The problematic word in this phrase is *lliurat*, a transitive verb meaning "to hand over, to surrender," in a mild-mannered way; the word is etymologically linked to the Latin *mansuetudo*, tameness or mildness.

Again at the closure, their variance is striking: Bogin has "beneath the sky's eternal clasp," where Raffel has "here under the silent, closed eternity of heaven." While I dislike the latter's intrusively weighty "heaven," his "closed eternity" is both there in the original and better poetry than saying "the sky's eternal clasp," which leads the reader to question whether the final word is a noun or a verb. We are fortunate to have each of these translations, and where they can be read in tandem, the rewards are multiplied.

Dana Gioia's translations of the hermetic Eugenio Montale's suite of twenty love poems composed in the late 1930s, *Motetti* (Graywolf Press, 1990), are reasonably accurate, sturdy, and surprisingly more interesting than the translator's own poetry. Generally, a poet who translates goes to school on his or her poetic elder, but Gioia's poems bear no discernable handprint of Montale's style or vision. Having associated himself with a kind of *nouveau* formalism propounded by Wyatt Prunty, Frederick Turner, and others, and which produces literary criticism that is mean-spirited and ill-informed, Gioia's versions of Montale nonetheless find a lovely movement in time and structure not at all at odds with the original Italian. But they are not a substantial improvement on the versions presented by William Arrowsmith

in his translations of the larger *The Occasions* (Norton, 1987). Gioia's version
of the second poem reads:

> Many years, and one of them a little harder
> on a foreign lake burning in the sunsets.
> Then you came down from the mountains to bring me
> back
> Saint George and the Dragon.
>
> If only I could print them on the banner
> rising and falling in the brutal wind
> of my heart—and descend for you
> into a chasm of fidelity, forever.

Why he has made a line of the single syllable "back" is difficult to figure;
Montale has two quatrains. But his treatment is direct, the movement of the
translation registering perceptions and rhythms carried over from the original.
Arrowsmith offers:

> Many years, and one year harder still on the foreign
> lake aflame with the setting sun. Then
> you came down from the hills, you brought me back
> my native Saint George and the Dragon.
>
> If only I could print them on this blazon
> thrashing under the lash of the northeaster
> in my heart . . . And then, for your sake, sink
> in a whirlpool of fidelity, undying.

I do not understand the "my native" tag applied to George and the Dragon;
it does not appear in the original. But Arrowsmith has a startling ear for the
poetry in English, especially in the second quatrain. Where Gioia's "banner"
is merely "rising and falling" in a calm breeze, Arrowsmith wishes to print
"on this blazon/ thrashing under the lash" of the northeaster, his sounds and
images much more consistent with the turmoil the poet is feeling when he
says "*che s'agita alla frusta del grecale* . . ." The Italian *frusta* is "lash," and the
wind is blowing in from Greece.

The narrative linking these lyric poems tells the tale of "impossible love,"
in Gioia's terms, between the poet and an American Dante scholar, Irma

Brandeis, and account for Montale's allusions to Dante within the suite. Gioia, in his note on the translation, refers us not only to the sense of the original, but to its spirit, arguing on behalf of versions unencumbered by footnotes. In this, he largely succeeds. But any conscientious reader must surely read both translations, and, with luck, perhaps someone will reprint Charles Wright's earlier limited edition from Windhover Press in 1981, giving us three solid versions of this important work.

Montale's reputation as a "hermetic" poet has no doubt cost him a larger North American audience. Gioia compares him to Eliot, but that would be the Eliot of *Four Quartets* rather than the Pound-influenced and edited Eliot of *The Wasteland*. Montale is musically and philosophically sophisticated, as Arrowsmith's substantial scholarship (at the *back* of the book—where it belongs) makes clear. But Montale needs none of the apparatus one needs to get through, say, *The Cantos*. He simply requires an attentive reader, one whom he rewards generously whether in the original or in translation.

W. S. Di Piero is a fine poet, an excellent essayist, and earned his spurs as a translator for his work on Giacomo Leopardi's *Pensieri*. He has also brought us a generous *Selected Poems of Leonardo Sinisgalli* (Princeton, 1982), which attracted little or no attention upon publication. Sinisgalli clearly follows in the Hermetic tradition of Eugenio Montale, but is at heart a poet of small objects, "kin to scorpion, fly, ant, and toad," a poet for whom experience is located in particular detail and observation, the whole body alert to sensual data. Here is the poem "Old Grief" entire:

> Grief comes easily to old people.
> At midday
> sitting in a corner of an empty house
> they burst into tears.
> Infinite despair
> catches them by surprise.
> They lift a withered slice of pear
> to their lips, or the pulp of a fig
> baked on roof tiles.
> Even a sip of water
> or a visit by a snail
> helps to ease a crisis.

In the original, "Even a sip of water / helps to ease a crisis / or a visit by a snail." Di Piero's inversion of the order of perception does not impede the poem. It in fact sharpens the focus. His English rhymes heighten the sound and intensify the melopoeic properties of his version, demonstrating an enviable ear for poetry: long *e* and "ear" sounds; lift-lips-sip-visit; surprise-slice-tiles-crisis.

Born in the mountains of Lucania southeast of Naples in 1908, Sinisgalli was an advertizing and design director for Olivetti and other companies. He was also a gifted watercolor painter. He founded Italy's most influential graphic arts journal, *Civilta delle machine,* which he directed for six years. A lifelong student of mathematics and science ("the prosody of the invisible"), it was this scientific turn of mind which turns his poetry away from the glorification of self and personality toward poetry of cool surfaces, uncluttered observation, as though the poet spent a lifetime taking notes as the world rolled by. Di Piero calls him a pilgrim who conjures the past, working in the grammar of time. "That scansion of the moment," Di Piero says in his introduction, "gives a structure to knowledge."

I'll Come to Die

Here's where I was meant to live.
I'll come to die by these streams,
vineyards, stones
shaped like hammers or hearts,
stones they call "changers"
because they've been filed down
by thousands of years.

In a translated afterword, Sinisgalli says, "To the Poet, existence is a constant wonder. Yet his song, his boredom, his weariness and sudden energy are all fatally subject to banal meteorological routine. The history most meaningful to him is that told by a lunar cycle or the ticking of a clock."

Also from Italy, but a generation older, Diego Valeri was born near Padua, but his poetry will be forever identified with Venice. A number of his poems bear an interesting resemblance to those of Sinisgalli, especially "Blade of Wind," written in the 1950s:

The dark roads, and the sunlight in the courtyards,
and the world . . . And the infinite
spaces and silences.
And the human ghosts. And time, like a smooth blade
of wind along the edge of everything.

Valeri bridges the gap between the neo-classicism of 19th century Europe and the modernist revolution. His poems tend to turn on moments of epiphany, as in the closing couplet above. Educated at the University of Padua and at the Sorbonne, he became professor of modern French literature at the University of Padua, and translated, among other things, *Madame Bovary*. Certainly, he would have been intimately conversant in the work Paul Valéry.

What attracted both Valeri and Sinisgalli to Paul Valéry's writing is, in part, a scientific attitude which locates the poem within the body. In "Analecta," Valéry says, "The nervous system, among other properties or functions, possesses that of linking very different orders of magnitude. For example: it joins what belongs to the chemist with that which belongs to the mechanic. Physics today considers *masses* so infinitely small that even light has nothing to do with them. Whatever images we may conceive of them *have no bearing, can have none,* on what they are supposed to represent." It is a second, other, body which we and others see, which has form, Valéry says, and "Indeed it is this body that was so dear to Narcissus."

This more scientific attitude toward poetry and art, toward life, brought a renewed sense of humility, but also a deeper sense of connection to the world. Valeri, found guilty of anti-Fascist activities, fled to Switzerland for the remainder of the war. In the 1970s, shortly before his death, he composed an essay, "The Old Poet and His Book," and he compiled a collected poems. "In my book," he said, "there is no pose, there is no trickery, there is no conformity, there is no anticonformity, there is no ideological enthusiasm for any part or point of view, there is no modish experimentalism, there is no lying of any kind, either moral or artistic." It is the sort of statement we often read and dismiss, but which should be examined more closely, perhaps through the eyes of a Gioconda Belli or a Rosario Castellanos.

Michael Palma's translations of Diego Valeri, *My Name on the Wind* (Princeton, 1989, $12.95 paper), generally reflect the clarity of the original without attempting to capture a close equivalent for its exact sound. Valeri is a "nature poet" without the paraphernalia of much Romantic poetry, nature poetry with a more scientific attitude, much as Jeffers and Rexroth and, later, Gary Snyder, would bring to North American nature poetry. Some of the poems lose rhyme in translation, but the images remain crisp. In others, the retention of rhyme produces less than wonderful results, as in:

Fredda ancora l'aria

Fredda ancora l'aria, i cieli duri.
Ma gia la terra fuma, soffocata
da desideri oscuri:
sotto il velo dell'erba appena nata,
brucia e suda, e rabbrividisce nuda.

The Air Still Chilly

The air still chilly, and still harsh the skies.
But the earth is already smoldering with suppressed
and dark desires:
under the veil of newborn grass it burns
and sweats, and shivers in its nakedness.

That awkward phrase, "still harsh the skies" found its way into Palma's translation because of its slant-rhyme with "dark desires." But as the opening line of a poem, it sounds contrived; it sounds, well, *translated*. And with the "earth smoldering or burning," *terra fuma,* weak "suppressed" finds its way in, replacing the powerful *soffocata* of the original only because of its rhyme with "nakedness" at the closure. Here, a kind of low-grade melopoeia has been rescued at the direct expense of phano- and logopoeia. Generally, Palma is closer to the imagery and thinking of the original, often capturing the elegiac tone and the directness of expression very well.

Another poet deeply wounded by World War Two, a survivor of the death camps, Dan Pagis was born Bukovina, Romania in 1930. In 1946, he moved to Israel and began writing poetry in Hebrew and became a teacher in a kibbutz. He later taught at Harvard and at the University of California. He is credited with bringing to Hebrew poetry a colloquial diction and a direct style infused with classical mysticism.

His selected poems, *Variable Directions* (North Point Press, 1989, $21.95 cloth), is translated by Stephen Mitchell. Unfortunately, none of the poems is presented in the original, so it is impossible to sit with a dictionary and worry out a poem or two. Mitchell's English versions seem sensible, but slightly literary considering Pagis's reputation for colloquial language:

The Portrait

The little boy
keeps fidgeting,
it's hard for me to catch the line
of his profile.
I draw one line
and his wrinkles multiply,
dip my brush
and his lips curl, his hair whitens,
his skin, turned blue, peels from his bones. He's gone.
The old man is gone. And I,
whither shall I go?

Two troubling instances in the translation: 1) why "whitens" over "turns white" when the latter is indeed the way we would say it in American English? 2) *whither* shall I go? *Whither*? It sounds arch; it sounds almost archaic. A poet would ask, "Where shall I go" or "where shall I turn."

But for the most part, these English versions read very cleanly. Mitchell's equivalents are most often simple and direct. Emptiness is a recurrent theme, and the empty page signifies for Pagis the core emblem of our struggle to leave a mark on the world. In "A Small Poetics," he provides a brief *ars poetica:*

You're allowed to write everything,
for example, *and* and *and.*
You're allowed with all the words you find,
all the meaning you plant among them.

It's a good idea, of course, to check
if the voice is your voice
and the hands are your hands.

If so, lock up your voice,
gather your hands, and obey
the voice of
the empty page.

Writing in Hebrew two hundred years ago, Nachman of Bratzlav said in "The Torah of the Void," "All speech is bordered by the five limits of the mouth. All creation is a limiting in three dimensions and in time and in substance: 'In wisdom hast Thou made them all.'" Pagis, schooled in the classical Hebrew mystics, finds that by first granting permission and then setting limits, one can engage "creativity," one can engage the "unwisdom" of the Void.

Mitchell, perhaps best known for his translations of poems by Ranier Maria Rilke, has also translated the *Tao Te Ching* (Harper and Row, 1988), the ancient Chinese masterwork attributed to Lao Tzu. Given an enormous advance for the work ($130,000) despite his inability to read the original, Mitchell has connected this Taoist masterpiece to his own zen practice, a folly capable of being committed only by a westerner. Mitchell also sees fit to drop an entire chapter (No. 50) and to replace it with his own "improvisations on the passage's theme." Elsewhere, he has rewritten, paraphrased, or invented whole lines and passages and completely misinterpreted others, often applying his version of a "zen" interpretation which could not possibly have existed until hundreds of years after Lao Tzu. Elsewhere, he injects all sorts of modern paraphernalia, bombs outside the city and so forth.

While both Taoism and Buddhism (the sources of Zen) embrace an unnamable insight, their philosophical roots are different. Buddhism declares codependent origination; Taoism declares a harmony found between appositional *yin* and *yang* bound by a third mysterious force. Because Harper and Row has invested so heavily in this translation, Mitchell's publisher will be determined to make this *the* translation of our age, and, should it succeed, a new generation will come to fundamentally misunderstand early Chinese culture and a masterpiece. Anyone wanting a reliable English translation should turn to the Peguin edition translated by D. C. Lau or other recent translations.*

Born a generation or two before Dan Pagis, Aleksander Wat was born in Warsaw on May 1, 1900, the son of a pious student of the Kabbalah who also read Kierkegaard and Plotinus, and filled the young poet with the Jewish intellectual spirit and tradition without imposing a traditional religious education. As is so often the case is Eastern Europe, Wat grew up in a polylingual household, reading Polish, Russian, and French. While still in his teens, he co-founded a Futurist writing group and published his first volume of poetry. A second volume would wait until 1957 to appear.

---

*My translation of *Tao Te Ching* was published by Shambala in 2005. —SH

Wat's sense of responsibility and his acceptance of ordeal is clearly evident in an early poem, "Childhood of a Poet":

Melos whispered words in his ear,
their meaning was incomprehensible.
Weaving them by twos, by threes
she would crown his forehead
with thorns.

She fed his heart with bitterness.
Till, overflowing with nausea, it exploded in a spasm
of joy
shared with nobody
nobody
nobody.

That was a sad childhood.
Sounds, remembrances, dreams
in which he always soared one inch above earth.
Then he fell.
The fall of a child . . .
The levitation of a poet.

Czeslaw Milosz, co-translator of Wat's selected poems, *In This Skin* (Ecco Press, 1989, $17.95 cloth), with Leonard Nathan, quotes the poet's autobiography as saying he simply reached a philosophical dead end with his early Futurist/Dadaist verse. "Values had lost their foundation and their meaning, " Milosz says. Although he never officially joined the party, Wat edited the influential party magazine, *The Literary Monthly,* between 1929-32, when it was shut down. Wat spent several months in prison, then went to work for a publishing house until Hitler's invasion in 1939, whereupon he was arrested and passed through several more prisons. He was accused of being a Trotskyite, a Zionist, even an agent of the Vatican. He lost all track of his wife and child and they were deported.

Wat spent months in starvation in a prison is Saratov, but was eventually released, and reunited with his family in 1943, and they returned to Poland in 1946. He again took up his literary calling, only to be again labelled "a hostile element" and silenced in 1949. He suffered a stroke and for several years was in and out of neurology clinics. During the political "thaw" of 1956, he returned to his poetry, and his 1957 volume of verse (*Poems*) made a celebrity of him.

Wat's tragic humor is altogether capable of handling complex philosophical problems, usually relying on a narrative structure to provide a resolution. His poems are populated by prisons, hotels, hospitals, and city streets, all bearing somehow directly upon human fate.

Like the other Futurist poets, Wat must certainly have been influenced by the poetry of Anna Akhmatova, who wrote, "Our sacred craft has existed/ for thousands of years . . ./It is the light of the world even in the darkness." Richard McKane's hefty (320pp) *Selected Poems of Akhmatova* (Bloodaxe Books, 1989) is published on the centennial of her birth. In her lifetime, she was championed and condemned, persecuted, and reviled as "half nun and half whore," only to emerge as the premier Russian poet of this century. Her poems have been translated numerous times with varying degrees of success, but are probably and justifiably best known in the United States through the brilliant translations of Stanley Kunitz and the late Max Hayward published by Atlantic Monthly Press in 1973. Here is their version of her 1924 poem, "The Muse" in its entirety:

All that I am hangs by a thread tonight
as I wait for her whom no one can command.
Whatever I cherish most—youth, freedom, glory—
fades before her who bears the flute in her hand.

And look! she comes . . . she tosses back her veil,
staring me down, serene and pitiless.
"Are you the one," I ask, "whom Dante heard dictate
the lines of his *Inferno?*" She answers: "Yes."

But for one word, "glory," one might very well believe this to be an original Kunitz poem. It is a wonderful poem in English, full of noble diction and honest fear and love. And the Kunitz/Hayward translations are presented bilingually so that one might trouble out a few of Akhmatova's with a dictionary and comparative translations.

Lyn Coffin's 1983 edition published by Norton gives the poem this way:

When at night I await the beloved guest,
Life seems to hang by a thread. "What is youth?" I demand
Of the room. "What is honor, freedom, the rest,
In the presence of her who holds the flute in her hand?"
But now she is here. Tossing aside her veil,

> She considers me. "Are you the one who came
> To Dante, who dictated the pages of Hell
> To him?" I ask her. She replies, "I am."

What an enormous difference in the opening line between these two versions! Coffin gives away her translation with "beloved guest," which asks the reader to determine whether it's said "beloved," or "belovéd," and in either case, the language sounds artificial. Kunitz sets up a powerful tension in his opening. Coffin translates words while searching for a rhyme.

Richard McKane's version:

> In the night when I wait for her to come
> life seems to hang on a strand of hair.
> What are honours, what is youth, what is freedom
> before the dear guest with the little flute in her hand?
>
> There, she has entered. She threw back her veil
> and looked at me inquisitively.
> I ask her: 'Was it you who dictated
> to Dante the pages of the *Inferno*?' She answers: "It was I."

McKane, like Coffin, misses the possibility of a dynamic opening line, settling for a literal. But his diction is in general superior to that of Coffin, permitting him to draw rhymes from the interior, as with *hang, strand,* and *hand,* and also settling on subtle slant-rhymes like *come* and *freedom.* Still, the poems often feel self-evidently translated. How unsatisfying is McKane's "It was I" at the closure after reading Kunitz's simple, scary "Yes." And only Kunitz brings us face-to-face with a muse who is "serene and pitiless," a muse which is believable, unlike the more purely literary muse of Coffin and McKane and others. Like her great compatriot, Akhmatova has been unevenly served by her translators, but she alone has an English-language equivalent which is certifiably great of itself.

Richard McKane's translations are good. They are reasonably literal, and without the amount of dead language and arch rhymes of the Coffin versions, with the added benefit of including many, many more poems than any other English selected poems. He has also included her long poems, "Requiem," "The Way of All the Earth," "By the Sea Shore," and "Poem without a Hero," poems which enlarge and enhance our understanding of her sweep of knowledge and her lifelong dedication to vision and craft. Nonetheless, the more translations I read, the deeper my appreciation for the supreme accomplishment of Stanley Kunitz and Max Hayward.

But we no longer must settle for only a selection of Akhmatova's poems. Judith Hemschemeyer's decade-long struggle with *The Complete Poems* (2 vols. cloth, $85.00, Zephyr Press, 1991) will surely reward any reader wanting a full assessment of Akhmatova's poetry in English. While Hemschemeyer hasn't Kunitz's renowned ear, her translations are more literal and are sturdy, reliable, utilitarian translations. A major accomplishment by any reasonable estimation, Hemschemeyer's treatment refuses to warp the poems into forced rhyme, preferring rather to tackle a literal—but not unpoetic—translation, the result being what should become *the* Akhmatova in translation for our time.

Roughly contemporary with Anna Akhmatova, Marina Tsvetaeva was born in Moscow in 1892, and published her first book at the age of thirty. A friend and correspondent of Boris Pasternak and Rainier Maria Rilke, they called her "our only equal in strength," and she lived most of her adult life in exile, in abject poverty, in Prague and Paris. In 1933, she wrote her friend, George Ivask, "My husband is ill and can't work. My daughter earns five francs a day. . . and on this, . . . four of us slowly starve to death." Her husband, Sergei Efron, was eventually exposed as a Soviet agent, and the family returned to Moscow in 1939, only to have her husband charged with offenses against the state and executed, apparently in the summer of 1941. Alone and again in hopeless poverty, Marina Tsvetaeva hanged herself on August 31 of that year. She was not yet fifty years old, and, with Akhmatova, the greatest Russian poet of the century. No one attended her funeral.

She was a notoriously difficult character who felt completely abandoned in the world, claiming to have cared for nothing except poetry. In a letter to Rilke, she demanded of poetry "the truth of this moment." She sought to connect to other souls through poetry and once stated, "The word is all I want. . . . he who kisses me misses *me*." Her alienation and frustration are everywhere evident in her poems, and "The Muse," from her first book, makes a kind of parallel with Akhmatova's poem on the same theme:

She has neither rights, nor forebears,
Nor a handsome falcon.
She walks on—wrenches away—
So distant!

The gold-winged fire lit
Under her swarthy eyelids.
With her rugged hand
She takes and forgets.

Her skirt untucked,
Scraps laid bare.
Neither wicked, nor kind,
But merely distant.

Neither weeps, nor complains:
Draw her up close—she yields.
With her rugged hand
She gives and forgets.

Then, with the guttural
Spouting, with the screech . . .
Take care, O Lord,
Of this distant one.

Tsvetaeva could find no community of artists, no companionship in a society which had no place for the aesthetic imagination. Tsvetaeva's poem predates that of Akhmatova by three years. She leaves herself out of the poem completely, choosing rather to simply describe the one who "has neither rights, nor forebears," as her muse "wrenches away" to remain in the distance. In "Under the Shawl," she saw "woman" as carrying the future under her shawl, because "you widen in secrets as in shawls,/ you last in shawls as in secrets." These translations, *In the Inmost Hour of the Soul* (The Humana Press, 1989), are presented in English only. Nina Kossman seems to have captured much of the lyric density and movement of the original, the obdurate, passionate, solemn personality of the poet apparent at every turn. Perhaps it is best to let Tsvetaeva's epitaph speak for itself; it is drawn from a poem she wrote in 1934:

My veins slashed open: unrestrained,
Unrestorable, my life gushes forth.
Hold steady your plates and your bowls!
Each bowl will soon be shallow,
The plates—too flat to contain it.
Up the brim and *over*

Staining dark earth nourishing reeds.
Irreversible, unavoidable,
Unrestorable, the poem streams.

There are poets for whom poetry is autobiography or therapy or simply the dance of the intellect. But for Tsvetaeva, the poem was evidence of supreme *being-aliveness* experienced in the moment, a song from the soul to the soul.

Two generations younger than Tsvetaeva, Johannes Bobrowski was born in the spring of 1917 in East Prussia, growing up on "both sides" of the River Memel, the son of a railman and the grandson of a Lithuanian farmer. As a 24-year old German soldier on the Eastern Front, he witnessed the "slavering wolves" of the SS commit their murders in Kaunas and wrote:

Kaunus 1941
. . .
Did my eyes avoid yours
brother? Sleep struck us
at the bloody wall. So we went on
blind to everything. We looked
like gipsies at the villages
in the oak-wood, the summer
snow on the roofs.

I shall walk on the stone banks
under the rainy bushes,
listen in the haze of the plains.
There were swallows upstream
and the woodpigeon called
in the green night:
My dark is already come.

Captured and held prisoner of war in Russia until 1949, he worked as a coal miner. Many of his poems are rooted in historical allusions and parallels, and although his poems often ring with a touch of darkness reminiscent of his German contemporary, Georg Trakl, his style is far less impenetrable, his structure more openly lyrical, owing something to the 18th century poet Klopstock, and to Hölderlin. His poem, "Russian Songs," is an elegy for Tsvetaeva which concludes:

I sleep—
you give me a grain of salt
scooped from an uncrossed
sea, I give you
a drop of rain
from the land
  where no one weeps.

Like Tsvetaeva before him, he died before reaching 50, partly the result of his war experiences and generally poor health. Translators Ruth and Matthew Mead have chosen only lyrical poems for their selected poems, *Shadow Lands* (Anvil Press Poetry, 1984), leaving out a great many composed in classical meters. Presented in English only, the result is a large collection of powerful lyrics by a poet virtually unknown in North America.

Born five years after Tsvetaeva, George Trakl grew up in Salzburg, Austria, attending Catholic teacher preparatory school in the mornings and receiving Protestant instruction in the afternoons. Twice refused promotion in the *Staatsgymnasium,* he turned, in 1905, to private instruction, beginning a five-year apprenticeship in a Salzburg apothecary, where he began to chronically abuse drugs, a practice that lasted throughout his life. In the years before the war, he became a favorite of Kurt Wolff, who offered to publish a volume of Trakl's poems, a project that was delayed until after the poet's death by cocaine suicide in November of 1914 in Cracow, Poland, where he had been sent for treatment of severe chronic depression. He was housed in a cell shared with an officer suffering delirium tremens. At Grodek, a few months earlier, following a disastrous defeat, he had been left in charge of ninety wounded and dying men, an experience from which he never recovered.

Trakl had been an unstable personality all his life. His poems are full of intimations of incest and nightmare visions and voices from unreality. As I learned first-hand while translating a dozen or so of his poems years ago under the direction of a brilliant tutor, Trakl's German is dense, almost impenetrable at times, making him one of the most difficult poets imaginable for any translator, his madness or near-madness lending his poems odd angles of vision and a haunted undertone. Daniel Simko's translations, *Autumn Sonata* (Moyer Bell Limited, 1989), received the Poets House Translation award and certainly deserves it. While staying very close to the original, he has worked the poems into a demotic American English. He opens "De Profundis," one of Trakl's most famous poems, this way:

There is a stubble-field where a black rain is falling.
There is a brown tree that stands alone.
There is a hissing wind that encircles the empty shacks.
How melancholy this evening is.

Near the village
A gentle orphan gathers sparse corn.
Her eyes widen, round and golden in the dusk,
And her womb awaits the heavenly bridegroom.

On their way home
The spepherd found her sweet body
Rotting in the bushes. // . . .

And while the simple English rendering loses the density of the original, it reads splendidly. But we get to lines like *"Auf meine Stirne tritt kaltes Metall/ Spennen suchen mein Herz./ Es is ein Licht, des in meinem Mund erloscht.// . . ."* and read, in English:

Cold metal steps on my forehead.
Spiders search for my heart.
There is a light that dies in my mouth. // . . .

"Cold metal steps on my forehead" is, to be sure, what the poet said. But in literal translation, it sounds out of sync; it sounds awkward. There are lines throughout Trakl's oeuvre that simply must sound translated—like Chinese poets when they are speaking of particular people and places and events— lines that are the result of a most peculiar mind, a tormented, driven mind struggling not to simply collapse.

Trakl once shared a patron's largesse with Rainier Maria Rilke, only to learn later that his benefactor was Ludwig Wittgenstein. Rilke came to love his poems, as did James Wright, who also translated some Trakl. Here are Wright's opening lines from "De Profundis":

It is a stubble field, where a black rain is falling.
It is a brown tree, that stands alone.
It is a hissing wind, that encircles empty houses.
How melancholy the evening is.

Beyond the village,
The soft orphan garners the sparse ears of corn.
Her eyes gaze, round and golden, in the twilight
And her womb awaits the heavenly bridegroom.

And what does Wright do with the "cold metal" image later? "Cold metal walks on my forehead." Of the more than half-dozen versions of Trakl on my shelf, the translations of James Wright, and now Daniel Simko, stand alone. Trakl had a vision and a world. These translations make that vision eloquently available.

Utilizing the talents of a rather large number of translators, Kimon Friar and Kostas Myrsiades have selected from fifty years of work to compile their huge anthology of poetry by Yannis Ritsos. This *Selected Poems* (BOA Editions, 1989) includes 444 poems gathered from 43 books, and includes 17 different translators. It is impossible to make an adequate assessment in a brief space, but I note with particular pleasure the presence of Emund Keeley whose translations of George Seferis and Yannis Ritsos have nourished and inspired my own work for years and whose smaller selected, *Exile and Return* (Ecco Press, 1985) is a major achievement not represented in this anthology; Athan Anagnostopoulos, translator of Seferis's *A Poet's Journal* for Harvard; Minas Savvas, whose translations of Ritsos's *Subterranean Horses* and *Chronicles of Exile* should have been far more widely read. And Kostas Myrsiades has translated *Scripture of the Blind,* a large collection of Ritsos, with Kimon Friar.

Yannis Ritsos defies categorization. He is alternately political, tender, angry, lyrical, polemical, dramatic, religious, anarchistic, rebellious, —and author of 117 books of poetry (as of last year)! There are long poems, classical poems including a retelling of the *Philoctetes,* epigrams, erotic poems including a long suite, "Carnal Word," written in three days during 1981. Perhaps our current national passion for the tidy little book containing tidy little poems make this huge gathering appear at first more than a little unwieldy. It is. So is Whitman. And, for that matter, Dickinson. Here's is Kimon Friar's translation of "The Relation of the Unrelated" in its entirety:

Why should we speak? —he said—What's the use of many explanations
when, as you are hurrying to arrive in time
for friends awaiting you to discuss a matter
of much importance, which has to do with you and many others,
you suddenly stop in the middle of the street to look

at that bird serenely walking on the asphalt,
with its head raised ecstatically, more informed than you,
with a bus ticket in its long beak?

The lines comes in a rush, very much like conversational Greek, so that one can easily imagine the face of a friend speaking confidentially in the light of a village taverna, the moonlight on plane trees and olive groves in the distance.

From Yitsos's 1988 volume, *Slowly, Very Slowly in the Night,* Kostas Myrsiades gives us "Same as Always":

Houses and trees are bare. Birds
don't know where to perch. All day long
pedlars pass us by. We know them.
Cheap fabrics, cheap jewelry.
In the evening they leave, their wares unsold. And yet,
outside the coastal road, after the lights are lit,
large packs of wild dogs
still fight over a single bone.

BOA has included an extensive chronological index of published and unpublished work, and two brilliant essays, one on the short poems and one on the long, by Kimon Friar and Kostas Myrsiades respectively.

Living in Greece for a while several years ago, one of my favorite pastimes was listening to arguments in the tavernas over whether Odysseas Elytis or Yannis Ritsos was "the poet of our time." Elytis had just received the Nobel Prize. It is, of course, a fruitless but stimulating argument, much like the way Asians enjoying quarreling over Tu Fu and Li Po. If the Nobel selection committee had any nerve, they'd give him the Nobel Prize he deserves but hasn't received only because of his affiliation with leftist politics over many years.

From Anna Akhmatova to Gioconda Belli, from Rosario Castellanos to Johannes Bobrowski, the poets of this century have sought a means to identify the redemptive experience, to name and thereby transcend evils which have intensified decade by decade, speeding our sense of time and increasing our sense of temporality and our sense of loss of control over events shaping our lives. In some ways, the love and tragedy of Akhmatova rhymes with that of each of the other poets mentioned here. The people we call "the oppressed" remain oppressed; the color of their skin, their religion, their politics, —

these may change. But the suffering does not change. And we who learn from poetry, we for whom poetry is a measure of our lives? Our craft has existed for thousands of years, and our communal vision is measured by what we have retrieved from the shards and fragments of our journeys.

Nowhere in contemporary poetry are these shards more hazardous than in the poetry of the exiled Chilean poet, Marjorie Agosin. Her poems, translated by Cola Franzen (White Pine Press, 1988), speak openly of torture and barbed wire and the disappeared, because, she says, "they all wake me up at night to ask me not to forget them." How easy it is for us to doze off in front of the evening's sit-com, forgetting that the torture chambers and the death camps were our own inventions, that, as Agosin says, "The most unbelievable part,/ they were people like us/ good manners/ well-educated and refined./ Versed in abstract sciences,/ always took a box for the symphony/ made regular trips to the dentist/ attended very nice prep schools/ some played golf . . ."

Cola Franzen's translations are sturdy, adequate, but the half-page Introduction by Robert Pring-Mill is little more than a large jacket blurb, providing none of the particulars of the poet's life. The bi-lingual text reads like reports from any poet's war-torn front, Tu Fu during the An Lu-shan Rebellion, or the horrors Akhmatova faced between world wars. Agosin exposes the raw nerves of contemporary history as it is endured by women under totalitarian regimes the world over. I hope many more translations of her work will become available, and that an adequate introduction to her life and poetry will accompany same.

These poets and translators return us to the real work of poetry as it reinforces our need to transcend literary fads and academic understanding, bringing us again into the "real world" which exists, always, just beyond the distractions we cling to so desperately in our hopeless effort to escape the consequences of all our lives.

A culture which rejects history—as we have rejected our own history of genocide in the 18th and 19th and 20th centuries, and as we have rejected our own genocide against the Germans at the conclusion of World War Two when hundreds of thousands of German soldiers and civilians starved to death in camps, and as we have rejected our own genocide against the Japanese with the bombing of Hiroshima and Nagasaki—a culture which rejects history rejects memory, and its muse, Mnemosyne. Seeking a "Final Solution" to the "Jewish question," the Nazis modeled their concentration camps on those invented by the United States government to deal with "the Indian question" a century before. This news of Nazi inspiration has yet to reach our common understanding. Each family has its Oedipus, its Achilles heel. And, as Winston Churchill warned, we return into the bowels of history to repeat yet again our own redundant misery.

A Fool's Paradise

Michael Cuddihy, *A Walled Garden,* Pittsburgh: Carnegie-Mellow University Press, 1989
Eleanor Wilner, *Sarah's Choice,* Chicago: U of Chicago Press, 1989
Michael Hogan, *Making Our Own Rules,* Greenfield, NY: Greenfield Review Press, 1989
June Jordan, *Naming Our Destiny,* New York: Thunder's Mouth Press, 1989
Mary Jo Salter, *Unfinished Painting,* New York: Knopf, 1989
Li-Young Lee, *Rose* and *The City in Which I Love You,* Brockport, NY: BOA Editions, 1989
Christopher Merrill, *Fevers & Tides,* Santa Fe: Teal Press, 1989

In the third book of *The Dunciad,* Pope has his Goddess of Dulness transport the King to her temple where she curtains him with "Vapours blue" and prepares him to listen to Oracles and talk with Gods:

> Hence the Fool's Paradise, the Statesman's Scheme,
> The air-built Castle, and the golden Dream,
> The Maid's romantic wish, the Chemist's flame,
> And Poet's vision of eternal Fame.

Pope's wit here is about as gentle, about as subtle, as it gets. He *likes* these people, not despite their folly, but perhaps because of it. They are a people who prefer surface to interior. But, perhaps because of their earnestness, he offers a wry view, saving his more caustic wit for others. He makes an almost parallel image in his *Essay of Man:*

> See the blind beggar dance, the cripple sing,
> The sot a hero, lunatic a king;
> The starving chemist in his golden views
> Supremely blest, the poet in his Muse.

For all its parallels, this quatrain is interesting for its contrasts. Its people are *doers,* not dreamers, they are people who have gone beyond the mere surface, beyond the superficial, into lunacy, dance, starvation, into the most meaningful visionary expressions of being. A late 20th century reading of

Pope's lines invites a comparison with the naked jig of Dr. Williams, alone in his room, his dance and his poem and his breath and heart all pounding out the same tune.

The poem begins and ends in the body. The poet is a midwife; the critic is a coroner. Seen from the outside, the poet is a daydreamer with visions of superlatives dancing gracefully through his or her otherwise empty noggin. Examined from the inside, the fully-fleshed dynamics of living language incorporating heartbeat and breath becomes the measure of the poem: the poem, in order to exist, must make human noises. If the poet is a midwife, the body of the poet becomes pregnant with meaning; the voice itself becomes the body of the poem as it is delivered.

Michael Cuddihy demonstrates this point another way in his poem "This Body" in *A Walled Garden* (Carnegie-Mellon U. Press, 1989):

Each time breath draws through me,
I know it's older than I am.
The haggard pine that watches by the door
Was here even before my older brothers.
It's a feeling I get when I pick up a stone
And look at its mottled skin, the grey
Sleeve of time.
This body that I use,
Rooted here, this spur of hillside, leaves shaking in the wind,
Was once as small as a stone
And lived inside a woman.
These words, even—
They've come such a long way to find me.
But the sleep that translates everything
Moves in place, unwearied, the whole weight of the ocean
That left us here, breathless.

His lines fall almost weightlessly upon the breath, pauses falling completely naturally despite his carefully orchestrated rhyme and slant-rhyme. Experienced strictly as spoken music, the poem's "meaning" cannot be subtracted from its noises, it cannot be set aside to be examined as though it were something else somehow contained within the poem, like rhyme or alliteration. As somebody-or-other put it, famously: "A poem does not mean, but be."

Cuddihy does nothing fancy. He's not interested in being cute or in writing punch-lines to please the crowd. *A Walled Garden* is exactly what its title implies: a carefully tended interiority, a small world. In "First Name," the speaker is smelling mushrooms and onions and garlic "drift slowly out of the kitchen/ To become beyond intention:

> nourishment
> For others. The bowl we use
> Is ourselves, things and people touching
> Inside, the slow flesh peeled, palpable.
> There at the stove, an angel of steam
> Whispers past your ear, wordless,
> That first name, the one
> We listen for as we fall into sleep."

This must once again be that "sleep that translates everything," that interior, almost unconsciousness where Psyche's underworld and Paradise intersect. The act of listening becomes the poem's sacrament. Cuddihy's poems reveal the magic of mundane experience brought into crisp focus. Most often, they articulate sacramental relationships as they, in turn, define us. His poems are a quiet music of natural speech, more influenced perhaps by John Logan's music than that of his contemporaries, and there are also resonances from later Yeats. Later in *A Walled Garden,* Cuddihy says,

> . . .
> We are one flesh rending itself in ignorance,
> Signed with the same dust.
> Feelings we do not recognize
> Wash over us, rising into the air,
> Then stare back from the streaked mirrors.
> Impossible, our bodies
> We will wear them until they wear us out.

The paradox of ignorance and wisdom, morality and immorality, the sacred and the profane—Cuddihy's themes are as old as the *Tao Te Ching* and the Greek Anthology, and he returns us to their earnest simplicity, to the music of our collective unconscious as it sleeps, almost beyond time. His rhymes are subtle, coming from the interior so as not to call undo attention.

If Cuddihy's poems reflect an almost classical austerity, Eleanor Wilner's exhibit a rich mythological tapestry held together by an equally functional spoken line. Her imaginative ancestry follows a visionary tradition leading back through Yeats to Blake and on into pre-literate shamanistic practices. Her research along these lines, *Gathering the Winds* (Johns Hopkins University Press, 1975), is a study of "visionary imagination and radical transformation of self and society," and tackles visionaries as diverse as early Hebrew mystics and Native Americans like Wovoka and Smohalla as well as Blake, Beddoes, Marx and Yeats. Musically and syntactically, Wilner orchestrates almost baroque complexities as she explores a life of the mind. Her *Sarah's Choice* (University of Chicago Press, 1989) opens with "Coda, Overture," a poem to remind us that we are under a condition of music and more:

> She stepped out of the framing circle of the dark.
> We thought, as she approached, to see her
> clearly, but her features only grew more indistinct
> as she drew nearer, like those of statues
> long submerged in water. We couldn't name her,
> she who can't be seen
>
> except in spaces between wars, brief intervals
>
> when history relents, reflection
> intervenes, returning home
> becomes the epic moment—not the everyday event
> postponed in bars; . . .

and the images at first leave one confused—where are we? Who is this woman who is like a statue from underwater? Are we in the presence of a returning Ulysses, this one female? Behind us, there are burning cities, a frozen chorus, a "colonnade/ of salt, pillars like the wife of Lot, . . ." Here is a shield with the face of Medusa, a Goya portrait, the "Cyclops/ cramming nations in his mouth—

> an emptiness that nothing can assuage
> creates its mirror image in
> the gaping mouth, unfinished cry
> as the head and the body are severed—the horror
> on the hero's shield, the sound
> of hoofs trampling in the wind."

We are in the presence of a seer. The vision is orchestrated to shake the sleeper awake. The "hero" is a hero precisely *because* the vanquished cry remains unfinished.

After I sent a friend a copy of *Sarah's Choice,* he wrote back, "Medea! Oedipus! Medusa! Creon! Zoroastrians!" and quoted a line from one of the poems therein: "Jocasta/ in her chamber hung herself for shame." Eleanor Wilner's poems reflect the flights of a richly literate mind; her poems are peopled by gods and goddesses and suffering mortals who inhabit their wide heavens and their abysmal hells just like in "the real world" we all share; it is to her credit that she is on familiar terms with each. Moreover, these poems, like those in her marvelous earlier volume, *Shekhinah,* are full of splendid images and startling revelations, all turning slowly, carefully, in the meditative mind. She also exhibits a splendid ear for modulations and slant-rhyme and repeated vowel sounds. My friend had quoted from "Classical Proportions of the Heart," a poem that begins:

> Everyone here knows how it ends, in the stone
> amphitheatre of the world, everyone
> knows the story—how Jocasta
> in her chamber hung herself for shame
> how Oedipus tore out his eyes and stalked
> his darkened halls crying
> *aaiieeaaiiee* woewoe is me woe
>
> These things everyone expects, shifting
> on the cold stone seats, the discomfort
> of our small, hard place in things
> relieved by this public show of agony
> how we love this last bit best, . . .

which returns us, of course, into our own uncomfortable bodies in Pope's fool's paradise. The surface is hard, uncomfortable, there in the amphitheatre, but if we're there to be *seen* . . . .

> We feel a little superior, our seats
> raised above the circle where the blinded
> lion paces out his grief, . . .

Later, the crowd gone, only a shepherd remains, "he who disobeyed a King," and who carries a lamb into the night.

> . . . There is little drama
> in this scene, but still its pathos has
> a symmetry, because the lamb's small heat
> up close exactly balances
> the distant icy stars
> and when it senses home, and bleats,
> its small cry weighs against
> the wail of fallen kings.
> There is, as well, the perfect closure
> as the shepherd's gate swings shut
> and a classical composure
> in the way he bears
> the burden of his heavy heart
> with ease.

It is almost criminal to truncate a poem like this. Still, something of her obvious skill remains evident: a narrative power, a power to evoke, the ironic humor in the lovely line "Its small cry weighs against/ the wail of fallen kings," and a very sophisticated ear. In the title poem, she retells the story of Sarah and Isaac; in "Postscript," she offers a poem-as-letter-as-lyric. I love Eleanor Wilner's poems, especially her longer ones. The "returning home" of which she often speaks is a return into the body, a return into one's private, most secret life, a life shared—if at all—only within the cradling of an intimate voice. The imagination is only an expression of the thusness of the body, to put it in Zen terms. There are no words without silence.

Silence is rarely used to better effect than in Michael Hogan's poems. His *Making Our Own Rules* draws from fifteen years of publishing, beginning with pamphlets and chapbooks from Unicorn Press, Gallimaufry, and Turkey Press. A "new and selected poems," the more I read *Making Our Own Rules,* the more I wish Hogan had compiled a collected poems. Many of my old favorites—"Visitation Rights" and "After Mowing a Field," and others—are missing. Still, 60 pages of the best of Michael Hogan is very good to have. Here is "Ask and Ye Shall Receive":

> October and the monsoons are over
> the Pantano again a whisper

and the winds careless in
the downtown Tucson nights.
Snake, coming far in two seasons
from the Rockies to sunwashed Sonora
to Pima blades and broken bottles,
body scab-covered and scarred,
face a plateful of mortal sins.
Snake looking for his new skins
wakes in the alcoholic recovery bed
sick, and not for days this time,
but painful weeks of blood clots
secondary infection, palsy and fever
a liver the texture of pigskin.

He'd been as good as a play
but now the lights are down
the janitor sweeping.
Pain leaves him lucid
long enough to scream "God damn me!"
and God does.

In recent years, much has been written and said about the poetry of bearing witness to this world, and much of it has been written and said by people who strike me as more voyeurs in a Fool's Paradise than true witnesses. To watch is not enough. To see is not enough. To record is not enough. But to observe and to see clearly with the same eyes one uses to see inside one's own true self makes all the difference. Not simply to witness, but to testify—the terrible responsibility of a poetry capable of changing one's life. That's asking a lot of a short lyric, but if Rilke could find just such an experience in a short poem prompted by looking at a bust of Apollo, we who in our national madness commit genocide cannot afford to do less.

Hogan's unflinching portrait of a man's encounter with lucidity brought on by undeniable pain leaves the poet *out,* altogether out of the picture. He's not asking to be seen as a poet witnessing the suffering of a man who thereby becomes emblematic of suffering humanity. Hogan gives us only a man, one particular man, in all his particular and untasteful pain. Snake's agony is self-inspired. Perhaps in our reading of the poem, we make of him an emblem, we translate his agony into a *representative* agony. He gives us only the man himself. But his portrait is not ruthless. It refuses to exploit the character.

Perhaps because "God" damns Snake at the end of the poem, we cannot. I, at least, cannot. We become desensitized as we walk past the homeless on our city streets, but they are there by the thousands, by the millions, many of them mentally disordered, sick, hopeless. Hogan offers no solution. He simply paints what he sees—the human agony of the world's waste. Like Wilner and Cuddihy, Hogan appears to come more from a Yeatsian lineage than from the Modernism of Eliot or Pound. He speaks in the vernacular, his cadence unrushed, and he speaks from direct personal experience, as in "Florence, Arizona," another poem not included in his selected poems:

> Our work today is common to deserts.
> The curled hide of our hands
> laying cement block for the wall
> is one with the dust of those
> whose days built pyramids.
>
> Nothing changes. The desert holds
> all history in its bone-rich sands.
> To the north the Colorado
> flows through rich green places.
>
> I brush the sand from my clothes
> and stand, brown, bare-chested in the sun.

This poem comes from the poet's prison work crew experience. Convict labor is slave labor. Hogan's picture illustrates exactly what we've learned since building the pyramids when its comes to convict labor. And yet his poem offers no rage, no bitterness, only the moment when he stands (silence) brown (silence) bare-chested in the sun. Those two heavy silences in the last line carry enormous implications. Hogan's poems are virtually free of the ego and fake emotion, the public posturing and self-regard, that infects so much recent poetry. For Hogan, as for the others mentioned above, to undertake the poem is to undertake the possibility of radical transformation. The humility and compassion of his poems warms me when others leave me chilled to the bone.

June Jordan's *Naming Our Destiny* (Thunder's Mouth Press, 1989) spans more than 30 years of writing and includes some 50 new poems. She is a wise, passionate, compelling poet at work in the real business of poetry—the business of transformation, the business of naming names. In "Poem from

Taped Testimony in the Tradition of Bernard Goetz," she comes to meet the poem head-on:

I.

This was not I repeat this was not a racial incident.

II.

I was sitting down and it happened to me
before that I was sitting down or I was standing
up and I was by myself because of course
a lot of the time I am by myself because
I am not married or famous or super-im-
portant enough to have shadows or body-
guards so I was alone as it happens when
I was sitting down or let me retract that
I wasn't with anybody elsee regardless
who else was there
and I know I am not blind I could see
other people around me but the point
is that I wasn't with them I wasn't
with anybody else and like I said
it happened before two three
times it had happened that I was
sitting down or I was standing up
when one of them or one time it was
more than one I think it was two
of them anyway they just jumped
me I mean they jumped on me like
I was chump change and I know
I am not blind I could see they were
laughing at me they thought it was
funny to make me feel humiliated or I don't
know ugly or weak or really too small
to fight back so they were just laughing
at me in a way I mean you didn't
necessarily see some kind of smile
or hear them laughing but I could feel
it like I could feel this fear take
me over when I would have to come into a room

full of them and I would be by myself
and they would just look at you know what
I mean you can't know what I mean
you're not Black . . .

This poem, which runs several pages, is a tour de force underscoring the power of the idiomatic, the power of the colloquial, showing the reader just what might pass through a mind like that of a Bernard Goetz, but in a Black woman's experience. There are a number of truly extraordinary poets writing in colloquial speech now: Hayden Carruth, Etheridge Knight, and David Lee have been pushing at those boundaries in narrative poems for many years; Lucille Clifton and Judy Grahn write a spoken voice most forcefully. June Jordan is in the forefront, but not limited by, that oral tradition.

Too much poetry of recent years has been bogged down in reflective, reflexive meditations of isolated dreamers in air-built castles. Elsewhere, the world over, governments are falling and democracy growing *because of the work of writers.* Jordan's poetry is deeply engaged, as she is, in daily history. She reminds poets of their authentic duties. In her hands, history is not a passive entertainment, but the immediate product of our daily lives. It is consequential.

In a response to Yeats's "Leda and the Swan," she offers "The Female and the Silence of a Man," and her Leda, with lacerated breast and clawed heart,

sinks into a meadow pond of lilies and a swan.
She floats above an afternoon of music from the trees.
She vanishes like blood that people walk upon.
She reappears: A mad *bitch* dog that reason cannot seize:
A fever withering the river and the crops:
A lovely girl protected by her cruel/incandescent energies.

The poem is lovely in its formal dress, and as "true" and as powerful as any written by those who profess adherence to a "formalist" credo.

Jordan's passionate commitment to a search for justice and for compassion is everywhere evident within these pages, never more powerfully than in the closing autobiographical poem, "War and Memory," which runs nearly 8 pages. Near the end, she declares,

I fell in love
I fell in love with Black men White
men Black

women White women
and I
dared myself to say The Palestinians
and I
worried about unilateral words like Lesbian or Nationalist/ . . .

and I wrote everything I knew how to write against apartheid
and I
thought I was a warrior growing up
and I
buried my father with all of the ceremony all of the music I could piece together
and I
lust for justice
and I
make that quest arthritic/pigeon-toed/however
and I
invent the mother of the courage I require not to quit.

This poem makes use of what in others is so often a weakness—from the first person pronoun to the choice of "telling" over showing—but finding a music to carry the poem song-like on the expansive voice of its speaker, she gets away with it, makes it work. The poem is packed with cultural icons and historical snippets like Afros, the Viet Nam War, the "War on Poverty" that we must also have lost, Victory Rations, and more. The poet remembers calling the police to ask them "to beat my father up for beating me/ so bad/ but no one listened . . ." Hers is a poetry that thrives on memory and commitment and an oral tradition with roots in "giving testimony" whether in affirmation or before the Inquisition.

June Jordan returns us to the real work of poetry. She refuses to indulge in the easy equation. Hers is poetry of passionate courage and enormous compassion, a poetry that speaks on behalf of the world's oppressed and dispossessed and disenfranchised, and does so with great clarity without the pandering to propaganda and cheap emotional tactics that too often mar the work of lesser poets. I might contrast her political poems with a poem from the much-lauded Mary Jo Salter, whose collection, *Unfinished Painting* (Knopf, 1989), was the Lamont Poetry Selection. If June Jordan is engaged, Salter is aloof; if Jordan is passionate, Salter is cool; if Jordan is raw and gutsy, Salter is merely cunning. In a poem called "Chernobyl," she manages to write about a major catastrophe while remaining perfectly cutesy-pooh-smug:

Once upon a time,
the word alone was scary.
Now, quainter than this rhyme,
it's the headline of a story

long yellowed in the news.
The streets were hosed in Kiev,
and Poles took more shampoos.
The evacuees were brave.

Under the gay striped awning
of Europe's common market,
half-empty booths were yawning
at the small change in the pocket.

As far away as Rome,
unseen through weeks of sun,
the cloud kept children home.
Milk gurgled down the drain.

In Wales, spring lambs were painted
blue, not to be eaten
till next spring when . . . Still tainted,
they'd grown into blue mutton.

Then we had had enough.
Fear's harder to retain
than hope or indifference. Safe
and innocent, the rain

fell all night as we slept,
and the story at last was dead—
all traces of it swept
under the earth's green bed.

There is nothing to recommend this poem. From its entirely predictable
meter and rhyme down to its last clank and groan, this poem embodies an
appalling insincerity, the rigidity of the form reflecting a smug state of mind.
The poem actually trivializes Chernobyl. Like June Jordan, Salter has chosen

a "telling" rather than a "showing" approach, but there all similarities end. When she says, "Fear's harder to retain/ than hope or indifference," I know that I am listening to someone who has lived a very sheltered, a very protected life. Unfortunately, I do believe that—for her, at least—fear *is* harder to retain than indifference. She inhabits a world where fear is something momentary or something that happens to someone else. "The Poles took more shampoos" indeed! And wasn't Auschwitz a kick in the pants!

The poet, I suspect, learned nothing from the making of this poem. Her strategies reduce poetry to mere craft displaying wit or intellect. On the jacket copy, Joseph Brodsky declares, "Mary Jo Salter's work embodies the marriage of superb craftsmanship to the tragic sense of reality, which is the formula of true poetry." I was not aware that poetry came in a formula, nor can I attest to any great tragic sensibility at work in these poems. Technical skill, yes; necessity and conviction are another matter.

At rock bottom, I simply don't believe Salter. Hers is a poetry of surface. Confusing artifice with art, she settles for writing verse. Her poems are "schemes" not vastly dissimilar to those of Pope's Statesmen, hers a fool's paradise where no confrontations rattle our comfortable nests and the world, despite its disasters, remains tidy. I cannot fathom the thinking of the Academy of American Poets when they continue to take this kind of stuff seriously and praise it to the heavens and load it with laurels.

Li-Young Lee provides another antidote. The poems gathered in his *Rose* (BOA Editions), are autobiographical, thoughtful, and wonderfully engaging. His father is a dominating figure, and Lee struggles with his memory of that strict, almost forbidding figure of a minister. In a beautiful poem, "Eating Alone," the poet has pulled the last of his onions from his garden, washed them, and remembers his father and a particular silence:

> It was my father I saw this morning
> waving to me from the trees. I almost
> called to him, until I came close enough
> to see the shovel, leaning where I had
> left it, in the flickering, deep green shade.
>
> White rice steaming, almost done. Sweet green peas
> fried in onions. Shrimp braised in sesame
> oil and garlic. And my own loneliness.
> What more could I, a young man, want.

James Wright struggled for years before he learned to get his poems this direct, this plain, and this true. It's not merely the poignancy of Lee's poem, but what lies behind it: to be young in America is to fear loneliness above all else. Lee not only embraces his loneliness, he welcomes it, and, with it, that hard-earned wisdom most poets gain, if at all, only in middle or late career.

Born in Jakarta, Indonesia in 1957, Lee fled with his family to escape Sukarno's prisons, living in Hong Kong, Macau and Japan before coming to the U.S. To his credit, his worldliness is far more intimately *felt* than advertised in his poems, although they do celebrate his ethnicity, often using anecdotes to illustrate family relationships. His maturity as a poet is simply astonishing. In "Mnemonic," he offers a kind of *ars poetica*:

> I was tired. So I lay down.
> My lids grew heavy. So I slept.
> Slender memory, stay with me.
>
> I was cold once. So my father took off his blue sweater.
> He wrapped me in it, and I never gave it back.
> It is the sweater he wore to America,
> this one, which I've grown into, whose sleeves are too long,
> whose elbows have thinned, who outlives its rightful owner.
> Flamboyant blue in daylight, poor blue by daylight,
> it is black in the folds.
>
> A serious man who devised complex systems of numbers and rhymes
> to aid him in remembering, a man who forgot nothing, my father
> would be ashamed of me.
> Not because I'm forgetful,
> but because there is no order
> to my memory, a heap
> of details, uncatalogued, illogical.
> For instance:
> God was lonely. So he made me.
> My father loved me. So he spanked me.
> It hurt him to do so. He did it daily.
>
> The earth is flat. Those who fall off don't return.
> The earth is round. All things reveal themselves to men only gradually.

I won't last. Memory is sweet.
Even when it's painful, memory is sweet.

Once, I was cold. So my father took off his blue sweater.

If Salter's is the voice of the status quo, if she is the embodiment of complacency, Lee goes quietly, methodically, about the business of stripping away layers of the psyche, digging into the deepest interior to reveal his soul. In his familial poems, Lee risks sounding like all the many thousands of MFA poets remembering their own vanished youth; but he doesn't. His humility is rare and refreshing. His voice and his people are particular, each unique, and he has none of the complacency—which is, after all, a form of cowardice—of so many of his contemporaries. His poems are made *from* his life *with* his life, his poems are earned. He dares to be simple. And he is surely among the finest young poets alive. Lee's second book, *The City in Which I love You* (BOA Editions, 1990) is the most recent Lamont Selection, and as such redeems the Academy of American Poets. If his more recent poems retain a kind of raggedness, it is a lack of polish well-suited to rough-hewn craft. Perhaps his recent popular success has distracted him, but *The City in Which I Love You* also seems more wordy, more casual than the poems of *Rose. City* is, nonetheless, a powerful and engaging book.

Assuming that the best way to make a poem is to place perfect words in perfect order, the next question is, "Shall we place more importance on getting at some greater truth or upon making a beautiful object?" This is the basic argument between open and closed forms. The predetermined form sometimes, perhaps even often, forces the poet to see things from a fresh perspective; but it also presents times when certain kinds of truths become modified in order to accommodate a syllabic count or a rhyme. The closed form works wonderfully within a narrative frame, or in traditional song. The open form, revealed only as the poem reveals itself, cannot be separated from the poem, and admits a grander variety and places greater emphasis upon a poet's vision. Open forms also tend to conceal the weaknesses of those who remain relatively unskilled either in versification or in the use of poetic energy. What makes "regular meter" interesting is the way our language bucks *against* regularity; nothing would be duller than a perfect iambic. Our best poets draw strengths from both traditions.

In *Fevers & Tides*, Christopher Merrill, another young poet, demonstrates his lessons well. He tends to like a formal stanza, and in poems like "Old Wives' Tales" each becomes almost a poem unto itself. Many of his lines measure a regular meter. His poems join a light surrealist touch with a deep feel for the natural world. His literary ancestry would be more along the lines of André Breton and Wallace Stevens than the Williams school of Modernism. Sometimes he sounds almost like a young Robert Frost. The opening poem of *Fevers & Tides,* "Words" is composed in a loose pentameter.

> Paint blistering on the ceiling of the den:
> Excuses gathered speed, helping no one.
> So I walked up the same mountain as before.
>
> Passed the same barbed wire, broken glass, tire tracks.
> Then vetch, and penstemon, and the rusted water
> Pipe coursing down through stands of scrub oak, aspen.
>
> In the dry creek: a rattlesnake, coiling,
> Guarding the rocks and ripped oak roots, head swaying,
> Shaking its only bead, like a fanatic . . .
>
> I know the little ones can kill: their venom's
> Pure as the fury of the lovers' first
> Attempts at cruelty, before they learn
>
> What words or gestures will end an argument
> Without destroying everything again
> And yet I stood there for a while, listening
>
> To a woodpecker addling an aspen,
> A mule deer thrashing in the underbrush,
> And near the city thunder rumbling . . .
>
> Some rattlers grow to be as long as humans.
> This one I sidestepped in the end, and headed
> Up the steep part of the trail, holding my tongue.

In the first line of the final stanza, there are two essentially dead words: *to,* and *be.* Rattlers grow as long as humans. But in order to maintain his regular rhythm, he needs those extra syllables. In the last line of the penultimate stanza, the nine syllables count to ten when the ellipses is included. Working with ten or eleven syllables to the line, Merrill's cadence is very natural. If he tends toward the meditative, he at least carries within his poems a sense of the embodiment of history and the power of *things*. And he won't be tied down by Dr. Williams's dictum, "No ideas but in things." He looks for ways to represent the imagination at work or play, often with surprising results. He asks, "What shall we call that constellation of spy/ Satellites hanging from Orion's Belt,/ Like keys?"

Merrill establishes and maintains a thoughtful earnestness throughout *Fevers & Tides* as he did in his first volume, *Workbook*. He manages to be delicate without being showy or precious. His poems bear the handprint of a journeyman.

At any point in history, most of the poetry being written is vapid. But there is also, constantly throughout history, poetry being written by relatively unknown writers who care a great deal more for their literary undertakings than for their literary reputations. For some, the poetry is evidence of the vision quest. Classical Chinese poetry is full of scornful lines about poets dreaming of eternal fame. Cuddihy, Wilner, Hogan, Jordan, Lee, and Merrill—one could hardly find a more diverse anthology; yet each rewards the reader with intelligence and warmth and with a wide sweep of understanding.

At no time in its history has North American poetry offered more. There are dozens, perhaps even hundreds, of the finest poets ever to write in the American tongue alive today. Poetry in the late 20th century is no fool's paradise, not when it has demonstrated once again its ability to transform the world.

Writing Re: Writing

In his Introduction to *The Wedge* in 1944, William Carlos Williams began a major redefinition of poetry, a definition that includes more than it excludes, one that *projects* a totality of experience within a field of action or energy. "The war is the first and only thing in the world today," Williams said. "The arts generally are not, nor is this writing a diversion from that for relief, a turning away. It *is* (author's emphasis) the war or part of it, merely a different sector of the field." And, a little later, "When a man makes a poem, makes it, mind you, he takes words as he finds them interrelated about him and composes them—without distortion which would mar their exact significances—into an intense expression of his perceptions and ardors that they may constitute a revelation in the speech he uses. It isn't what he *says* that counts as a work of art, it's what he makes, with such intensity of perception that it lives with an intrinsic movement of its own to verify its authenticity. . . . There is no poetry of distinction without formal invention, for it is in the intimate form that works of art achieve their exact meaning, in which they most resemble the machine, to give language its highest dignity, its illumination in the environment to which it is native. Such war, as the arts live and breathe by, is continuous."

Several years later (1951) in his *Autobiography,* Williams goes one step further, including as a chapter a chunk of Charles Olson's 1950 essay, "Projective Verse," with illustrative comments by Williams himself centering on the necessity of working with "essentials" when it comes to composition. "Nothing," Williams says, "can grow unless it taps into the soil."

Poets have been articulating "apologies" for and techniques and metaphysics of poesis for as long as there have been poets. But I daresay William Carlos Williams, for all his essays and articles on poetry, remains a fairly misunderstood or taken-for-granted poet and theorist.

T. S. Eliot, whose poetics stood a polar 180 degrees from Williams, became an institution within academia with essays like "Tradition and the Individual Talent," an eminently "teachable" essay because of its abundance of opportunities for further explication and comment. Williams remained all the while a lonely searcher for an *ars poetica* rooted in purely American idiom, a poet indeed without a large audience until the 1950s, by which time Eliot's "career in letters" had long since ended.

When New Directions published *The Collected Poems of William Carlos Williams* in a two-volume definitive edition annotated and edited by Christopher MacGowen in 1986 and 1988 respectively, almost no one took note of the various translations from Spanish and (in collaboration with David Raphael Wang) classical Chinese late in Williams's life; almost no one took note of Williams's variations on Sappho. And despite the fact that *most* of his last poems were written in fairly conventional lines rather than in the triads so many readers nowadays assume to be Williams's greatest contribution to American poetry, most of us continue to this day to categorize Williams wrongly, simplistically, continuing to misunderstand his decades-long struggle to re-invent an articulated line. We tend to lump together the "Pound-Williams" line of American poets as though it were a self-evident, self-contained movement, as though David Ignatow's deep critical appreciation of Williams could be juxtaposed with that of Allen Ginsberg, Robert Creeley, Marvin Bell, or Denise Levertov, all arriving at the same fundamental conclusion.

Two decades after Olson's "Projective Verse," two decades after publication of Williams's *Autobiography,* Denise Levertov began one of her major essays, "On the Function of the Line" (*Light Up the Cave*, New Directions, 1981), with the following observation: "Not only hapless adolescents, but many gifted and justly esteemed poets writing in contemporary nonmetrical forms, have only the vaguest concept, and the most haphazard use, of the line. Yet there is at our disposal no tool of the poetic craft more important, none that yields more subtle and precise effects, than the linebreak if it is properly understood."

And now, decades after Levertov's essay, the same problem remains. The sloppy, the ill-considered, the thoughtless, the vaguely formal, the end-stopped or the run-on or the indeterminate line tends to be the natural order when one peruses the many quarterlies and journals.

Levertov begins with a fundamental understanding of the *musical* structure of formal, metrical verse: "A sonnet may end with a question; but its essential, underlying structure arrives at *resolution* [author's emphasis]. 'Open forms' do not necessarily terminate inconclusively, but their degree of conclusion is—structurally, and thereby expressively—less pronounced, and partakes of the open quality of the whole." It was this property exactly—having to do with essential musical structures—that Williams began to articulate in his Introduction to *The Wedge* and further refined in his *Autobiography.*

"Open" forms locate a poesis in which the poem, despite being a made thing, tends to eschew formal "closure" in favor of identifying an *instance* of opening—so that the poem "opens out" into experience itself rather than merely referring to such. Charles Olson's "The Kingfishers" begins his volume *The Distance* with, "What does not change / is the will to change," and concludes, seven pages later:

> I pose you your question:
> shall you uncover honey / where maggots are?
> I hunt among stones.

Olson sought a way to heal "the impossible distances" through "transporting poems and inscriptions" from Mayan and Sumerian cultures, and his correspondence with Robert Creeley, now published by Black Sparrow Press, traces this development.

Introducing Olson's *Causal Mythology,* Robert Duncan says, "Some things in poetry are matters of appreciation; literary values or social values or aesthetic values that do not vitally concern me. And some things are matters of taste, of my liking or not liking them in part or in total. These have no solid ground in the truth of things for me. . . ." And then he quotes Shelley: "One great poet is a masterpiece of nature which another not only ought to study but must study." Early in that lecture, Olson observes: "One of the reasons why I'm trying to even beat the old dead word 'mythology' into meaning is that I think it *holds more of a poet's experience* than any meaning the word 'mysticism' holds. The principle would seem to be that the only interest of a spiritual exercise is production."

If our understanding of Williams suffers as a result of sloppy and/or lazy scholarship, we pass on that fundamental reductive "appreciation" through the use of textbooks (like the Norton anthologies) which reflect narrow, highly arbitrary and uninformed opinions formulated not by leading poets (practitioners) but by scholar-professors who specialize in this poet or that— at the expense of omnibus surveying, and at the expense of first-hand authentic experience in composition. The brief, the simple, and the "explainable" are preferred to the long, the dense, or that which defies explanation. I have no anthology on my shelf in which I can find a complete "Asphodel, That Greeny Flower," for instance.

Nonetheless, we have a large and growing body of writing re: writing written by poets, much of it engaging, much of it luminous and articulate, some of it merely contentious, some pretentious and pernicious. But nowhere in all this recent prose on poetry is William Carlos Williams more victimized by reductive thinking than in Robert Bly's attack in "A Wrong Turning in American Poetry," an essay gathered in his recent *American Poetry: Wildness and Domesticity* (Harper & Row, 1990). Bly quotes the endlessly quoted "No ideas but in things!" and observes, "His poems show great emotional life mingled with the drive of the intelligence to deal with outward things— but no inward life, if by inward life we mean an interest in spiritual as well as psychological intensity. Williams was a noble man, of all poets in his generation the warmest and most human. Still, his ideas contained something destructive: there is in them a drive toward the extinction of personality. Williams's 'No ideas but in things!' is a crippling program. Besides the ideas in things there are ideas in images and in feelings. . . . Williams asked poetry to confine itself to wheelbarrows, bottle caps, weeds—with the artist 'limited to the range of his contact with the objective world.' Keeping close to the surface becomes an obsession."

"No inward life"? No interest in spiritual intensity?

Bly's essay is dated 1963, one year after publication of *Pictures from Breughel,* a book that includes the 1954 "The Desert Music" in which Williams says:

> Only the poem.
> Only the counted poem, to an exact measure:
> to imitate, not to copy nature, not
> to copy nature
> NOT, prostrate, to copy nature
> but a dance! to dance
> two and two *within* him—
> sequestered there asleep,
> right end up!
> A music
> supersedes his composure, hallooing to us
> across a great distance . .
> wakens the dance
> who blows upon his benumbed fingers!
>
> Only the poem
> only the made poem, to get said what must
> be said, *not to copy nature,* sticks
> in our throats .

[my emphasis] "The Desert Music," written following a devastating stroke, is an attempt by Williams to regain his imaginative powers, a long descent into the core of his own being. "What," he asks, "in the form of an old whore in / a cheap Mexican joint in Juarez, her bare / can waggling crazily can be / so refreshing to me, raise to my ear / so sweet a tune, built of such slime?" The poet sits in passive observation while seven guests are seated at his table, including a couple of drunken cowboys. One of the dinner guests will ask, "So this is William / Carlos Williams, the poet." And the inevitable question arises: "Why / does one want to write a poem? / Because it's there to be written. / Oh. A matter of inspiration then?/ Of necessity." Later, walking back over the bridge leading into the U.S., Williams continues to reflect on his curt replies, only the music itself still engaging him, until he declares, "I *am* a poet! I / am. I am. I am a poet, I reaffirmed, ashamed . . ." And the linebreaks *are* the "meaning" as much as the words themselves. Segregating the "parts" of a poem is a little like segregating the parts of an engine: pull out the pistons and they are still pistons, but the engine doesn't run. Like an engine, the whole poem measures time and issues an energy, a force.

Pictures from Breughel closes on "Asphodel, That Greeny Flower," certainly one of the great spiritual poems of the century. Bly, with a pre-determined program of his own, takes a line Williams wrote 50 years earlier, leaves all context behind, and deliberately misinterprets, seeking a straw man to belittle in order to assert his own ego. Williams would be the last poet to ascribe to the demolition of the personality; but he was not, unlike his exasperating friend Ezra Pound, entirely ego-bound. Williams would, Zen-like, be free of ego in order to arrive at a truer personality entirely his own. The "things" Williams spoke of were the real things of the real world, the *stuff* of late 20th century American poetry *and experience*—wheelbarrows and broken bottles—just as Dante insisted upon a living vernacular tongue. Williams was as "modern" as the ancient Greek poets from whom he learned the nuts and bolts of craft. Bly's *reductio ad absurdum* misses the whole point.

American Poetry collects Bly's various reviews and essays from his magazine, *Fifties,* et cetera, and concludes with an interview in which Bly, hindsight perfectly focused, includes Williams among the very few "knots of wild energy" from the 1950s. While *American Poetry* is full of good, interesting, and useful ways of thinking about poetry, Bly's habit of making a personal attack his *modus operandi* grows tedious and irritating. He says Denise Levertov's poems "have no ideas in them," only to proceed by quoting any number of poems that close with the very opening of enormous ideas; Bly then goes on to praise her music and the perfection of the sound of her own distinct voice. Elsewhere, he quotes "two gruesome lines" from Levertov's "Matins":

> The authentic! I said
> rising from the toilet seat.

"There is a tone of triumph about the lines," Bly says, "as if she were Maria Callas singing *Aida.*" Bly then mocks her by quoting a parody written by Felix Pollak, and *then* proceeds to say, "No one should mock the seriousness of her search for the authentic, nor the fact that looking for it immediately around you is a more fertile mental effort than looking for it in sunsets or Platonic ideas." [No ideas but in things?] "Still, there is a ponderous solemnity about it all, an utter lack of humor about herself," Bly concludes. A solemn lack of humor? Ponderous? If I were Robert Bly, I'd accuse Robert Bly of being humorlessly anal retentive. Levertov's couplet *is* humorous, *is* profound, is in fact a perfection of the idea of no ideas but in things. It is the "field of action." *Flush! Gurgle!* Levertov's couplet is a perfect articulation of Zen. It *is* Maria Callas singing *Aida.*

In Bly's estimation, "Robert Lowell's Bankruptcy" lies at the heart of *For the Union Dead.* "Because the ideas behind the book are decrepit, Lowell has no choice but to glue the poems together with pointless excitement. The persistence of bodiless excitement derives from a second bankrupt tradition, which is centered on the notion that an artist must never be calm, but must be *extreme* [author's emphasis] at all costs." This bourgeois notion, Bly says, comes from both right-wing and left-wing sources, "Tate and the *Partisan Review.* . . Lowell has always had a poor grasp of the inner unity of a poem. In *Imitations* he often inserted violent images into quiet, meditative poems— his translations of Montale, for example— realizing that the sensational images had destroyed the inner balance of the poems. In *For the Union Dead* he does the same thing to his own poems."

In "Where Have All the Critics Gone," Bly says, "When we read the magazines, we *feel* [author's emphasis] there is little criticism around. . . Reviews appear, but with not much energy. . . fewer critics look dispassionately at the whole spectrum. *APR* . . . does not cover the spectrum. Instead of running reviews that might cause dissension, *APR* prints a twenty-page article simply patting the feathers of some established poet, articles so boring that even graduate students can't read them without weeping." Bly includes *The New York Times, The Nation,* and *The New Republic* on his list of boring offenders. It *is* a problem that merits serious attention. He offers a useful, practical suggestion: "that every person publishing poetry or fiction in this country take a vow to review two books every six months." But does his habitual use of insulting language aid his case? Sometimes Bly, in all his passionate intensity, is his own worst enemy.

In "James Dickey: Imaginative Power and Imaginative Collapse," Bly uses Dickey's "Slave Quarters" from *Buckdancer's Choice* to illustrate a "paralytic imagination," one dominated by racist attitudes. From the same book, he examines "Firebombing" and concludes that the author uses "everything, dogs, cats, cows, people," as mere "objects to use power on," and continues with "The Fiend," declaring Dickey guilty of "pointless violence." It is a passionate and articulate reading.

Passion is—of itself—neither honorable nor dishonorable; however when pugnaciousness and personal nastiness intrude into one's critical apparatus, this reader's "appreciation" is frustrated, even when the core ideas hold significant appeal. Robert Bly is by turns rude, wise, shrewd, blind, infuriating, insightful, and always passionate. All in all, much of this book falls somewhere between literary criticism and instant pathography. Bly rarely bothers to fully illustrate his contentions. But he is challenging, his own ideas often deserving of a more thoughtful sounding out than he himself appears willing to give them.

His more recent essays are more carefully presented and provocative in the best sense (is Robert Bly risking *maturity*?), and his appreciations of Etheridge Knight, John Logan, Thomas McGrath, and others are perhaps reward enough in themselves. It is curious to note that this spokesman on behalf of "The Great Mother" has almost nothing to say about recent poetry written by women. Aside from a few allusions to Marianne Moore, Levertov seems to be the one women poet he's read, and even in this his reading is sloppy and ungrateful.

Sherman Paul is among the most knowledgeable and articulate scholar-critics following the "Pound-Williams-Olson line" and his 1963 "biography of a poem" ("Desert Music"), *The Music of Survival* (University of Illinois Press, 1968), is a major contribution to Williams studies. His new collection of essays, *Hewing to Experience* (University of Iowa Press, 1989), is another grand contribution to the field. Paul remarks in his introduction that he "entered the conversation" in the study of New Criticism with the first edition of *Understanding Poetry,* an enormously influential work Paul sees in retrospect as "a road no longer taken."

Paul describes his own book quite clearly in his introduction: "The first section is prefatorial and sets out the contexts of poetry and the insistences (not themes, because they emerged in encounter) that I discuss: 'open' as against the judgmental practice of criticism, the crisis of criticism at the present time, the poetics of 'projective verse,' the ideogram and the serial poem, poetry and old age, ethnopoetics, the gift exchange of the imagination, canon-making, and nature poetry. Rereading this section now, the essays and reviews seem to me to belong to a single discussion in which criticism is (re)aligned with the 'American' tradition that runs from Emerson and Whitman to Williams and Olson. This tradition may be said to be 'American' because it accords primacy to experience, the 'original relation' that Emerson called for in *Nature* and the 'nakedness' that Olson called for in *The Maximus Poems.*"

"Projective Verse" was largely a response to New Criticism and its fundamental devotion to, as Robert Duncan remarked, "devices and ornament, taste, reason, rationality, rule, . . . and rule must be absolute." Paul reminds us that Olson described "projective" as a kind of answering music [not unlike that advocated by Lu Chi in his early 4th century *Art of Writing*] calling "attention to the *self-action* involved in open poetry—the energy, the speech-force, that enables it, and also the stance, since, by way of the allusion to Keats' criticism of the 'Egotistical Sublime,' it speaks for 'negative capability,' the projection of self outward to things that is the condition of being open to them, openness itself the condition insisted on as privilege by D. H. Lawrence. Open poetry requires that risk, the self-action by which one moves oneself, 'puts himself in the open.'"

In an assessment of Robert von Hallberg's *American Poetry and Culture 1945-1980,* Paul points out that von Hallberg "omits the very things literary history should remark: this 'poetry of changes' (the phrase is Jerome Rothenberg's) and a poetic task involving the 'will to change' (the phrase is Olson's) that made the work of poetry both cultural and political in significance. The task of poetry in these and subsequent years had been, and continues to be, to open the openable and encourage the 'symposium of the whole' (the phrase is Duncan's)—not to encourage consensus but all the voices excluded by it. This inclusivity characterizes the poetry of the last forty years; this *panharmonicon,* which Emerson said abrogated 'stiff conventions' and, admitting everything, abandoned the 'tame' [see Robert Bly on the "domestic"], the 'ineffectual,' and the 'decorous.' It is simply not true," Paul observes, "that 'beginning in 1960 the poetic avant-garde has been drawn into the mainstream of American literary life.' Nor is it true that 'civic virtues are not the responsibility of the avant-garde,' for what is striking is the extent to which this avant-garde demonstrates, if not 'civic virtues,' a more primary concern for the 'great household' (Duncan's phrase) and for the *polis* (Olson's as well as Hannah Arendt's term)—in sum, a concern for what Olson spoke of as 'the initiation of another kind of nation.'"

In one of his most stimulating pieces, Paul addresses M. L. Rosenthal's essay on "Problems of Robert Creeley," insisting upon Rosenthal's inability to deal directly with Creeley's "nakedness" which reminds us of the body, "and the physical aspect of his poetry." Paul quotes Creeley's remark that "nakedness" means to stand "manifestly in one's own condition, in that necessary *freshness*, however exposed, because all things are particular and reality itself is the specific content of an instant's possibility." Paul closes his argument noting Creeley's tendency to recognize the very act of writing as a declaration of a love that may win "forgiveness," seeing in Creeley an attitude similar to the Williams of "Asphodel." Rosenthal, author of *The Modern Poets* (Oxford, 1960), *Poetry and the Common Life* (Schocken, 1983), and other books, and editor of selected editions of Yeats and Williams, is not treated as a straw man in Paul's essay, but rather provides an opportunity to explore an alternate reading.

Paul is especially illuminating in his remarks on H.D., Williams, Creeley, the Creeley/Olson correspondence, and, surprisingly, on Gary Snyder and Barry Lopez. He takes a much longer, broader view than Robert Bly, his prose is far more fully developed, more clearly articulated, as passionately *felt*, and he will probably sell—at best—one tenth the number of copies. It's unfortunate, because Sherman Paul is a brilliant critic with an impressive body of work including *Hart's Bridge, Olson's Push, The Lost America of Love*, and *In Search of the Primitive*. He merits, as much any any critic now writing, an audience of poets. He is worth serious study, and worth quarreling with.

A Government of the Tongue (Farrar, Straus and Giroux, 1989) collects selected prose by Seamus Heaney written since *Preoccupations* (1980). Heaney brings up the subject of another kind of projection in a wonderful essay, "The Impact of Translation," where he says, "In the case of heroes, it is not so much their procedures on the page which are influential as the composite image which has been projected of their conduct. That image, congruent with the reality, features a poet tested by dangerous times. What is demanded is not any great public act of confrontation or submission, but rather a certain self-censorship, an agreement to forge, in the bad sense, the uncreated conscience of a race. Their resistance to this pressure is not initially or intentionally political, but there is of course a spin-off, a ripple effect, to their deviant artistic conduct. It is the refusal by this rearguard minority which exposes to the majority the abjectness of their collapse, as they flee for security into whatever self-deceptions the party line requires of them. And it is because they effect this exposure that the poets become endangered: people are never grateful for being reminded of their moral cowardice."

Heaney examines "the professionalized literary milieu" and finds "the poet in the United States, for example, is aware that the machine of reputation-making and book distribution, whether it elevates or ignores him or her, is indifferent to the moral and ethical force of the poetry being distributed. A grant-aided pluralism of fashions and schools, a highly amplified language of praise which becomes the language of promotion and marketing—all this which produces from among the most gifted a procession of ironists and dandies and reflexive talents, produces also a subliminal awareness of the alternative conditions and an anxious over-the-shoulder glance toward them."

Translated poetry, Heaney asserts, brings news that stays news from "a road not taken in poetry in English in this century, a road traveled once by the young Auden and the middle-aged Muir. Further, because we have not lived the tragic scenario which such imaginations presented to us as the life appropriate to our times, our capacity to make a complete act of faith in our vernacular poetic possessions has been undermined. Consequently, we are all the more susceptible to translations which arrive like messages from those holding their own much, much farther down the road not taken by us—because, happily, it was a road not open to us. When we read translations of the poets of Russia and Eastern Europe, 'We are on the very edge . . . And still the interrogation is going on.'"

As readers, we have tended to see in translated poetry a music of highly intensified exigencies, an experiential vocabulary that appears to be derived from a life more "fully lived" than our own, especially when that poetry comes by way of formerly Eastern Bloc countries. The American literary establishment remains, for instance, far more conversant with the old-guard metrical twaddle of Joseph Brodsky than with the impassioned musicality of Nicaragua's Gioconda Belli or—until the events of Tiananmen Square in 1989 made them fashionably "newsworthy"—the poetry of exiled poets from China.

In a review of the Czech poet Miroslav Holub, Heaney outlines a "fully exposed" poetics. He begins by drawing our attention to current trends: "In spite of a period of castigation about the necessity for 'intelligence' and 'irony', poetry in English has not moved all that far from the shelter of the Romantic tradition. Even our self-mocking dandies pirouette to a narcotic music. The dream's the thing, not the diagnosis. Inwardness, yearnings and mergings of the self toward nature, cadences that drink at spots of time—in general the hopes of poets and readers still realize themselves within contexts like these. We still expect the poetic imagination to be sympathetic rather than analytic. 'Intellect' still tends to summon its rhyme from Wordsworth's pejorative 'dissect'." He argues on behalf of a poetics that "quarrels with classicism in the same spirit as Czeslaw Milosz quarrels with it in his resolute book *The Witness of Poetry,* where he detects the constantly threatening 'temptation to surrender to merely graceful writing' as a disabling part of the heritage of classicism. "Classicism," Heaney asserts, "in this definition, becomes a negative aspect of the Horatian *dulce,* a matter of conventional ornament, a protective paradigm of the way things are, drawn from previous readings of the world which remain impervious to new perceptions and which are therefore deleterious to the growth of consciousness."

In the title essay, Heaney professes on behalf of Osip Mandelstam's magnificent fantasia, "A Conversation about Dante," an essay in which the Russian poet argues in favor of an organic structure originating *within* Dante rather than the more customary academic view that Dante's "threes"—triadic stanzas, thirty-three cantos to the book, three books to complete the whole—were an exterior imposition. Mandelstam (and Heaney) "subverts the age-old impression that his work was written on official paper, and locates his authority not in his cultural representativeness, his religious vision or his sternly unremitting morality but rather in his status as an exemplar of the purely creative, intimate, experimental act of poetry itself."

Heaney also finds in Elizabeth Bishop's "At the Fishhouses" a most reticent, "mannerly" poet creating a "slow-motion spectacle of a well-disciplined poetic imagination being tempted to dare a big leap, hesitating, and then with powerful sureness actually taking the leap." Completing his appreciation of her poem, Heaney calls up Yeats's phrase, "to hold in a single thought reality and justice," and reminds us that this is exactly what authenticates poetry, gives poetry its governing power.

The essay "Lowell's Command" might be read against Robert Bly's brief piece. Heaney, like so many others, calls "For the Union Dead" and "Waking Early Sunday Morning" "two of the finest public poems of our time." Heaney believes the "relaxed poetry in *For the Union Dead* prefigures the achievement of the best work in *Day by Day.* It wakens rather than fixes." Other essays, on Sylvia Plath, on Kavanagh, on Auden, are equally engaging.

Both stylistically and by subject, Heaney falls somewhere between scholarly academic criticism and that which we have come to expect from our poets—the more personal appreciation of old masters and/or contemporaries. Somewhere in the midst of all of this, I wrote a few remembered lines from

Pound's *Canto XVI* in the margin of *The Government of the Tongue* : "They were all ready, the old gang,/ Guns on top of the post office and the palace,/ But none of the leaders knew it was coming. . . ." Pound was of course talking about the Bolshevik Revolution, but something about Heaney reminds me of the most institutionalized poets of the U. S., our own old guard from the academy to the textbook anthologies that serve our poetry so very poorly. As interesting, as deeply engaging as Heaney's essays are, he nonetheless articulates a poetics of white, college-educated, university-fed, bourgeois male sensibilities: Bishop and Plath and Lowell and Auden and Larkin; in *Preoccupations,* it was Yeats and Hopkins and yes, Kavanagh and Lowell: interesting and articulate, but . . .

Commenting on Heaney's earlier prose, *Preoccupations,* W. S. Di Piero reveals perhaps more than he intends when he says, "A poet often writes prose to articulate an investigative technique or explanatory procedure, by which his intended discovery, probably initially intuited, may be claimed and justified. An exhibition of need and will, it is also an act of self-declaration. The essays in *Preoccupations* demonstrate Heaney's aspirations, his awareness of his own position in the poetic tradition, and an account of those patterns of exploration which comprise the nervous system of his verse."

Di Piero sees in Heaney a "crucial distinction" between what gets called craft ("skill of making") and what gets called technique, that which "involves not only a poet's way with words, his (sic) management of metre, rhythm and verbal texture; it involves also a definition of his stance toward life, a definition of his own reality. . . ." Heaney's definition of technique makes use of that "projectivist" term, *stance.* But his own techniques as a poet bear little resemblance to a projective stance. Praising a number of Heaney's poems, Di Piero takes a cautious approach to the more recent work. "A number of poems," Di Piero says, "demonstrate the triumph of rhetoric over theme, or mere good writing over investigative vision. By 'mere good writing' I mean exclusive attention to the sheen and noise of language, such that flamboyance and invention, however sincere and in service to however serious a theme, come to displace clarity and integrity of feeling." Closing his assessment, Di Piero warns, "A poet's career is always in the making—or remaking—and one must be careful not to mistake fine craft for true feeling, deft mechanics for the intricate felt life of forms." Di Piero's warning should be memorized by every poet who wins a major fellowship or book award, by every poet who has ever settled for merely good writing.

In another essay gathered in *Memory and Enthusiasm* (Princeton University Press, 1989), "On Translation," Di Piero, himself a gifted translator of Italian as well as a poet, offers yet another admonishment, this time against one of the major literary fads of the 1970s, the "international style" of poetry advocated by, among others, former U.S. poet laureate, Mark Strand. "Young people in writers' workshops who read widely in translations done in a world language or international style are themselves influenced by that style (or nonstyle); they claim it as their own and Americanize it. They become influenced not by poetry but by a translation *product* [author's emphasis]. Thus a rootless, denatured style comes to be accepted as an American style. Back of this stands the desire to become internationalists."

In the final essay, "Work," Di Piero gets down to one irreducible fundamental: a poetry defined in part by its *techne,* that is, by its practice or performance. He returns us to a truer sense of Poet as Maker, one with roots in the early Greek *tekton,* a builder or form-giver, providing us with a grander sense of a poet's work beyond mere craft or mere good writing. "Poetry," he says, "is neither diminished nor debased by the new model (though it is debased by the *inauthenticity* and *professionalism* the new model encourages) so long as it does not surrender its techtonic life, its complex and elusive thought-character, for this is what makes it the most human of the arts [my emphasis] . . . To believe that poetry is a task in reply to living in a world of things, and that the poet's work is to receive the object world, may induce a sustaining fluency, at least for a while."

"No ideas but in things." As Levertov says in "An Admonition," we learn to read the universe, to identify *meanings* in things. Ernest Fenollosa noted that metaphors do not spring from subjective processes, rather they tend to follow along "lines of relations in nature herself." Dante's *selva oscura,* that "dark wood of the self," lies half-hidden within a poet's field of experience, composed of interwoven "meanings" which beg for illumination, for articulation, for—in Duncan's phrase—the annunciatory act. When, in "Poem beginning with a Line by Pindar," Duncan says, "I too / that am a nation," he is identifying that field wherein mythos, history, metaphor, and personality merge, commingle; wherein—as *literature*— he locates "a text for the soul in its search for fulfillment in life and takes the imagination as a *primary instinctual authority*" [my emphasis]. Such an act of annunciation ennobles and empowers by naming, approaching the aforementioned requirement of Yeats: "to hold in a single thought reality and justice."

But *whose* reality? *Whose* justice? Stanislaw Baranczak, a Polish poet/ writer presently teaching at Harvard, addresses this problem from an East European perspective in his *Breathing Under Water* (Harvard University Press, 1990). In the title essay, he establishes his field of action: "I wonder, for example, what my reaction would have been had I picked up today's newspaper, dated August 25, 1989, from my doorstep seven years ago, just months after the imposition of martial law in Poland and more than a year after my arrival in this country. What would I have made of the news about a million people forming a human chain in Lithuania, Latvia, and Estonia to demand independence for their Soviet-annexed countries? About the thousands of East Germans fleeing to the West across Hungary's newly opened frontier with Austria. . . . *The Gulag Archipelago* being printed in a literary journal, . . . about the election of a Solidarity activist as prime minister and the formation of Poland's first non-Communist government since World War Two?"

Beginning with a wonderful comic piece, "E.E.: The Extraterritorial," Baranczak looks at America through the eyes of an immigrant, then examines émigré antitotalitarian perspectives on the West, the profundity of Václav Havel, and composes an essay on censorship, "Big Brother's Red Pencil," that is particularly interesting in light of the abundant and mordant attacks on the National Endowment for the Arts by various pseudo-populist politicians in recent years.

Baranczak examines "The State Artist" and finds a bundle of contradictions in an art that had "the best of both worlds: it could enjoy both the privileges of power and the legitimizing conceit of serving the people." And in his review of Czeslaw Milosz's *The Land of Ulro,* Baranczak identifies a search for *unde malum,* the origins of evil, Milosz's rejection of "secular humanism," and his concern with the complex issue of "how civilization should deal with the individual's sense of insignificance in the universe."

Like many another exile, Baranczak brings his new audience fresh perspectives. His observation on the nature of poets is beguiling: "An outside observer has every right to treat the poets' complaints with utter suspicion. Logically speaking, if writing is really such a pain in the neck, it must be recompensed with some kind of pleasure—otherwise, who would bother to write poems at all? And, since there are apparently thousands of contemporary poets and none of them can seriously count today on any of the more tangible rewards (such as making money or winning a Maecenas' favor), the very joy of writing is most probably the only compensation for the pain of writing." His own poems, *The Weight of the Body* (TriQuarterly Books, 1989), are full of ironic knots, startling observation, and luminous narrative lyrics. His balancing of "reality and justice" equips him with a powerful sense of paradox.

Adam Zagajewsky, an exiled Polish poet presently living in Paris, has written a remarkable suite of essays, *Solidarity, Solitude* (Ecco Press, 1990), careful meditations on the nature of a poet's work, musing over differences between poets in totalitarian countries and those who speak as anti-totalitarians. "In Denmark a twenty-year-old poet undergoes great agony because he does not know what he should write about. He feels in himself the pressure of artistry, yet this artistry seeks embodiment. He writes a poem about Alexander the Great. The next day about the language. On the third day he writes an erotic poem. He lacks unity, something that would tie together his inspirations and that reviewers could cite as the 'unifying principle.' The twenty-year-old poet suffers terribly. He reads old masters, leafs through magazines, takes walks along the flat Danish earth. He hears the singing of the lark. In the evening a pockmarked moon shows itself. In him alone grows a need for love, desire, longing. He reads Marx, understands the anger of the proletariat. He thinks about death. He comes across *The Gulag Archipelago:* from that moment on, he hates the Soviet system. He reads Pascal, but also Danish poets somewhat older than he. He ponders the accuracy of the analysis to which Pasolini subjects a society of consumers. . . . A twenty-year-old poet finds himself in an exceptional situation: because he has not yet decided which reality he will express, he is capable of hearing many voices."

Only later, following long periods of intensified *listening*, can Zagajewsky's imaginary Danish poet begin to fathom "the trauma concealed in expression: in articulating one reality, he must forget about the others; he has to betray some of his own experiences in order to express others more forcefully." Expression, Zagajewsky says, is monotheistic. His poet must choose. And only later, much later, when the poet is forty, he writes about "trees and skylarks."

But in Cracow or Warsaw, his poet's task in entirely different; his whole reality is entirely different. "The world is ordered, it has been ordered by totalitarian slavery." This is not entirely an order imposed by exterior totalitarianism, Zagajewsky is quick to point out, but one that can best be understood only through metaphor—he offers the image of "a corset that stifles the organism of reality." The corset may be imposed entirely from without—by the bureaucracy, say—but certain discomforts are identified only from within. He claims spiritual kinship with anti-totalitarianism, and, because he does claim such kinship, begins to think about it critically "because I believe one should sometimes think against oneself."

He finds a "disturbing facet of anti-totalitarianism is that one of its greatest sources of strength, its splendid spiritual tension, depends upon placing all the world's evil in one place: totalitarianism." So thinking, he says, "We become a little like angels. . . . They, the totalitarians, are evil. We are good and innocent. Order reigns in the world, even though it is extremely unjust: they keep us enslaved, we oppose them." Finally, "Anti-totalitarianism does not allow me to think against myself." It makes of the poet a "quasi-angel" incapable of thinking against self-originated metaphors and such instances as might prompt him or her to become otherwise (*other* -wise). Consequently, we are tempted to indulge in "demonizing" whoever *they* happen to be, *they* the totalitarians. Cavafy's great poem "Waiting for the Barbarians" addresses this very attitude.

Besides offering a great deal of insight into his own social-historical situation, Zagajewsky's essays provoke fresh insight into the "antitotalitarian" poet —American or otherwise—especially the poet who insists upon certain kinds of political "correctness" in verse, the angelic poet with an inflexible program incapable of accommodating any "thinking against oneself."

The idea of thinking a metaphor backwards receives an impressive albeit brief treatment in an essay by Judy Grahn, "Drawing in Nets," included in a large collection of essays by contemporary poets, *Conversant Essays* (Wayne State University Press, 1990), edited by James McCorkle. Grahn insists that a metaphor is drawn, both in the sense of magnetically drawn and in the sense of geometrically drawn. (All words, Aristotle insists, are metaphors.)

She cites the woman who draws at her doorway a figure who magically repels malevolence. "This meaning of drawing," Grahn says, "to draw by means of cleverness and knowledgeable construction of one's imagery, so irresistibly that a power otherwise loose in the free-form universe is now captured and exerting its force in the context of human lives, never ceases to engage me whenever I think of art and how it works. That it works like a vessel or plumbing system with which we capture water. That it works like a hexagram on a barn wall to repel unwanted forces. That it works like the barn to secure the cows of our desiring." Grahn points out the double motion of the metaphor, arguing, "If I wish the death of some quality in human behavior that I also say is 'wolf,' I effect the death of wolves." She calls for a greater attention to care and precision and accuracy of emotion and thought: "lest the artist catch something in her drawing that she really did not intend to catch."

Gloria Anzaldúa contributes an essay, "Metaphors in the Tradition of the Shaman," in which she underscores exactly how, coming into possession of precise metaphor, we "protect ourselves," and how "the resistance to change in a person is in direct proportion to the number of dead metaphors that person carries. . . . *En poseción de la palabra.*" Read in conjunction with Olson, this essay reminds me that it is equally true to observe, "What does not change / is the resistance to change."

Conversant Essays is a hefty read, nearly 600 pages of tight, small type (horribly designed with a typeface that has no respect whatever for the function of letter-forms), including essays by some fifty poets. It is an anthology that attempts to represent six "topical constellations": the sufficiency of language, questions of form, readings, tracing the personal, histories, and speculations. Among the poet-critics, there are voices from the "language" poets, new formalists (or whatever they're called this week), Iowa Workshop poets (whatever that means), "organic line" poets (or whatever they are called this week). There are a number of excellent essays by women. (Why have anthologies of critical writing taken so long to include feminist criticism?)

Besides the above mentioned, there are many more delightful contributions: Emily Grosholz's deep reading of *The Witness of Poetry* in "Milosz and the Moral Authority of Poetry"; Denise Levertov's "On Williams' Triadic Line; *or How to Dance on Variable Feet*"; Sandra Gilbert's essay on Levertov herself, "Revolutionary Love: Denise Levertov and the Poetics of Politics"; Alicia Ostriker's provocative "Dancing at the Devil's Party: Some Notes on Politics and Poetry"; a difficult, intriguing essay, "Otherhow," by Rachel Blau DuPlessis; Irena Klepfisz on Jewish American poetry.

Brad Leithauser contributes an essay, "The Confinement of Free Verse," in which he bases much of his observation on the pseudo-science of Frederick Turner's *Natural Classicism: Essays on Literature and Science* (Paragon House, 1985), a tome that contains a great deal of ambition and not a little pretension, including this: "Whole groups of writers, dramatists, philosophers, artists, and scientists have sometimes arisen, energized by natural classical principles: the paradigm case is obviously classical Athens, but we may identify such groups as the circle of Tu Fu and Li Po in China . . ." But in fact no such "circle" existed. Tu Fu met Li Po certainly not more than *twice*. In his lifetime. Is Turner suggesting that Li Po (the elder) and Tu Fu *created* T'ang culture? Or were they as much an *expression* or annunciation of that culture? Turner includes in his list "the American Renaissance that surrounded Emerson." If that small group of writers constitutes a Renaissance (capital R), in what way does it compare with the cultural development of the Greek *polis*? "In such periods," Turner continues, "the artists, sages, or shamans *seem to have the confidence* [my emphasis] to rise to a conception of their work as performative fiat." How, one must wonder, does Turner account for the "confidence" of a Pasternak, a Zbigniew Herbert, a Milosz, a Solzhenitsyn? In plain self-evident fact, much of the greatest art has arisen out of solitary individual existential protest.

Leithauser quotes Turner: "Metrically experienced poets can readily recognize the LINE (sic) divisions of poetry in languages they do not know, when it is read aloud." Presumptuousness if not arrogance abounds. Even Leithauser admits Turner's "theories are apt to sound shaky or thin. But his preliminary findings strongly suggest that something innate within the matrix of the human body—some complex concatenation of heartbeat, respiration, and, especially, synaptic firings within and between the two hemispheres of the brain—contrives to impose on any sort of poetry demands that run deeper than the language of their composition. . . . Poets will gravitate toward those prosodies amenable to the demands that the body brings to the task of assimilating a line of verse" and so on. Until he quotes Turner again: "If this hypothesis is accurate, meter is, in part, a way of introducing right-brain processes into the left-brain activity of understanding language; and in another sense, it is a way of connecting our much more culture-bound (and perhaps evolutionarily later) linguistic capacities with the relatively more 'hard-wired' spatial pattern-recognition faculties we share with the higher mammals." Leithauser then observes, "The reading of *Paradise Lost,* then, or any other densely metrical poem, would be an ongoing act of neurological synthesis. And the centrality of this synthesis would also help explain poetry's curious conservatism."

But: if "music" is a function of the right brain, is that music necessarily limited to *metrical* music, or are more open forms also a product of those particular synapses? What are the synaptic possibilities of the five-tone scale? Such questions apparently never even occur to Turner and Leithauser.

Leithauser, like some of his neo-formalist *confreres,* condescends to admit a certain "charm" in certain poems as a result of "their looseness, their unlabored ease," but argues on behalf of a poetry that is "made to suffer" in its construction. *"A poem should undergo just as much prosodic suffering as does not actually kill it, "* he declares in italic, paraphrasing John Berryman's adaptation of the ancient Greek cliché "What does not actually kill me strengthens me." To underscore his argument on behalf of formal traditional prosody, Leithauser calls on—of all people—Ezra Pound—from a 1932 issue of *The Criterion.* Pound, fed up with "Amygism, Lee Masterism," calls for "rhyme and regular strophes." But it doesn't suit Leithauser's predilection to comment on the architecture of the line in *The Cantos,* so none is offered.

Anyone who actually believes "suffering" a necessary condition in the making of art suffers a Romantic naiveté. Quite to the contrary, the healing properties of art—including its making—have been renowned since antiquity.

The problems of these kinds of "movements" in poetry are further evidenced by the opening sentence of Dana Gioia's "Notes on the New Formalism"—"Twenty years ago it was a truth universally acknowledged that a young poet in possession of a good ear would want to write free verse." Students of Donald Justice at the University of Iowa will no doubt be surprised to learn this absolute truth. Indeed it was just twenty years ago that Howard Nemerow won both the National Book Award and the Pulitzer Prize for Poetry for his *Collected Poems.* I could go on at great length rebutting this utterly uniformed observation. Like Bly, Gioia is over-fond of setting up the straw man. These kinds of movements are almost always rooted in reactionary behavior, whether they are rooted in totalitarianism or in devout faux-antitotalitarianism, whether their particular final solution is prosodic or political. As Nemerow once observed, "Rhymed or unrhymed, you can't polish a turd."

There is little that is new within the ranks of the "new" formalists. They represent, in some ways at least, an advance to the rear. Which is fine as long as one of them—now and again—comes up with a decent poem. The problem with their criticism is that it thrives on devastating straw men, is selfish and arrogant, and often arises out of narrow and ungenerous reading. The problem of arrogance and condescension is enormous: "Most free verse," Gioia says, "*plays* with the way poetic language is arranged on a page and articulates the visual rhythm of a poem in a way early method verse rarely bothered to." Thereby reducing the poetry of all "free versifiers" to mere typographical play—the way a child might "play poet" by arranging "poetic language" imaginatively. This is smug condescension at its arrogant worst.

William Blake—who knew something about various kinds of prosody—observed, "Genius is not lawless." There, somewhere between his heaven and his hell, he included, presumably, non-metrical as well as metrical genius. Gioia makes any number of other bizarre exclamations, including the notion that metrical poetry is somehow a "more predominantly oral tradition." He goes on to scold "these young poets" by saying, "For them poems exist as words on a page rather than sounds in the mouth and ear." This is a criticism that should more appropriately be addressed to Helen Vendler's massive critique of Keats wherein sounds in mouth and ear are never mentioned. The whole point of Olson's "Projective Verse," Levertov's essays on the line,

Williams's prosodic edicts, and so forth, is *exactly* what happens with the sounds of poetry—in the mouth and ear. Poetry is composed by ear.

Like Bly, the *nuevo formalistes* do themselves a disservice by being so deliberately ungenerous, so deliberately arch, so devoted to a program. Much of what they have to say is interesting and invigorating, but they are so determinedly stating a cause—hoping to create a *cause célèbre* perhaps?—that they alienate those who would learn from their scholarship. They would become the new totalitarians of poetry. Artistic movements are made up largely of sycophants. It was true of New Criticism, Agrarianism, the original New Formalists of thirty years ago, and it was true of the Beats. And it was true of McCarthyism. Most of them are camp-followers who in no time at all dissolve into puddles of Amygism or Masterism or Edgar Guestitis. The same is true of literary antitotalitarian totalitarians demanding political correctness. Most of the people who go to great lengths to bad-mouth "language" poetry don't know a damned thing about it. One gets more attention by being infant-like and throwing a noisy tantrum.

Turner, Leithauser, Gioia, and a great many other poets could probably learn something useful by attending to Jerome Rothenberg's ground-breaking work in ethnopoetics, especially *Technicians of the Sacred, Shaking the Pumpkin, Symposium of the Whole* and *Exiled in the Word*. Rothenberg remains completely open to diverse poetics, understanding that each is "both a method of composition and a stance toward reality." This "stance toward reality" remains virtually undefined in the vocabulary of new formalists.

Rothenberg advocates a "field of experiment and change" which creates, juxtaposed to "traditions," a marvelous paradox. He invokes imageless and wordless poetry; *musique concrete*; that greatest paradox, "free verse"—two words with mutually exclusive meanings; nonsyntactic or asyntactic poetry; and so on. Professing on behalf of these kinds of explorations, Rothenberg says, "If we can say that now—and more!—we are not made shamans thereby—or priests or magicians—but our own resemblances to and differences from those others are the hidden theme of most of what we do. . . . the new paradigm . . . is still only partial, as the disintegration of the old imperialism/ethnocentrism is (we now know) also only partial."

One of the supreme accomplishments of American verse in the twentieth century is its ability to assimilate diverse influence while retaining its own character—a character in constant becoming, to be sure—musically resourceful far beyond the limits of any single imagination, able to accommodate the formal and the informal, the outlandishly experimental and the ultraconservative, lines capable of achieving a flexible polyphony.

Robert Duncan pointed out the following as re: enjambment as expression of certain kinds of temperament: Creeley enjambs and Olson doesn't; Ginsberg doesn't enjamb, Pound doesn't enjamb, Pope doesn't; Shakespeare enjambs all the time; Jonson doesn't enjamb. If I say that A is better than B because A enjambs and B doesn't, no one would give it a thought. To say that Nemerow is "better" than Duncan *because* Nemerow end-rhymes is not only meaningless, but destructive of the ability to appreciate both.

Formal metrical structure mirrors certain kinds of musical structure, from Bach to the blues, in which a melodic theme is stated, variations on that theme are explored, and a conclusion is reached through resolution. Open forms are, intrinsically, neither better nor worse. They are simply made (and not necessarily made simply) of an entirely different measure. If the *stuff* of poetry did not transcend even the words themselves, nothing could be translated.

Williams admonishes us to work according to our talents and the will that drives them. "The secret of the poetic art," Duncan wrote in the *H. D. Book*, "lies in the keeping of time, to keep time designing or discovering lines of melodic coherence. Counting the measures, marking them off, calculating the sequences; the whole intensified in the poet's sense of its limitation."

If a laziness or sloppiness mars much of our poetry as Levertov, Gioia, and many other poets agree, it is rooted in a failure to articulate a functional sense of measure, open *or* closed. It is a problem with roots in education. Children are regularly taught that "anything can be a poem," and that any "poetic" expression of self-awareness is instance enough for the occasion of poesy. And there is some small truth in that. Entering our colleges, would-be poets often face college creative writing classes taught by professors who are narrowly specialized and who remain, in a broad sense, in an intercultural sense, functionally illiterate. The *techne* is often ignored in favor of the more abstract—and therefore less threatening—notion of *poesis*.

One solution is to make use of anthologies like *Conversant Essays*. And to insist upon a scholarly core literature that would include both historical and cultural depth. Understanding Matthew Arnold's critical vocabulary, a young poet may then use Arnold's tools in evaluating his or her own poem. Moreover, the student becomes aware of historical development, progression, or cycle. This is a very *practical* kind of scholarship. Writing re: writing is only a footnote, perhaps, to the endless conversation that is great literature. But it is also a dialogue with directly applicable uses, a dialogue that is stimulating and enlightening.

Alas, it has also been a dialogue with a notable absence of humor. Robert Peters has written a "compendium of new poetic terminology," *Hunting the Snark* (Paragon House, 1990), that is both hilarious and instructive. Alphabetically arranged, he cites categories of poetry that are sometimes serious and often funny, as when, under the category "Chintz," he offers: "Chintz, like the cloth from which cheap curtains are made, refers to those flat, sprawling, pretentious, enervated phrases dropped into poems, giving the illusion of intellectuality, culture, and charm. Robert Pinsky sometimes writes chintz poems. His 'The Unseen' lacks discernible, convincing emotion, and comes off as 'writing.' The piece is designed in flashy triplet stanzas, much as a miser's guineas might be arranged in piles of three. The rhymes seem fashioned rather than felt. A riff on *air* scampers throughout the first four stanzas, accompanied by much fancy diction, diction easy to see through, like chintz." *Et cetera.*

There are "Fulbright Poems" written "mainly by poets holding academic appointments who teach undergraduate English literature and world literature courses, with a smattering of art or music history thrown in. The 'academic abroad' poem hit the market in epidemic proportions following World War II when veterans returning to academe extolled the fountains of Rome." Peters identifies Iowa Workshop poems, Dazzle poems, Cope-and-mitre poems, Homophobic poems, Homosexual poems, Snigger poems, You poems, and many more. He is trenchant and opinionated and receptive to an astonishing range of things, and he seems to have read everything. Myth poems, Poultry poems, Nuclear poems, Political poems,—how could I not encounter a few of my own weaknesses as a poet time and again while "hunting the snark?"

Equal parts satire and scholarship, spiced with provocation, *Hunting the Snark* is not without its limitations. In his comments on Pinsky quoted above, for instance, why does Peters insist that writing in triplets is "flashy" rather than recognizing in the triplet a formal measure of time? Under the category "West Coast Poems," he devotes nearly the entire entry to the San Francisco area writers, adding a concluding paragraph about Los Angeles. This is a Californian's map of the coast, to be sure. Seattle, Portland, Eugene and such do not exist and there are no poets outside of cities on the coast. San Diego, of course, is by now part of Mexico. Only farmers and bureaucrats live in Sacramento? Nevertheless, after a very long exploration of recent writing re: writing over the past year, Peters is a breath of fresh air.

I close as I began, with the William Carlos Williams of *The Wedge*: "There is no poetry of distinction without formal invention, for it is in the intimate form that works of art achieve their exact meaning. . . to give language its highest dignity, its illumination in the environment to which it is native. Such war, as the arts live and breathe by, is continuous." Now the Cold War has ended; Germany is again Germany; Solidarity is a major force in democratic Poland; Estonian poets will speak freely and a new body of critical vocabulary emerge. Poets exiled from China will write the poetry of life in exile. The whole planet teeters of the brink of ecological suicide. A half million American troops return from the Persian Gulf and Kuwait continues to burn. And the struggle "to hold in a single thought reality and justice" remains the same struggle: for poet, pacifist, critic, and soldier alike, as each speaks from a different sector of the same battlefield.

A Poetry of Daily Practice

Adrienne Rich, S. J. Marks, Dorianne Laux

"What you do every day is as important to the soul, to the revelation of the soul, as what your parents did to you, or what you were like when you were five or ten."
—James Hillman

"Re-vision—the act of looking back, of seeing with fresh eyes, of entering an old text from a new critical direction—is for us more than a chapter in cultural history: it is an act of survival. Until we can understand the assumptions in which we are drenched we cannot know ourselves. . . . I feel in the work of the men whose poetry I read today a deep pessimism and fatalistic grief; and I wonder if it isn't the masculine side of what women have experienced, the price of masculine dominance."

I first read Adrienne Rich's comments in a fragment from the essay, "When We Dead Awaken," more than fifteen years ago in a standard college anthology containing 23 male and 3 female poets. With the growth of publishers like Alicejames, Beacon, Seal Press and other independents, and with the influence of feminist studies within the academy and without, poetry and criticism written by women has flourished over the last two decades as never before.

In the complete essay (in *On Lies, Secrets and Silence,* Norton 1979), Rich also says, "Now, to be maternally with small children all day in the old way, to be with a man in the old way of marriage, requires a holding-back, a putting-aside of that imaginative activity, and demands instead a kind of conservatism. I want to make it clear that I am *not* saying that in order to write well, or think well, it is necessary to become unavailable to others, or to become a devouring ego. This has been the myth of the masculine artist and thinker; and I do not accept it. But to be a female human being trying to fulfill traditional female functions in a traditional way *is* in direct conflict with the subversive function of the imagination. The word traditional is important here. There must be ways, and we will be finding out more and more about them, in which the energy of creation and the energy of relation can be united. . . ."

Rich was calling for, searching for—and in fact had already established within her own poetry—a poetics of the mundane, a poetics of daily political, social, moral, and imaginative life in which Woman is depicted neither as abstract mystery personified nor as tragic victimized heroine, neither as temptress nor as redemptress, but as fully human, in short a poetry of "real life." In a subsequent collection of essays (*Blood, Bread, and Poetry*, Norton 1986), she says, "The critique of language needs to come not just from women who define themselves as writers but from women who will test the work against their experience—who, like Woolf's 'common reader,' are interested in literature as a key to life, not an escape from it." Critics who test work against personal experience and who turn to poetry—to paraphrase Robert Duncan—for evidence of the real are rare in either gender.

If the traditional roles of mother and father, wife and husband, become intolerable, destructive constraints, what happens to marriage as an institution, what happens to "the traditional family" as most of us imagine it? First of all, the "traditional family" is largely a product of a nostalgic imagination. The first shelter for battered women opened its doors in 1974. Domestic violence is undoubtedly less of a problem now than in the past simply because it is out of the closet and there are places for people to turn for help for the first time. In the traditional family, violence was power. And if the traditional American family of, say, the fifties, held to such high moral values, how do we account for our political behavior over the past forty years of almost continuous murder abroad and social stratification within? Traditional family values kept the homosexual community in the closet, society segregated, the world supplied with arms, and the same wealthy white males in power.

When I turn back to the poetry of the sixties, seventies, and eighties, I suddenly realize that most of the male poets who wrote those anthology poems of domestic life and love are no longer with the same partners—they are divorced, separated, exiled in some way or another, often removed even to the margins of their own emotions, and I begin to see in poetry written by men a deep pessimism, a mounting sense of grief amplified, compounded in part, by the failure of institutions like traditional marriage.

Much of the poetry of the last quarter century has explored through personal detail the very questions Rich raises. It has done so with varying degrees of success, but there is almost nothing else like it in the annals of verse, this sudden opening into a polyphony—cultural, ethnic, philosophic— of voices, nearly each of which is dominated by the personal mode, a poetry of confession and self-revelation in almost relentless pursuit of personal redemption. Adrienne Rich—along with Carolyn Kizer, Robin Morgan, Susan Griffin, Olga Broumas, Judy Grahn and others—brings urgent daily practice to the forefront. Over the past three decades, her stubborn truthfulness, her private politics and public passions, and her unwavering quest for a poetry of authentic experience have made her one of the essential poets of our time. I have returned to her poems over those years as one turns to a revered but critical teacher: as a constant source of personal transformation.

Rich's new book, *An Atlas of the Difficult World* (Norton, 1991), is yet another departure, a major accomplishment by any reasonable standard. The title poem is "a map of our country" that extends her already impressive sweep of understanding, providing a glimpse into her own self-transformations:

> A dark woman, head bent, listening for something
> —a woman's voice, a man's voice or
> voice of the freeway, night after night, . . .
> . . . If you had known me
> once, you'd still know me now though in a different
> light and life. This is no place you ever knew me.
> But it would not surprise you
> to find me here, walking fog, the sweep of the great ocean
> eluding me, even the curve of the bay, because as always
> I fix on the land. I am stuck to earth. What I love here
> is old ranches, leaning seaward, lowroofed spreads between rocks
> small canyons running through pitched hillsides . . .
> These are not the roads
> you knew me by. But the woman driving, walking, watching
> for life and death, is the same.

This first of thirteen movements sets the stage. The tone is conversational, almost casual, meditative. The scene itself could have been lifted from Steinbeck. Neither poet nor landscape is unfamiliar territory, yet Rich brings a fresh perspective. She moves quickly to a "Sea of Indifference, glazed with salt" and

> . . . the desert where missiles are planted like corms . . .
> suburbs of acquiescence . . .
> whose children are drifting blind alleys pent

between coiled rolls of razor wire
I promised to show you a map you say but this is a mural
then yes let it be these are small distinctions
where do we see it from is the question

Her canvas is large, her initial gestures sweeping. I love her use of corm—a *corm* being the bulb of a plant like a crocus, an image presenting a nearly perfect counterbalance to the severity of its subject, the corm so graciously optimistic in its utter contrast with the deep pessimism of nuclear weapons.

Aristotle says metaphor represents the poet's greatest attributes and is the one thing that cannot be learned from others, and here as so often elsewhere Rich demonstrates her genius for what Aristotle called "intuitive perception." She sees within the "breadbasket of foreclosed farms" many ghosts, she hears the reverberations of many public lies. Continuing her meditation on a night porch in New England, she notes,

. . . That wind has changed, though still from the south
it's blowing up hard now, no longer close to earth but driving high
into the crowns of the maples, into my face
almost slamming the stormdoor into me. But it's warm, warm,
pneumonia wind, death of innocence wind, unwinding wind,
time-hurtling wind. And it has a voice in the house. I hear
conversations that can't be happening, overheard in the bedrooms
and I'm not talking about ghosts. The ghosts are here of course but they speak plainly
—haven't I offered food and wine, listened well for them all these years,
not only those known in life but those before our time
of self-deception, our intricate losing game of innocence long overdue?

She notes a spider spinning its web beside her, and responds:

. . . she will use everything,
nothing comes without labor, she is working so
hard and I know
nothing all winter can enter this house or this web, not all labor
ends in sweetness.
But how do I know what she needs? Maybe simply
to spin herself a house within a house, on her own terms
in cold, in silence.

Like the spider, Rich weaves a world within a world, but unlike the spider, must overcome the silence, must speak clearly to define her struggle. She must define her own terms. She surveys a continental terrain composed of junked cars, truckstops, chain-link fences, and poisoned watershed:

Waste. Waste. The watcher's eye put out, hands of the
builder severed, brain of the maker starved
those who could bind, join, reweave, cohere, replenish
now at risk in this segregate republic
locked away out of sight and hearing, out of mind, shunted aside
those needed to teach, advise, persuade, weigh arguments
those urgently needed for the work of perception
work of the poet, the astronomer, the historian, the architect of new streets
work of the speaker who also listens
meticulous delicate work of reaching the heart of the desperate woman, the desperate man
—never-to-be-finished, still unbegun work of repair—it cannot be done without them
and where are they now?

The tone and imagery are reminiscent of Ezra Pound's early poem of exile, "The Rest." This poem also brings to mind the pedagogy of Pound on the nature and function of metaphor: the use of concrete imagery to convey the meaning of immaterial relations—his famous misunderstanding of Aristotle's *Poetics*.

Rich juxtaposes image with image, often building lists like Whitman's— carried by the phrasing, the incantatory music of her speaking voice. Her deep sense of responsibility and encompassing vision are Whitmanesque in scope. She is, she says, "bent on fathoming what it means to love my country." In contrast with the poets, teachers and weavers exiled and silenced in the above passage, she presents an indelible image of an archetypal contemporary male, a man struck dumb, numbed by the circumstances of his life:

On this earth, in this life, as I read your story, you're lonely.
Lonely in the bar, on the shore of the coastal river
with your best friend, his wife, and your wife, fishing
lonely in the prairie classroom with all the students who love you. You know some ghosts
come everywhere with you yet leave them unaddressed
for years. You spend weeks in a house
with a drunk, you sober, whom you love, feeling lonely.

You grieve in loneliness, and if I understand you fuck in loneliness.
I wonder if this is a white man's madness. / . . .

Rich extends her meditation to include the word *soledad*, loneliness or solitary retreat, bringing into play a small chapel, *La Nuestra Senora de la Soledad* and the California prison made infamous during Black Power movement days. She achieves a compassionate tone toward troubled men that is very refreshing and deeply moving:

> From eighteen to twenty-eight of his years
> a young man schools himself, argues,
> debates, trains, lectures to himself,
> teaches himself Swahili, Spanish, learns
> five new words of English every day,
> chainsmokes, reads, writes letters.
> In this college of force he wrestles bitterness,
> self-hatred, sexual anger, cures his own nature.
> Seven of these years in solitary.Soledad.
> . . .
> where the kindred spirit touches this wall it crumbles—
> no one responds to kindness, no one is more sensitive to it
> than the desperate man.

This is an excruciatingly accurate portrait of a man I have been. And in the years I taught in prisons, I met this man over and over again. Her poem underscores the truth of slogans many of us uttered twenty-five years ago as we marched in the streets to demand social change and an end to the Viet Nam war. It is a poem of great compassion and love and controlled anger closing, fittingly, on a generous note of dedication to her readers.

An Atlas of the Difficult World is a magnificent book written, as Rich says in a poem for a friend, from the marrow. While we have come to expect from Adrienne Rich a new poetry with every book, it is surprising when a poet's second book can withstand comparison. S. J. Marks writes from the bleak nostalgic heart of the American male as he searches his soul to identify the demons he must confront in a solitary, lonely, struggle for redemption. *Something Grazes Our Hair* (University of Illinois Press, 1991) is an often harrowing journey through the grief of separation.

Cherries

I am lying here alone in the dark house
and where you are you are putting out the light,
and it is evening.

Your face, quiet with dreams,
the small mouths of sleep—
I watch you with quiet trembling,
and what I feel for your softness
comes back.

Between your eyelids,
the dreams open their eyes like
rotted cherries,
and when you die, I will not know it.
Always the wind blows. We speak
to make ourselves remember.

This is not exactly the "masculine pessimism and fatalistic grief" Rich saw twenty years ago, but it *is* the second generation of that grief. Marks uses the sense of loneliness in "Cherries" in a zen-like fashion: his loneliness is a longing *in the soul* rather than merely the longing for companionship. "When you die," he says, "I will not know it." The statement is tautological, self-evident, but it cuts both ways at once: it is painful to say, painful to hear, painful to realize at either end; but despite all that, it is just such cognition that must be achieved if the poem (or the poet, or the mate) is to rise into epiphany. Coming to understand grief, we can then overcome it, live through it into the "new life."

His work of memory, his re-vising of his psyche, explores the very high price of the passive-aggressive male, showing the disastrous results of a kind of typical behavior without indulging in self-recrimination or self-pity, without bitterness or rage. This is a portrait of a man with good intentions:

Before the End of Summer

When we were waiting,
I lived in a room along
the hall, and I saw inside

my eyelids at night. An
open skull, claw hands,
sparse hair, dying skin.
We ate bread with lumps
of unbaked flour and blackberry jam.
Always hungry,
sometimes we stole.
She was a dark
girl, with a pointed face.
What would happen?
She couldn't know.
I dreamed of food: ham,
turkey, rhubarb.
She dreamed of beetles.
And woke
to waiting. Nothing
came from anywhere for her.
I had plans. We did not talk.
Her dark eyes
watched me, I thought,
and I look away.

The woman in the poem dreams, but wakes only to waiting. "Nothing came from anywhere" suggests that she is passively waiting for someone else, some *other,* to fulfill her dreams. He meanwhile is disturbed by dreams of claws and skulls, images of violence and death, images generated perhaps by his own intuitive feeling of decay from within. Are her dark eyes *really* watching him, or does he grow paranoid out of a sense of impotence and inevitable failure? Perhaps both.

In her striking 1982 book, *The Anatomy of Freedom* (Doubleday), Robin Morgan suggestions that life shared between woman and man becomes almost physically impossible because Woman must live—like Man—for *herself* first of all, and learn "to act instead of reacting, taking responsibility for life on this planet *without* taking on any attendant guilt." She would have to be willing, Morgan observes, "to leave everything familiar behind, be willing to believe she knows that way out . . ." if she is to attain self fulfilment. A woman willing to live "for herself" requires her mate to re-evaluate the whole relationship. "Despite all attempts to tighten familial bonds into ropes of bondage, family forms continue to change and grow, like living organisms:

through interaction and in context of the whole. That 'whole' has something to do with human need—for warmth, intimacy, endurance, trust, a shared history." Marriage fails when there is no "shared" history.

In a pamphlet issued in 1977, *Women and Honor: Some Notes on Lying*, Adrienne Rich had written, "Men have been expected to tell the truth about facts, not about feelings. They have not been expected to talk about feelings at all." The emotionally vulnerable male often retreats into silence. "Lying," Rich wote, "is done with words, and also with silence." In a poem from his "Zen Sequence," Marks reflects the change in the man when he broaches the subject of masculine silence again, from another perspective. Here, hindsight provides the context.

> Driving home,
> the voices of many people drift through me,
> nothing is what it was:
>
> "I like the uncertainty,
> the threat of losing. . . ."
>
> There are things I didn't tell you,
> but I loved you.

The enormous tragedy of this poem lies in the speaker's learning to speak— too late. The closing couplet is a direct echo—conscious or otherwise—of Nazim Hikmet's "There are things I didn't know I loved." And who exactly likes the uncertainty, the threat of losing? Perhaps the absent lover. Perhaps the poet is remembering something he himself said. Nevertheless, the poet is left with the dead weight of the unstated, a gift given too late.

Rich asks whether masculine isolation is one of the inevitable results of masculine power, and of course the answer is yes. Those who rule are isolated, remote from the lives of ordinary people. A man who exercises tyranny in the home assaults himself with a loneliness that is in proportion to his tyranny. The loneliness of Richard Nixon is prototypical. The criminal who exercises illegal power over another soon learns the lessons of prison loneliness— loneliness among masses.

Marks achieves the kind of vulnerability, the kind of risk, that results from confronting and naming one's own underworld. It is a world where the living and the dead are one. In "To the Ocean" he addresses masculine silence and hardness. "People ache. They can't manage to tell / their experiences. They have nothing to give. / No words. . . ." He aches to

> touch the people I love
> and can't do without.
>
> I love them so much.
>
> Even the dead.
> One must let the dead live within one.
>
> I return to life deprived of all
> I thought it impossible to do without.

Why "touch" the people he loves? Because touch is a primary language; touch because it is so much more simple and direct than than struggling with words. This is dangerous territory. That "I love them so much" is as flat as a line can get unless it is somehow *earned*, but Marks earns his statements as well as his metaphors. He also writes from the marrow. He dares to make honest, beautiful poetry from the raw interior of a man coming to grips with the lessons of our recent history, a region where the personal reflects the social, wrestling the very demons Rich pointed out in her essay.

Marks, a family therapist, completely avoids the ugly jargon and self-centered generalities of pop psychology while laying his own psyche utterly bare. If the subject matter of his new book is painful, the overall work exhibits a tenacious love of life and a willingness to undergo ruthless self-scrutiny in order to clarify his commitments and his need to continue to make his gift. Often harsh, these poems nonetheless achieve a compassionate grace that is in itself redemptive. His poems will show you a lot more about the sensitive intelligent contemporary male soul than any weekend whacking drums and hugging in the woods.

Equally gutty in its use of daily practice, daily grief and joy, Dorianne Laux's *Awake* (BOA Editions, 1990) has held me in its grip for a year now, too enthralled to think about it in any critical way. This is one of the best *first* books I have ever read. These are poems of remarkable maturity, comfortably unapologetic in admitting their influences. "Ghosts" is a better revision of Philip Levine than any by those who merely imitate him. Laux learns something about technique, as she amply demonstrates, but the music and the vision are entirely her own. The title poem offers within it a few lines undoubtedly inspired by lessons in craft learned from Jack Gilbert, but once again the sensuous language and vision are entirely her own. "On the Back Porch" might be read in the context I have presented with Rich and Marks, another commentary on masculine silence:

> The cat calls for her dinner.
> On the porch I bend and pour
> brown soy stars into her bowl,
> stroke her dark fur.
> It's not quite night.
> Pinpricks of light in the eastern sky.
> Above my neighbor's roof, a transparent
> moon, a pink rag of cloud.
> Inside my house are those who love me.
> My daughter dusts biscuit dough.
> And there's a man who will lift my hair
> in his hands, brush it
> until it throws sparks.
> Everything is just as I've left it.
> Dinner simmers on the stove.
> Glass bowls wait to be filled
> with gold broth. Springs of parsley
> on the cutting board.
> I want to smell this rich soup, the air
> around me going dark, as stars press
> their simple shapes into the sky.
> I want to stay on the back porch
> while the world tilts
> toward sleep, until what I love
> misses me, and calls me in.

Another traditional domestic harmony poem? Not quite. There are certain traditional roles: daughter in biscuit dough, the domestic scene under her control as when she says, "Everything is just as I left it." But things are changed slightly. He is tender toward her. But his implied silence nonetheless fills her with momentary longing. Her poem shows something about the post-feminist evolving family. The poet is perfectly comfortable in her role, and her longing is momentary, suggesting partnership and shared responsibility—in short, a developing shared history.

Laux's ear is a delight. I love the noises her poems make, the rhymes and slant-rhymes and alliteration, the audible potential of her line.

In "The Tooth Fairy" she remembers the quarters her parents slipped beneath her pillow at night. But harsher memories intrude: "It's hard to believe / the years that followed, the palms / curled into fists, a floor / of broken dishes, . . ." managing by the poem's closure to find tenderness and affection despite bitter experience. "Quarter to Six" is a searing poem of two women surviving the wards of an asylum, living through the shock and grief of physical and sexual abuse, all of its terrors finally resolved in power and hope.

For Laux, the act of re-vision is a source of self-transformation rooted in part in the power of simply naming. This is a quality she shares with a lot of women (and men) who write about sexual or domestic violence and incest and other personal and familial terrors. This is a way of overcoming "the assumptions in which we are drenched." Surviving terror and abuse, Laux is enobled by her ability to transcend justifiable rage.

In "When We Dead Awaken," Rich quotes a question posed by the classical anthropologist Jane Harrison, "Why do women never want to write poetry about Man as a sex. . . ?" Laux certainly isn't the first woman to do so, but she does it like no one else:

China

From behind he looks like a man
I once loved, that hangdog slouch
to his jeans, a sweater vest, his neck
thick-veined as a horse cock, a halo
of chopped curls.

He orders coffee and searches
his pockets, first in front, then
from behind, a long finger sliding
into the slitted denim the way that man
slipped his thumb into me one summer
as we lay after love, our freckled
bodies two pale starfish on the sheets.

Semen leaked and pooled in his palm
as he moved his thumb slowly, not

to excite me, just to affirm
he'd been there.

But this man pressed his thumb
toward the tail of my spine
as if here were entering
China, or a ripe papaya,
so that now
when I think of love
I think of this.

This is a fearless, passionate erotic imagination, the poet herself remaining beautifully vulnerable, full of good humor and ripe memory, tender and tenacious. The lovemaking in the poem is friendly, nonviolent and nonthreatening. The poem turns not on the objectification of the lover, nor on explicit detail, but on a quality of most-coital languor in which memory and imagination create parallel associations—as they say, "just like in real life."

Kenneth Rexroth advocated a poetry stripped of superfluous artifice, a poetry of "fidelity to objectively verifiable experience." Laux works within close proximity of such a poetics, her daily life in the world everywhere offering inspiration. Again in "The Laundromat" she allows her erotic imagination to present a world in which the poet can indulge in "animal kindness," wanting to "hump every moving thing," to "lie down in the dry dung" like a buffalo to scratch, to "grow lazy in the shade." All this while folding her underwear.

Awake is a formidable book. Dorianne Laux makes her poems from the stuff of a lived life, from the daily practice of seeing the world—being *in* the world—with a true poet's eyes. In an essay/review in the September 1991 *Ms.* magazine, Adrienne Rich once again discusses the importance of "poetry for daily use," saying: "I want, for daily life, a passion that subverts the cool blankness, the manic speech, of the buyers and sellers who are our 'leaders'— passion that can't be managed, packaged, or freeze-dried into group therapy formulas. I want voices speaking from lives and landscapes not necessarily known to me yet sharing boundaries with mine."

S. J. Marks and Dorianne Laux extend and explore just such boundaries. One may glimpse in their work the mutual enrichment that is a result of "feminist" literature and criticism. Neither offers formulas, each speaks with a barely controllable but disciplined passion. Marks refuses to sink into pessimism despite the depth of his grief. Stubbornly compassionate, Laux overcomes the terrors of what could have been a bitter life.

"There must be ways," Rich says, "and we will be finding out more and more about them, in which the energy of creation and the energy of relation can be united. . ." Rereading "When We Dead Awaken," I remember how depressed I felt when I first read these words: "No male writer has written primarily or even largely for women, or with the sense of women's criticism as a consideration when he chooses his materials, his theme, his language." Fifteen or twenty years ago, it was not unusual for me to receive an anonymous curse in the morning mail: after all, a *man* couldn't possibly be a feminist. Fifteen years ago, I drove all the way to Portland, Oregon, to hear Adrienne Rich read her poems, only to be turned away at the door: no men allowed. But even then, and certainly all during the years between, I have written as much for women as for men, have written with feminist criticism in mind. Separatism is no longer in vogue. But most of the socio-political problems remain. What used to be called "women's issues," like domestic violence or family planning are no longer seen in such a narrow light, and yet the Clarence Thomas hearings demonstrated how little attitudes have changed among the privileged white males who rule.

I don't see how any poet in the country can, any longer, ignore the fundamental arguments of feminist criticism or ignore the consequences of passively acquiescing to those who rule. For me—as a poet and as a man—as for so many American poets of the last two decades, the poetry and criticism that matters, that is of daily use, is born in the spirit of subversive generosity. I go to school on Rich, Marks, and Laux precisely because by doing so, I believe, I become a better man. That's why I read poetry: to change my daily practice.

Body and Song

The Poetry of John Logan

No one read anything silently until two or three hundred years ago. Sometime after Gutenberg, when reading became more widespread through the growth of education and the availability of "texts," some anonymous schoolteacher in some anonymous town or village somewhere discovered "silent reading" and began a fundamental change in our perception of literature. "Don't move your lips when you read," the teacher says to the third-grade class, thereby missing the primary *form* of all literature: the noises it makes.

The Greeks and Romans taught slaves to read aloud so that they could relax and listen, or listen while attending to other things. One of the foundations of Jewish culture, the oral tradition presented not only poetry, but history and theology and social persuasion, drama, and philosophy–all in rhythms and measures designed to make them accessible through *memorization*. John Milton, his eyesight failing, taught his daughters to *pronounce* Latin—with little or no comprehension. He wanted his ears full of the sound of it, and their understanding of the "text" meant nothing to him. In ancient China, poets and audience alike gathered for "poetry-and-wine" festivals that included poetry writing contests and the chanting of works judged best. Formally "reading" a poem is comparable to "reading" a Bach sonata or a great tune by John Coltrane: the "educated" may draw "informed" conclusions, but will invariably turn to theory rather than to the emotional, the gut-level—the very foundation of art—in order to respond.

When John Coltrane first began performing "My Favorite Things," a jazz critic somewhere (in *Downbeat?*) transcribed a solo from a Carnegie Hall performance, then showed the transcription to Coltrane at the beginning of an interview. Coltrane looked at it long and hard, squinting as though listening to black smudges of ink that covered several pages. Then he looked up. "Can't play it," he said. That was *all* he said. Later, after listening to a recording of his performance, Coltrane realized that he *had* played it, and played it exactly as it had been transcribed. His body possessed a knowledge far greater, far deeper, than even his own mind could conceive. John Coltrane was a poet, and had a poet's *ear.*

Speaking about poetry, we often permit ourselves to return to third grade, to sit and read squiggles and ink-smudges in silence, completely unaware of how the poem might engage, might propel or compel our physical bodies. A hundred years ago, there were Tennyson and Browning societies who gathered to listen to poetry in the same way some people now gather at bookstore or college campus poetry readings. It is doubly unfortunate that so many university literature courses continue to "teach" poetry silently, stuck in *logos,* the "reason" of the poem, and stuck in *phanopoeia,* the imagery of the poem. Our insistence upon a way to "explain" the poem often denies us the truest experience of the poetry. From the very beginning, the notion of poetry as a gift of and from the body is apparent. The Greeks believed that by emptying ourselves of ourselves, we may draw into our bodies the breath of one of the Muses—inspiration; becoming inspired, we become pregnant with meaning; pregnant with meaning, we make a song by *listening;* listening attentively, we make sounds with the body, and a poem is born, a poem we then give away in order to become empty again, in order to become inspired. The song, the spiritual exchange, is the fundmental experience of poetry. The lyric poem itself exists *only as a condition of music,* whether that music be flatly spoken or whether it be an aria, and it cannot be properly understood without being heard.

Rhyme became a fundamental part of poetry because it is a mnemonic device. Mnemosyne is the mother of the Muses. More people "remembered" the poems of Robert Service than T. S. Eliot because, in part, the former used predictable meters and predictable rhymes—Service is easy to remember. When I was a teenager memorizing "The Love Song of J. Alfred Prufrock," I bought the Caedmon recording of Eliot and "learned" the poem the exact same way I learned a new recording by Miles Davis or Elvis Presley: by saying it as I listened. I learned every nuance in the voice, every pause. Learning to recite "Prufrock" was the first step toward my own self-definition as a poet. It was the equivalent of a musician's struggle with a Bach or a Coltrane. One must have "masters" in order to become a student. I had learned to recite Wordsworth, Shelley, Keats, Longfellow, Service, and others as a child. But "Prufrock" taught me to listen to other qualities of the poem, it freed me of predictable rhyme and meter, and by doing so, returned me to rhyme and meter with a better ear. Through *listening,* I learned to see language through a modern lens for the first time, and to realize that I had enormous choices to make whenever I make a poem. Formal meter and rhyme don't often accommodate the idea of the *mot juste*. But I did not want to abandon the formal characteristics of poetry altogether.

Any poet who excludes *any* possibility within a poem as a result of allegiance to a set theory of composition is foolish. Almost any generalization one makes about poetry can be persuasively argued, except this: poetry is sound issued from the human body. "Concrete" poets may argue. I respond with a *koan:* "Why is the white horse not a horse?"

All elucidation regarding "form" or "content" or "craft" are *after the fact* of the poem itself, after the presentation of a carefully ordered series of sounds and silences which we call poetry. A sonnet is more than a form, it is a sensibility. It resists, among other things, narrative; but it also invites narrative through sequential composition. It is difficult if not impossible to bare a poet's soul in the octosyllabic couplets of Hudibrastic verse, and yet we can find something of the soul of Auden in his "New Year Letter." But we can't find a sonnet until its syllables have been sounded; we can't count out the syllables of a line until we've heard it.

Donald Hall has a delightful essay on poetry and the body and pleasures thereof in his most recent collection of essays, *Poetry and Ambition* (University of Michigan Press, 1988), from which I quote: "At school sixty years ago we learned by memorization and recitation, the famous rote-learning we affect to despise. We memorized not only *amo amas amat,* but also, 'There is no joy in Mudville, mighty Casey has struck out.' Nor is memorization the issue; the issue is performance. If father and mother did not read scripture aloud they read Dickens. At school we listened to athletes of elocution compete on prize speaking day. After school we met at Lyceum or Oratorical Society or local Chataqua, to sing songs and speak pieces. By 1930 this out-loud culture was mostly dead and there's no point in whining about it. But in the 1930's American poets forgot how to scan; *Understanding Poetry* is a gravestone over the corpse of meter. Connections between print and mouth are largely canceled."

Hall argues for tasting and licking and rolling sound in the mouth, for carrying it on the wings of breath. "When Helen Vendler wrote three hundred pages on Keats's Odes, paraphrase-and source-hunting," he writes, "she did not consider it worthy of remark that these poems occur in lines, in meter, in stanzas, with rhythm, assonance, consonance—or that they make a noise when spoken aloud."

Donald Hall has published several books of essays with University of Michigan Press including *Goatfoot Milktongue Twinbird,* and *The Weather for Poetry.* In the above, I think he is exactly right. Being a product of what

Hall describes as a 1920s-or-earlier education, having grown up speaking poetry almost daily, having been frightened by my father's recitation of "The Raven" and soothed by "The Village Blacksmith," I have never known how—even in a library—to read a poem silently; I cannot read a poem without moving various parts of my body besides my eyes and fingers: my breath is borne (read: born) on the first line, and muscles begin moving,—lungs, spine, the many, many muscles of the human face and throat working to make sound. This was the single greatest gift my adopted parents could possibly give. It was a gift that has—over and over—literally saved my life.

How can I make such an outrageous assertion? Locked behind bars or in the trenches or in whatever appeared to be hopeless situations, I found solace and hope and expressions of love and anger in the words of poets I learned; when the outer world offered only pessimism, I found nourishment and hope in the *sounds* other men and women brought into my often ravaged body. The gift of poetry is the gift of music; it is a dance. Thus the poetry of China and Eastern Europe, of Russia and Chile, of Mexico and Japan: its very intonation has been a tool for shaping culture, which is a shaping, a defining, of human proportion. It's all there in the resonance, in the assonance and consonance, in the etymology of the sound of syllable joining or bumping or buckling syllable, in the rhyme, in the rhythm, in the meter. Poetry goes to the heart by way of the ear, and to the conscious brain later, *after* the poem.

Alone in a cell in solitary confinement, the prisoner is not alone; he or she—given poetry—has a power no one can take away except by taking life itself away. Perhaps it takes a Jacobo Timmerman, an Irina Ratushinskaya, a Faiz Ahmed Faiz to understand the importance of poetry *to the body.* It is impossible to demonstrate this power of poetry to anyone who has never been under extreme duress. How can one understand turning to poetry in the face of death without facing death?

For some, poetry is a connection to "suffering humanity" that cannot be broken. John Logan put it this way: "The poet is an anonymous lover, I believe, and his poetry is an anonymous reaching out, which occasionally becomes personal—when there are those present who care to listen. At the personal moment a mysterious thing happens which reminds us of magic, and hence the power of Orpheus: the loneliness each of us feels locked inside his own skin, and the anonymous reaching each of us does, therefore, becomes a *bond* and hence we are neither alone nor anonymous in the same sense as we were before." The Orphic power is there even when no one cares to listen, a power—born of sound—that prepares us not only to face death, but for death itself. The transcendent and transformational powers of poetry go back at least as far as the seed syllable, the mantra, or the first single note we imitated from animal sounds in the wild. The art of the visionary, the art of the shaman, is "called up" from the very language others use almost thoughtlessly.

Logan has a great deal to say on poetry, and his essays and reviews, *A Ballet for the Ear* (University of Michigan Press, 1983) are a pleasure and instructive to read. But more than his essays, his poems demonstrate aural qualities any lyric poet would admire, if not envy. He says this in one of his best early poems, "A Century Piece for Poor Heine,"

3

He called his mother a dear old
"Pussy Cat";
His wife was a "wild cat";
She was the stupid Cath-
Olic opposite of the Jewish
Other—and cared even less
For his verse, being unable
To read and listening little.
Which is worse. Their need for love
So shocked him, he ran away
To a princess friend—like his sister
A rather crystalline dolly
Charitable toward sexual folly.

Listen to the shifting sounds of *princess, sister,* and *crystalline;* Logan's marvelous off-rhymes contribute directly to the sound (the *meaning*) of the poem. There are multiple interior and well as exterior rhymes: *Worse, verse; friend, crystalline.* Elsewhere, Logan seeks a poetry "that charms the exile/ of listeners into a bond" and his own voice is indeed a bond. To be incapable of listening is worse than to be illiterate. And those who become accomplished listeners? They too become exiles as a result of the *quality* they invest, they become artists.

During the Greek War of Independence, there was a great general named Makryannis, born in a poor village and uneducated. Because of the circumstances of his life, he never really had an opportunity for schooling, but he became a military and a moral leader of his people. Late in his life, he felt an urgency, a necessity to tell his story. All his life, he had listened. But he had never learned to write. So he learned a basic phonetic alphabet and wrote a great autobiography *phonetically,* an autobiography that was then "translated into Greek" and became a source of inspiration for poets like George Seferis and for many others. "What I write down I write down," he says, "because I cannot bear to see right stifled by wrong. For this reason I learned to write in my old age and to do this crude writing . . ."

The same kind of courage and humility is abundant in the poetry of John Logan, now available in a *Collected Poems* (BOA Editions, 1989). He shares a similar passion and a similar sense of the tragic. I discovered John Logan's poetry in the early 60's after hearing Kenneth Rexroth read "Century Piece for Poor Heine" at one of those famous evenings where Rexroth held court for hours on end with his passionate erudition and astonishing ability to memorize poetry in several languages. The book I found was Logan's second, *Ghosts of the Heart.* Advised by a judge to enlist in the U.S. Marine Corps or plan for a life in prison, I enlisted, signing on for duty in Japan. After Boot Camp, I packed for Asia, and John Logan's book, still unread, went into my duffle bag.

Once in Japan, I began learning some Japanese and studying Zen, *Ghosts of the Heart* still buried in a foot locker under my bunk. Months went by, maybe even a year. I extended my stay. Finally, one late autumn day, I took that book and walked up a hill in the sunshine and sat under some trees with a bottle of saké and read it. "Byron at Shelley's Burning" brought a chill down my back. I had grown up on the Romantics and had always tried to imitate my foster father's deep rich voice when I told the poems, and I was utterly captivated by the story of Shelley's heart that would not burn and by Byron's drowning.

Byron at Shelley's Burning

The brain of Shelley cooks
Inside its smoking case;
The bones and flesh fall off
And show the seed of Shelley's thought.

The wine of Byron fumes
Inside his cup of skull;
The lengthy hair of Percy
Streams on his romantic pyre.

The scissor legs of Byron
Swim where Shelley drowned
In wine romantic seas
Of Italy. And Byron notes

The wine red beauty
In the sheets of flame
Of Shelley, as he sees
The body burn upon the beach.

But Byron's brain could not
Foresee how *he* would die
In Greece, his blood ebbing
Into his eye out of a drunken leech.

I had not heard eloquent American English in a year or more. My ears were full of military jargon like, "Where's your lid, marine?" (meaning "Where's you're hat; you're out of uniform.") and the racist, sexist bar-talk of young men full of intentional machismo and braggadocio. My life was a mess. I'd been in more jails than I could remember, had no home to "go home" to, and felt utterly ashamed to be wearing a Marine Corps uniform in occupied Okinawa. I was struggling with the idea of conscientious objection for the first time in my life, and my timing—as usual—could not have been worse. We all knew what was going on in Southeast Asia in 1962, although very few of us had heard yet of Viet Nam. I was ashamed of my country and ashamed of myself and I was in every way an exile.

John Logan's little lyric filled my ears with the music of being alive. And it returned me to the Romantics who returned me to the Greek war of independence, inspired by General Makryannis, a poor, illiterate country bumpkin who survived prison and led his people's revolution before he "learned to speak" in written words. Compared to Makryannis, I had no problems at all. I set about memorizing Logan's poem that afternoon, and late that night, in a G.I. bar full of noisy, drunken post-adolescents, I recited it to some poor, cornered fellow inebriate who, no doubt, had never heard of Logan, Byron, Keats, Shelley, or the "goddamned Greek War of Independence, General Macaroni, but no shit, that's great *stuff!*" And maybe we wandered off arm in arm to get a case of crabs from some village lovely who, we believed in all sexist innocence, made military life worth living.

Saying that poem out loud made life worth living that day. In its music, in its consonants and vowels, rhymes and slant rhymes, I found a desire to be a poet, to make *this kind* of music. I wanted to make that kind of sense of the world someday. And now nearly thirty years have passed, and John Logan is dead, and this large (500pp) book, *John Logan: The Collected Poems,* opens in my lap, and there's that "Heine poem" again, and I can almost hear Rexroth's voice—which always reminded me of W. C. Fields—caressing the sounds, and here's the poem that left me stunned in Okinawa, and they are just the beginning. Whole *books* of poems: *Spring of the Thief* and *The Zig-zag Walk.* From the latter, I look up a poem I read aloud to one of the first friends I made after moving to Port Townsend sixteen years ago:

Two Preludes for La Push

1
Islands high as our inland hills
rise clean and sheer above the chill
April seas at La Push.
In a hush
of holy fog
the lean trees along their tops
(inaccessible to be climbed)
are offered up in flames of salt and wind.
And at La Push
the white, furious waves mass and rush
at each earthen island base.
These waves
are sudden, violent, unpredictable as grace.
They change White then
Blue then Green
swift as in Raphael's great wing!
I've seen it here where it has always hid:
Light, the shadow of our ancient God.

2
In the late afternoon light
even our human feet
start halos in the sand:
soft flashes of mind.

From the occult shore where you can see or feel
only a few shells
(shattered) among the lively stones,
we walk home.
I follow my younger brother,
for I am the visitor.
He knows the maze of fallen trees
that back up the blasted beach
for blocks: whether
this path or another.
Here the logs lie like lovers,
short by long, benign,
nudging gently in the tide.

Further up all the logs have died.
We walk through graves of wood
which are so oddly
borne out of the fecund sea,
each piece a last marker for itself,
each tomb planted with bulbs and whips of kelp.
Now as the water light fades,
I feel the monsters rage
again in this abandoned wood—gray
on darker gray.
Sometimes the flesh of the drifted face
is almost white! They seem to lift
their awful limbs,
broken from their lost hands.
Now the grotesque, giant shapes all
whirl awhile!
In the final light
the hard knots
of eyes scowl and brood
above the smaller dead
animals of wood.
I am afraid.
My brother walks ahead,
I reach for land:
the driftwood logs heavily shake

underfoot, and I awake,
balancing between my youth and my age.

It may be helpful to learn something about La Push. People on the Olympic Peninsula, west of Seattle, refer to La Push and environs as "the West End." It is, like most of the villages on the peninsula, a backwater. But La Push is a "reservation," which, when translated out of government lingo, means Concentration Camp for Native Americans. When the Chimicum Indians on the east side of the peninsula couldn't be controlled, they were shipped off to the "West End" where they disappeared into other nations. La Push is near Forks, the peninsula logging capital and distribution point for clear-cut and old growth lumber, a town where every other vehicle is either a four-wheeler or a log truck. Astonishing in its beauty and heart-breaking in its ecological damage, the countryside around La Push climbs quickly into the Olympic Mountains with their snowy caps. Just down the road, there is an enormous rain forest so thick it is virtually impenetrable. And La Push itself is a fishing center, home to hundreds of gillnetters and trawlers and those who work the boats. Because it lies at the edge of the sea at the foot of mountains, it is rainy season there most of the year. And the sea is often wild.

The first Prelude is built entirely upon descriptive power until the penultimate line. The "religious" language of the poem is not in the least surprising considering the place itself, and considering Logan's lifelong struggle with Christian love and mercy. Nor is it surprising that the "ancient God" encountered there inspired in the poet some significant spiritual meditation which then brought the second Prelude, which continues the religious imagery with "halos in the sand," followed by the surprising and very Zen-like "soft flashes of mind." Suddenly, the shore is "occult," and "you can see or feel" invites us to consider our spiritual blindness, and the few shells are "shattered" and only the stones remain lively.

Not that it is of particular relevance, but Logan's physical description of the place is deadly accurate, even to the suggested tenderness of logs lying "like lovers,/ short by long, benign,/ nudging gently in the tide," only to feel "monsters rage" almost immediately thereafter. What are these monsters? Sea-serpents? Daemons of the dark woods? Or perhaps the ghosts of our own history, social and personal, brought together by the vision before our eyes. The death of human culture, the death of deep forest culture, the poisoning of the "fecund" sea—it is not surprising the poet bluntly states, "I am afraid." And poet and reader awaken together, balancing as the poet balanced climbing over huge driftwood logs washed up from islands of logs tugboats tow along a mile or so at sea. In "Two Preludes for La Push," as he does so often elsewhere, Logan wrestles with the twin angels Complicity and Compassion.

When a culture rejects its ancient mythologies, it must invent new ones to replace the metaphors borne by the old; otherwise, society loses its spiritual center. No one in our time has demonstrated exactly how this happens more clearly than Joseph Campbell. In La Push, Logan came face to face with the spiritual as well as physical poverty that is the result of Anglo-American contempt toward the spiritual metaphors, rites, and economies of more ancient Native American cultures.

Interviewing Logan in 1961, Marvin Bell asks, "Are you a religious poet?" Logan responds by quoting John Crowe Ransom: "Poetry is the secular form of piety," and then goes on to quote Rilke on the music of poetry: "True song demands a different kind of breathing. A calm. A shudder in the god. A gale." In the fishing village of La Push, on the northwestern coast of Washington state, Logan's breathing changed, and perhaps he felt his god shudder just a little as the song began to take form.

Later in the same interview, Logan says the shortcoming of poetry is "a certain tendency toward angelism: i.e., poetry tends to leave the earth and emulate the gods (whom the poets named). . . The true image of the poem is seen in the *tension* [Logan's emphasis] between Jacob and the angel—the *balance* of the two as they dance ("wrestle" is the vulgar word to describe what they were doing). Jacob corrects the timid and anarchic impulse to flight, while the angel exorcises the earth-bound impulse of Jacob. The result is a poem. . . ." In the "secular" piety of poetry, the poet accepts the dance of *whatever* angel as may appear—which is to say that the "true" poet is more a pantheist than a monotheist, recognizing in every gesture, the prayer at its root. In Hindu culture, as in certain religious communities, one might greet one's neighbor, palms raised and together in what is universally recognized at a prayerful attitude. It is, of course, a dance of the hands, a mudra. The gesture recognizes the "god" within the other, just as the Hindu sees the mind of god imagining everything; we are god. Mohandas Gandhi greeted everyone with that gesture because he recognized within everyone that which was within himself: good and evil, justice and mercy—the face of god.

In Gandhi's simple gesture, the violence of England against India, the racism of South Africa, the insane hatred of Muslim and Hindu and Christian are all confronted and overcome by the silence of placing one's palms together. Logan's piety finds expression in description and sound, like a kind of secular sutra, the poem identifying not a god *against* nature, but god *in* nature.

Leaving the beach, the driftwood logs "shake/ underfoot" like the earth itself trembling beneath a god we have grotesquely offended.

As a young man contemplating Conscientious Objection, I found in Logan's poetry the expression of piety I had not found in various religions. The metaphors of religion, I freely accept; its dogmas and its bureaucracy I must reject. In a short essay, "On the Inarticulate Hero," also in *A Ballet for the Ear,* Logan states, "The first problem of man [sic] is to learn how to utter his love, which is the articulation of himself as a person; the second problem is to learn how to shut up, which is the articulation of himself as a saint. Therefore both in the struggle to speak and the active quietness of the inarticulate hero we see ourselves in depth, and we reaffirm our hope of change and we experience through them, these superb incompetents, what Nietzsche so beautifully called 'metaphysical solace.'" This same metaphysical solace is also brought to us by the metaphors in our mythology, like Jacob dancing with the angel. Logan's early poems offered the formality of changed breathing together with vital metaphors, a balancing of sound and silence concluding in solace.

Dylan Thomas I could recite for the sheer sound alone. His poems are so heavily incantatory that even when he says preposterous things, the music carries one along. But in Logan, the music and the meaning are one, the expression of an insatiable spiritual longing. His use of assonance and consonance and rhyme are there as a condition of music, not simply as a mnemonic device or as mere artifice. He is not building in Procrustean beds.

We often use the word *song* as a metaphor for poetry, but every time we do so, we are forgetting that speaking is a form of song. When the television commedian blabbers gibberish fake Russian or Chinese, we are actually laughing at our own ignorance of music, reducing the song of a man or woman to reductive archetype which invites a racist, ethnocentric response: we laugh because we in our ignorance somehow believe that ours is the "true language" just as we have believed that ours is the "true religion." But language is a song under perpetual revision, and every language is true inasmuch as it continues to evolve toward a perfected definition. Poetry *is* song. The television commedian reproduces only an approximate song. But the song that is a poem has no room for approximations; poetry begins with naming, with particulars. And lyric poetry, by definition, is words *of* song. Logan, schooled in the "dead" languages of Rome and Greece, brought from these studies a highly trained ear and a taste for counterpoint in his music.

In the *Rig Veda,* early on, where language is first invented, it says, "When they set in motion the first beginning of speech, giving names, their most pure and perfectly guarded secret was revealed through love. When the wise ones [poets and seers] fashioned speech with their thought, . . . *then* friends recognized their friendships [my emphasis]. . . . A man that abandons a friend who has learned with him no longer has a share in speech." Those who use speech in bad ways "weave on a weft of rags, without understanding," but those who compose poems sit "bringing to blossom the flower of the verses," that is, they become the *embodiment* of speech, of wisdom. Rexroth said the poet "creates sacramental relationships that last always." But I prefer to believe that it's not the poet who creates these relationships, only the one who articulates their condition.

With Logan, it's not as simple as "we must love one another or die," that famous phrase that so unsettled Auden; rather, we must *articulate* our love, because the very act of speaking defines ourselves. In order to maintain our "share in speech," we must remain loyal to what we have learned *from* that speech—love and friendship and their embodiment, their articulation, in others. Otherwise our speech may have devastating consequences: we shall speak American English rather than Haida or Tlingit or Kwakiutl.

In another poem from his time in the northwest, "The Pass," Logan describes a visit to Deception Pass with his younger brother and some friends, where they

> all look down
> where gulls fall and rise over The Sound.
>
> The awful height stirs in me
> the huge easy
>
> gull
> of my own soul. / . . .

and the phanopoeia carries a heavy parallel to one of the most famous images in all of Chinese poetry, that of Tu Fu's gull in "Night Thoughts While Traveling," with its great closing couplet:

> Adrift, drifting, what is left for a lone gull
> adrift between earth and heaven.

If Tu Fu looks up to see the gull, Logan looks down from "the awful height." But for both poets, the gull represents a sense of being a misfit, a sense of profound longing and searching. Logan's poem concludes,

> I wait until the tug's
>
> completely underneath the span
> (by then
>
> even the wake of the younger boat is gone)
> and turn
>
> to walk back
> alone toward the rock.

His aloneness is understood through elemental images and through parallels like that of the disappearing wake of the "younger boat" as contrasted with the tug. But, phanopoeia aside, the rhythms of the lines are steady and irregular like the waves beating the sides of stone inlands carved by millions of tides, waters rushing through a narrow passage. His use of rhyme and off-rhyme are done with a completely relaxed, natural syntax. There are no inverted sentences, no dead words, no stacked adjectives to fill out a pre-determined measure.

Part of the argument between closed or pre-determined form and open or organic form is the appositional attractions of artifice and sincerity. One poet, the *maker,* becomes aware of the *object* a poem may be and is attracted to the idea of completely "finished" surfaces; another poet, attempting to connect with deep interior consciousness, wants to do away with artifice and surface completely, so that the poem becomes the process of self-revelation. Logan, having gone to school on traditional versification, draws on the powers of both traditions, overcoming the form versus content duality by sustaining both formality of speech by way of variable meters and use of sound, and by maintaining absolute sincerity of diction and of *logopoeia.*

Now John Logan is silent. In failing health, he fell to his death from the roof of the apartment house where he lived in San Francisco in 1987. We are left with this hefty *Collected Poems,* and with the many wonderful ways in which these poems move the body into song, the many ways they change the human heart and breath.

A Paradise of One's Own

Odysseas Elytis in English

Odysseas Elytis (the modern *a* replacing the older *u* in his first name at his suggestion) is a poet like no other in this world. Neither the leading figure in a literary movement nor a famous teacher of younger poets, he follows a line of individualistic visionary ecstatic poets leading all the way back to Sappho in the 6th century BCE.

He credits his art primarily to two moments of supreme insight. The first came one night in 1929 when the eighteen-year-old Elytis chanced upon a book by Paul Eluard, a moment reified in 1935 when Elytis, then a student at the School of Law, University of Athens, attended a lecture on surrealism by Andréas Embirícos. He left the university without his degree, and began a long friendship with Embirícos and association with other new Greek poets such as George Seferis and Nikos Gatsos. With publication of *Orientations* in 1939 and *Sun the First* in 1943, Elytis established himself as one of the great lyric voices of modern poetry.

What had attracted the young Elytis to surrealism was not its revolutionary rejection of traditional versification nor its stream-of-consciousness, but its faith in intuition and passionate exploration of the subconscious imagination. Imagination is as much "reality" as the temporal physical world around us. Surrealism was a means by which to return to the original source, a poetics that would reject the conventions of rational discourse in traditional verse, admitting dream, reverie, and dissociative imagery. The early poems shimmer with transparent light.

Kimon Friar, in his brilliant introduction to *The Sovereign Sun: Selected Poems* (Temple University Press, 1974) called them a "Dionysian exaltation not heard since the outpourings of Sikelianós, or the erotic optimism of Embirícos. Elytis showed himself in finer control of his technique, more translucent in his images, clearer in his expression. In *Orientations* and *Sun the First*, he became the foremost lyric poet of his generation; in him the deification of youth amid the legendary landscape and sweet reveries of the Aegean Sea received its apotheosis."

The second great revelation came after Mussolini invaded Greece in October, 1940, and the fall of Elytis's homeland, Crete, in 1941, beginning more than three years of Axis occupation. Elytis, a lieutenant in the First Army Corps, says in an interview with Ivar Ivask, "It became necessary for me to proceed toward that spear-point where life and death, light and darkness cease to be contraries. . . . Fear, the physical fear of war, the material fear of bombs and shells, annihilated within me all aspects of false literature and left naked the meaning of a true need for poetry. Fear was in turn annihilated in me by the salvation brought me, as a man, by a poetry made of nakedness and truth."

In the harsh Greek landscape, splendid as it may be, youth passes quickly, and the eighteen-year-old sun-dazzled boy-god was to convey the countenance of middle age by thirty. In 1943, Elytis composed *Heroic and Elegiac Song for the Lost Second Lieutenant of the Albanian Campaign*, a symphonic *tour de force* drawing on the powers of traditional demotic poetry, surrealist elements introduced with even greater restraint as the poet began to find a voice that would speak for an entire nation. His lyric was not of liquid sunlight on Aegean shores, but of how "agony stoops with bony hands." Years later, he would write in a letter to Kimon Friar, "I believe in the restitution of justice, which I identify with light. And together with a glorious and ancient ancestor of mine, that 'I do not care for those gods whose worship is practiced in the dark.'"

During the late nineteen forties and early fifties, he translated the poetry of Garcia Lorca, Brecht, Eluard, and Ungaretti, and wrote criticism, especially articles on surrealist art including pieces on Matisse, Picasso, Giacometti, and de Chirico. While living in Paris, he was associated with Breton, Eluard, Char, and others. Upon his return to Greece in 1953, he became a national figure in the cultural arena.

The poet would review the early part of that era in his only major prose statement on his art, *Open Papers* (a generous selection from *Open Papers* has been translated by Olga Broumas and T Begley, Copper Canyon Press, 1994). In "First Things First," he observes, "And yet from *what is* to *what could be*, you cross a bridge that takes you, no more, no less, from Hell to Paradise. Even more strange: a Paradise made of the very elements of Hell. The only difference lies in our perception of the arrangement of these elements, which is easy to understand if you imagine it applied to the architecture of ethics and emotions. . . . The common characteristic of all poets is their dissent from current reality."

Labeled early as a Dionysian celebrant of ecstasy, he responds, "This is fundamentally wrong. I believe that poetry on a certain level of accomplishment is neither optimistic nor pessimistic. It represents rather a third state of the spirit where opposites cease to exist. There are no more opposites beyond a certain level of elevation. Such poetry is like nature itself, which is neither good nor bad, beautiful nor ugly; it simply *is*. Such poetry is no longer subject to habitual everyday distinctions. . . . The final goal of every exploration is inescapably nature. This, obviously, is very much part of the Hellenic tradition."

The mature work of Elytis is marked by his depth of knowledge, his use of the "old, pure Katharevousa" (an artificially constructed language based on Attic Greek), along with modern demotic Greek, local and regional dialect, multiple voices, neo-logisms, and structural harmonies drawing from the strophic/anti-strophic composition of ancient liturgies and tragedies. And still his every chorus strives to achieve the realization of limpidity, the idea that within each image or idea is another complex image or idea, within which stand yet other images. His poetry amounts to a revelation of the working psyche as it becomes one with the poet's sense of commitment as he sings, in "Sun the First,"

I give my hand to justice
Transparent fountain source at the peak
My sky is deep and unaltered
What I love is always being born
What I love is beginning always

This, in the midst of World War II. If Kimon Friar's long out-of-print *The Sovereign Sun* was the best early general introduction to the poetry of Elytis, Olga Broumas's selection of his poems, *What I Love* (Copper Canyon Press, 1986), was the first to capture his lyric intensity. The *Selected Poems* edited and mostly translated by Edmund Keeley and Philip Sherrard (Viking Press/ Penguin, 1981) was also a noble achievement. Considering the enormous complexity of this "poet of limpidity," he has been wonderfully served by his various translators, each with individual strengths.

Complexity and depth of perception are reflected even in the poet's *nom de plume*, which recalls such classical Greek themes and ideals as *Ellas* (Hellas), *elpídha* (hope), *elefthería* (freedom), and of course *Eléni* (Helen). It also chooses a general rather than regional suffix to his surname. The poet nevertheless states, "Contrary to those who strive an entire life to 'fix' their literary likeness, I'm intent every hour and each moment on destroying mine, my face turned to prototype alone, whose nature is to be endlessly created, ready to begin again precisely on account of life and art's oneness, which exists far before or after the sashaying of salons and of cafes." His conviction to keep "the mechanisms of myth-making but not the figures of mythology" is a poetic equivalent to the Confucian instruction, "Worship the virtue of ancestors, not ancestors themselves," and bears considerable moral as well as aesthetic weight.

The challenge to his translators lies in capturing his powerful lyric intensity without losing his inner "correspondences" within the imagery, or stripping away his incantatory inventiveness. Just as we had to "go to school" on Pound and Eliot, H.D. and Williams, we must go to school on Elytis, "the most Greek of all Greek poets." For the American reader, ancient Greece—as interpreted through Roman classicism and the Italian Renaissance and Romantic poets from England—only gets in the way. As fellow Greek Nobel Poet George Seferis observed, modern Greek poets were forced "to destroy the traditional rationalism which lay heavily on the Western world" and "to regard Greek reality without the prejudices that have reigned since the Renaissance."

With publication of *The Axion Esti* in 1959, Elytis brought his mechanisms of myth-making to full fruition in what translators Edmund Keeley and George Savidis have described as "a kind of spiritual autobiography which attempts to dramatize the national and philosophical extensions of a highly personal sensibility. The poet's strategy—reminiscent of Whitman's in *Song of Myself* and Sikelianos's in *Prologue to Life*—is to present an image of the contemporary Greek consciousness through the developing perspective of a first-person persona who is at once the poet himself and the voice of his country." For this elaborate triptych, Elytis draws generously from the literary and historical Greece, including Homer, Heraclitus and Pindar, from Byzantine hymnographers and Greek Orthodox liturgy, from folk songs and the autobiography of the great (and illiterate) General Makryannis. To translate a poem of such length—80 pages of text—that is so intricately idiomatic and wrapped so snugly in Greek sound and rhythmic change is a nearly impossible task; and yet the Keeley/Savidis translation of *The Axion Esti* (University of Pittsburgh Press, 1974; presently out-of-print) achieves a maximum of poetry with few but excellent notes. It is a poem as monumental as Eliot's *Wasteland*, and probably the most widely read book of poetry in Greece since World War II, popularized in part by musical settings from the incomparable composer, Mikis Theodorakis. As much as anything else, *The*

Axion Esti established Odysseas Elytis as a Nobel Prize candidate to be taken very seriously.

In a series of poems written concomitantly with *The Axion Esti* and published as *Six and One Remorses for the Sky* (1960), Elytis confronts the idea of Beauty in a world of evil and finds in his personification an otherly beauty in which is revealed the real landscape to be seen:

> Where, near the river, the dark ones fought against the Angel,
> exactly showing how she's born, Beauty
>
> Or what we otherwise call tear.
>
> And long as her thinking lasted, you could feel it overflow
> the glowing sight bitterly in the eyes and the huge, like
> an ancient prostitute's, cheekbones
>
> Stretched to the extreme points of the Large Dog and of the Virgin.
>
> "Far from the pestilential city I dreamed of her deserted place
> where a tear may have no meaning and the only light be
> from the flame that ravishes all that for me exists.
>
> "Shoulder to shoulder under what will be, sworn to extreme
> silence and the co-ruling of the stars,
>
> "As if I didn't know yet, the illiterate, that there exactly, in
> extreme silence are the most repellent thuds
>
> "And that, since it became unbearable inside a man's chest
> solitude dispersed and seeded stars!"

With the acknowledged loss of innocence (illiteracy), comes the revelation of a deeper, truer landscape of the soul, mind solitary in its awareness, and yet connected to the seeded stars. "Beauty" may indeed be "otherly," she may stand alone in her "deserted place where a tear may have no meaning," she nevertheless remains for the poet a palpable albeit inexplicable presence. A few years later, in "Villa Natacha," Elytis would say, "I have something to say transparent incomprehensible/ As birdsong in hour of war." And, "I dream a revolution on the part of evil and of wars like that / made on the part of chiaroscuro and color shading, O Matisse."

He speaks for what insists upon remaining silent or unsayable. He struggles to reveal a Paradise—not the dogma of eternal life hereafter, but of a Paradise within, as though our inability to comprehend this Paradise lay at the root of all human suffering, a tragedy of enormous proportion, one that is itself the "other side" of Albert Camus's sense of the absurd. Just as Camus was not an existentialist, Elytis is not a surrealist. Both are Mediterranean pre-classic sensibilities, each representing a deep *humanitas*. While Elytis adores the moment of innocence, his is a search for the awakening moment, for "enlightenment,"—in his own words, for the "drop of light in the vast night of the soul." He remembers Matisse during the years of Auschwitz and Buchenwald "painting the most juicy and ripe, the most charming flowers and fruits which were ever made, as if the very miracle of life had found a way to coil within them forever." The lost second lieutenant of the Albanian campaign, the atrocities of war and the pestilence of cities—nothing can destroy the Paradise within. "Let them call me crazy / that out of nothing is born our Paradise."

In *Maria Nephele* (1978), he sets "parallel monologues" between a kind of punk *bete noire* filled with the post-adolescent ennui of disillusionment and an older male "Antiphonist," allowing "Mary of the Clouds" to become a figure for Helen, for Mary and for Antigone, achieving the "limpidity" that has become a signature of his poetry, one figure seen within the next, with yet another within that. Mary excoriates "the poets," accusing them,

> What can I do with you my eyes the poets
> who years now pretend invincible souls
>
> And years wait for what I never did
> standing in line like unclaimed objects . . . (sic)
>
> What if they call you—not one of you answers
> outside the world's a mess everything burning
>
> Nothing you claim—I wish I knew with what brain
> you rights in a vacuum!
>
> In times of wealth's worship o abandon
> you exude private property's vanity

Wrapped up in Palm leaves you go on holding
the wretched mourning-covered globe

And in the stench of human sulfur you become
the volunteer lab rats of the Holy.

MAN'S PULLED BY GOD
AS SHARK BY BLOOD.

The Antiphonist notes, "It is bigamy to love and to dream." And, "You 'fix' a truth / exactly as you fix a lie."

Kimon Friar has written of Elytis's mature work, "He has kept to a strict demotic base with taste and discretion, but he has also added to his lexicon, grammar, syntax, and rhythmic embellishments taken from all periods of Greek literature . . . . Throughout his entire career he has been primarily interested in the plastic use of language, manipulating words and images like a painter or sculptor, shaping and reworking them as though they were colors or material. He has shaken off the tyranny of the speech of the common man, together with that of the pseudo-educated, which are both strangleholds on the creative spirit. He has returned to the language of the poet-saint, the prophet who must utter his vision in a common liturgy."

Elytis's major work since winning the 1979 Nobel Prize in Literature is the epic *The Little Mariner*, published in 1984 (translated by Olga Broumas, first published by Copper Canyon Press in 1988), another conceptual *tour-de-force* alternating prose poems with charged lyrical passages separated by four "spotlights" drawn from Greek history and personal mythology and three "catalogues" of influences from throughout the centuries. His lifelong search for an inner Paradise culminates near the end of *The Little Mariner* with the observation that "Yes, Paradise wasn't nostalgia. Nor, much less, a reward. It was a right." Like *The Axion Esti* before it, *The Little Mariner* bears the undeniable handprint of genius, of poetic authority, of visionary enlightenment.

Earlier, in *Open Papers,* he had warned, "Don't think me exalted. I'm not referring to myself; I speak for whomever feels as I do and is not naive enough to confess it. If a separate personal Paradise exists for each of us, I reckon mine must be irreparably planted with trees of words the wind silvers like poplars, by people who see their confiscated justice given back, and by birds that even in the midst of the truth of death insist on singing in Greek and saying, 'eros' 'eros,' 'eros.'"

According to Hesiod, Eros is the first god to overcome humans *and* gods, and who instills within their souls all notions of beauty and anguish. Beauty and anguish, imagination and reality, Paradise and Hell—for Elytis, poetry, the truth of poetry, demolished such arbitrary distinctions, finding that "Paradise and Hell are made of exactly the same material." In Elytis's poetry, the major elements are air and water, both defined by light. "When I say 'Paradise,' I do not conceive of it in the Christian sense. It is another world which is incorporated into our own, and it is our fault that we are unable to grasp it." For the pre-Socratic imagination of Elytis, the *then* is found in the *now* just as the possible is seen within the impossible, the dream in the wakeful act.

On a visit to Athens nearly 15 years ago, I went to see the poet in his modest apartment where he lived for fifty years, devoting his life to poetry, thanks to a small inheritance. Over a glass of Jack Daniels—"I've never cared for ouzo or retsina"—I explained that Olga Broumas's *What I Love,* which we were then planning to publish, would not bring him much money. Even a recent recipient of a Nobel Prize wouldn't sell more than a few thousand copies of poems in translation in the U.S.A. Then I asked about his Greek publisher.

"My publisher prints about 25,00 copies," he said. "And then, after a few weeks, when they're all sold, it's reprinted in paperback. But that doesn't matter," he added. "A *real* poet needs an audience of three. And since any poet worth his salt has two intelligent friends, one spends a lifetime searching for the third reader," he laughed. He had written in *Open Papers,* "Not wishing to lose even a moment from your supposed Talent is like not wishing to lose even a drachma from the interest of the small capital donated to you. But poetry is not a bank. On the contrary, it is the conception which actually opposes the bank. If it becomes a written text communicable to others, so much the better. If not, that doesn't matter. That which must happen and happen uninterruptedly, endlessly, without the slightest irregularity, is anti-servility, irreconcilibility, independence. Poetry is the other face of Pride."

From among Elytis's last poems, Broumas has translated selections from *Outrock Elegies, The Garden with the Self-Deceptions,* and *West of Sorrow,* adding them to her previously published selections from all of Elytis's major works except *Axion Esti. Eros, Eros, Eros!* draws from the same literary and spiritual traditions as Elytis's original Greek. Nobody but Olga Broumas, born in Greece and into the Sapphic tradition, could so embody the sound and movement and spirit of the original while bringing these poems into American English.

If the *Elegies* are a result of facing his own declining health, and immanent blindness and death, *West of Sorrow* represents a kind of transcendence, ultimately an expression of gratitude for that Paradise within. Composed while visiting Porto Rafti in 1995, a year before his death, the poems of *West of Sorrow* are the final testament of a great visionary. In "As Endymion,"* the last poem in his final suite of poems, he concludes:

In a thousand sleeps one comes awake
but it's forever.

Artemis Artemis grab me the moon's dog
It bites a cypress and unsettles the Eternals
Much deeper sleeps whom History has drenched
Light a match to its alcohol
 it's only Poetry
Remains. Poetry. Just and essential and direct
As Adam and Eve imagined it—Just
In the pungent garden and infallible to clocks.

---

*Quoted from *Analogies of Light,* edited by Ivar Ivask U of Oklahoma Press, 1975). [Mike: Maybe we should look this up on *ours* translation.

Other sources includes *Modern Greek Poetry* by Edmund Keeley (Princeton U. Press, 1983), and *49 Scholia on the Poems of Odysseus Elytis* by Jeffrey Carson (Ypsilon Books, 1983).

The Poetry of Kenneth Rexroth

Introduction to *Complete Poems of Kenneth Rexroth*

"We have preferred the power that apes greatness—Alexander first of all, and then the Roman conquerors, whom our school history books, in an incomparable vulgarity of soul, teach us to admire. We have conquered in our turn . . . our reason has swept everything away. Alone at last, we build our empire upon a desert. How then could we conceive that higher balance in which nature balanced history, beauty, and goodness, and which brought the music of numbers even into the tragedy of blood? We turn our back on nature, we are ashamed of beauty. Our miserable tragedies have the smell of an office, and their blood is the color of dirty ink."

—Albert Camus

The year was 1948. Camus's relationships with Andre Breton and Jean-Paul Sartre had begun to feel the strain that would eventually lead him to disavow all ties with the existentialists. In North America, the official policies of the Cold War were under way. Senator Joseph McCarthy had recruited young politicos like Robert Kennedy and Richard Nixon to help him "purge the United States Government of communist infiltrators." School children were drilled in preparation for "atom bombs." And American poetry was divided between the conservative New Critics for whom T. S. Eliot was a standard bearer and those who followed William Carlos Williams's insistence upon "American idiom" and measure for poetry. The Bollingen Prize Committee meeting in 1948 included Eliot himself as well as elements from both camps (Conrad Aiken, W. H. Auden, Louise Bogan, Robert Lowell, Allen Tate, Karl Shapiro, and Léonie Adams) and was timed to coincide with Eliot's visit to the United States that fall. When they awarded the prize to Ezra Pound for his *Pisan Cantos,* a furor ensued. Pound was locked up in St. Elizabeth's Hospital for the insane, charged (but untried) with treason for his infamous radio broadcasts from Rome during World War II, writing his great poem and translating Confucius. The "runner-up" was *Paterson (Book Two)* by Williams. It had been the stated ambition of Pound and Williams to "break the back of the iamb," to liberate American poetry. Williams admired some of Eliot's poetry but despised his influence.

In San Francisco, the forty-three-year-old Kenneth Rexroth must have watched with interest. He had connections with many of those involved. Reading Ezra Pound's *Cathay*, translations from the eighth century poet Li Po, had first opened Rexroth's eyes to Chinese poetry while he was still a teenager. It was a huge awakening. In the early thirties, he corresponded with Pound, who provided insights into French and Chinese poetry especially, and who introduced him to James Laughlin, publisher of New Directions and Rexroth's lifelong friend and patron. The Pound/Rexroth letters conclude in political hostility and mutual animosity. Rexroth was then involved with the Wobblies and many left wing causes and despised "Pound's virulent, anti-Semitic doggerel." Pound was immersed in the economic theories of Major Douglas and Social Credit, and actively supported Mussolini. When Rexroth objected to including an Ezra Pound rant in *An "Objectivists" Anthology*, Pound responded that he would have nothing to do with the project if "dot Chew Bolschevick Rexwrothsky" was included.

Also in the thirties, Rexroth explored cubist art and poetry, eventually resolving his own differences with Tristan Tzara and Breton in a "cubist" poem, "Fundamental Disagreement with Two Contemporaries," (*The Art of Worldly Wisdom*, 1949). The exact nature of their disagreement remains for speculation. His experiments with cubist poetry were short-lived, although he would say years later that he gave them up only because so few people understood what he was doing. He returned to the spare style he had been evolving since his first poems.

Politically, he was a pacifist, like Lowell, William Stafford, and several other poets of the time. But Rexroth has been an almost solitary voice for pacificism throughout all the world's violence since World War I. Before the end of World War II, he wrote in his note to *The Phoenix And the Tortoise*, "If the shorter poems might well be dedicated to [D.H.] Lawrence, 'The Phoenix And the Tortoise' might well be dedicated to Albert Schweitzer, the man who in our time pre-eminently has realized the dream of Leonardo da Vinci. Leonardo died impotent and broken, all his projects half done. He proved that the human will is too small a door for the person to force through into universality. Schweitzer is an outstanding example of a man who found that door which is straight, and smaller than a needle's eye, but through which the universalization of the human soul, the creation of the true person, comes freely, as a guest."

One thing is clear: Rexroth, already a citizen of the world, believed that the "universalization of the human soul, the creation of the true person," may come freely, but only after enormous struggle to find that "door which is straight, and smaller than a needle's eye." The awakening he sought would lie in a poetry of increasing limpidity and deceptive simplicity. His search for that door would lead him through the history of philosophy, comparative religion, and the history of ideas. Like Pound, he was a neo-classicist engaged in the avant garde. He was a master of juxtaposition and polyphony. Along with the Greek and Latin translations in *The Phoenix And the Tortoise* are three poems by the T'ang dynasty poet, Tu Fu whom Rexroth would come to revere. He translated about forty of Tu Fu's poems over the years, calling him "the greatest non-epic, non-dramatic poet in history."

In the long title poem, "The Phoenix and the Tortoise," Rexroth incorporates paraphrases and translations of Japanese tanka from Gotoku Daiji, *Hyakunin Isshu*, Lady Akazome Emon, Emperor Sanjo, and many others. By 1948, his course and methodology were set. He adopted something similar to what has since been labeled the "ideogrammic method" advocated by Pound. All being becomes contemporary in his hands. He borrows, he layers, he juxtaposes, holding his poems together lyrically through the effective use of a roughly seven syllable line. Echoes and paraphrases and translations of ancient classics of the East and West become an integral part of the poem in progress, rewarding the reader with evocative and associative resonances. This practice also elevates the poetry out of the realm of the merely personal lyric or monologue, creating a historical context. Rexroth the poet is the contemporary of Sophocles and Sappho, Tu Fu and Reverdy, and literature is the bread of their communion.

Another clear example is "When We with Sappho," which begins with a direct translation of the Sapphic fragment, "About the cool water / the wind sounds . . ." but suddenly becomes an intensely personal love poem, a meditation that runs nearly four pages. Sappho becomes a presence opening the mind of the poet. A door. Rexroth's poetry incorporates the past as a presence in daily reality and evolving consciousness. What he reads is an essential element of mundane reality. Donald Gutierrez, in his study, *The Holiness of the Real: The Short Verse of Kenneth Rexroth*, has written of this poem, "Rexroth's verse sounds like an exalted experience undergone through words that have been rendered so plain, so 'artless,' and 'right' as to take on a transparency revealing the heart of the poem's life itself."

William Carlos Williams, reviewing *The Phoenix and the Tortoise* in *The Quarterly Review of Literature*, would say almost nothing about translation. And of Rexroth's philosophy he wrote, "I know nothing of mysticism . . . I'm going to try to take out the poetry, appraise it as best I can and leave the mysticism, as far as I can, intact. But first let me say that this is one of the most completely realized arguments I have encountered in a book of verse in my time." The title poem is rich in what Williams called mysticism. It begins with the geologic past of the California Coast Range, moving quickly and surely into "the falling light of the Spartan/ Heroes of the late Hellenic dusk," while considering various ideas of Aquinas, early Chinese philosophers, some ancient Greeks, and far too many other references and accretions to quote out of context. The net is cast wide. This "ideogrammic" style is common in Asian literature, and Rexroth knew it by the Japanese *honkadori*. The "dance of the intellect among the ten thousand things," as Tu Fu would say.

Rexroth received a Guggenheim Fellowship in 1948 and traveled in Europe, working on his long poem, "The Dragon and the Unicorn." Also in 1948, he added the finishing strokes to one of the most beautifully conceived and executed volumes of poetry since Pound's *Cathay*, *The Signature of All Things*. Most of the poems and poems-in-translation were composed to be sung, their melodies an essential part of the composition. Among these poems, two elegies stand out: "Delia Rexroth," a poem addressed to the poet's mother who died in 1916 when he was eleven; and "Andree Rexroth," an elegy for the woman to whom he was married for thirteen years and who died in 1940 following years of struggle with an inherited brain disease.

There is also a remarkable homage, "A Letter to William Carlos Williams," in which Rexroth observes, "And you're 'pure', too,/ A real classic, though not loud/ About it—a whole lot like/ The girls of the Anthology./ Not like strident Sappho, who/ For all her grandeur, must have/ Had endemetriosis,/ But like Anyte, who says/ Just enough, softly, for all/ The thousands of years to remember . . ." The poem illuminates the "sacramental relationships" that he had come to understand as essential to poetry, and does so at least in part by praising Williams's optimism. Rexroth held on to hope despite devastating personal and social losses and a struggle with deep-seated paranoia. But he was no wide-eyed optimist. He believed that love is the sacramental expression of hope and responsibility. Williams would claim later that the events described in the poem never actually took place, but what does that matter? The poem creates its own occasion.

Between Two Wars

Remember that breakfast one November—
Cold black grapes smelling faintly
Of the cork they were packed in,

Hard rolls with hot, white flesh,
And thick, honey sweetened chocolate?
And the parties at night; the gin and the tangos?
The torn hair nets, the lost cuff links?
Where have they all gone to,
The beautiful girls, the abandoned hours?
They said we were lost, mad and immoral,
And interfered with the plans of management.
And today, millions and millions, shut alive
In the coffins of circumstance,
Beat on the buried lids,
Huddle in the cellars of ruins, and quarrel
Over their own fragmented flesh.

"They have hope," Thales said, "who have nothing else." By age forty-three, Rexroth had survived the deaths of his mother and first wife; he had roamed the west during the Depression and written trail guides for the WPA; he worked as camp cook and roustabout in the Cascades and hiked through the Sierras. During World War II, he was a conscientious objector who worked in a hospital and personally provided sanctuary for Japanese-Americans. Upon the incarceration of thousands of Japanese-Americans at the outset of World War II, he declared his "disaffiliation from the American capitalist state" complete—and for the remaining years of his life, he would view American letters and history not as a disaffiliated passive bystander recollecting in tranquillity nor in bitterness, but as an alienated activist-poet, a devoted social commentator and agitator. He wrote literary journalism, "for money or for log-rolling for one's friends." He was one of the great essayists of his age, and some of his best were simply dictated, then transcribed from tape.

Rexroth's poems reflect an increasingly breathtaking sweep of understanding—of the languages and cultures he studied and his passion for naturalism and the poetries of pre-literate peoples. He delved into Kabbalah and Gnosticism. Reading the *Encyclopedia Brittanica* inspired his poem, "GIC to HAR." He read it, he said, "Straight through. Like a novel." He translated poems by Neruda and Lorca, Heine, classical Chinese poetry, Japanese classics, the French poems of O. V. Milosz and Pierre Reverdy; he studied Bakunin and the Anarchists, Buddhist and Taoist classics, the *Bhagavad Gita* and the Greeks of the *Anthology*; he wrote reviews on jazz, newspaper columns and composed a libretto for a ballet, "Original Sin," that was performed in San Francisco with music composed and lead by John Lewis of the Modern Jazz

Quartet. He edited an anthology of new young English poets, one of whom, Denise Levertov, he praised and promoted tirelessly even though they had never met. He also persuaded New Directions to publish Levertov and William Everson, who would later don the robes of Dominican Catholicism and publish as Brother Antoninus.

By 1958, the American political scenario had changed. Suburbia was spreading everywhere. Eisenhower warned of the growing threat of the "military-industrial complex," and much of the country enjoyed a feeling of well-being, but for the escalating Cold War. Poetry was the province of New Critics and the poetry establishment was firmly ensconced within the walls of academia. There were very few women poets and even fewer minority poets being published. But there were a few little coffee houses beginning to spring up in various cities where the hip crowd would read poetry aloud in public.

The San Francisco Renaissance was in full swing. Rexroth promoted poets on the airwaves at KPFA, including Lawrence Ferlinghetti, the surrealist Philip Lamantia, the young Gary Snyder, Philip Whalen, Levertov, Brother Antoninus, LeRoi Jones, Diane DiPrima, Bob Kaufman and many others. He helped found the Poetry Center at San Francisco State University and wrote his "Classics Revisited" columns surveying the literature of the world for *Saturday Review*, and later collected them in two volumes. Then Jack Kerouac's prose swept through a generation like a brush fire. Rexroth, although praising Kerouac's *On the Road*, would later claim (in a letter to Morgan Gibson) that he'd never even read *The Dharma Bums*, in which he is unflatteringly portrayed. And he bristled at being labeled, "father of the Beats." He and Kerouac didn't like each other.

Nevertheless, the publication and obscenity trial of Allen Ginsberg's "Howl" was the result of a poetry reading October 13, 1955, at the Six Gallery in San Francisco, organized in part and emceed by Kenneth Rexroth. Although the audience was tiny, the reading shook American poetry—indeed the poetry of most of the world—to its very core. In a white-washed 20 by 25 foot stall, the readers included Gary Snyder, Philip Whalen, Michael McClure, Philip Lamantia and Ginsberg, who read "Howl" for the first time, ending in tears to wild applause. When Lawrence Ferlinghetti published the book at City Lights, one of this country's great literary legal battles ensued. When called to testify in court, Rexroth confounded the prosecution by placing Ginsberg's poem directly "in the long Jewish Old Testament tradition of testimonial poetry."

It has often been suggested that the major inspiration for Ginsberg's poem probably was not as much Walt Whitman's model as Rexroth's lament upon the death of Dylan Thomas, "Thou Shalt Not Kill," written in 1953, with its heavy cadences and charged imagery.

They are murdering all the young men.
For half a century now, every day,
They have hunted them down and killed them.
They are killing the young men.
They know ten thousand ways to kill them.
Every year they invent new ones.
In the jungles of Africa,
In the marshes of Asia,
In the deserts of Asia,
In the slave pens of Siberia,
In the slums of Europe,
In the nightclubs of America,
The murderers are at work.

. . .

You killed him,
Benign Lady on the postage stamp.
He was found dead at a Liberal Weekly luncheon.
He was found dead on the cutting room floor.
He was found dead at a Time policy conference.
Henry Luce killed him with a telegram to the Pope.
Mademoiselle strangled him with a padded brassiere.
Old Possum sprinkled him with a tea ball.
After the wolves were done, the vaticides
Crawled off with his bowels to their classrooms and quarterlies.

. . .

The Gulf Stream smells of blood
As it breaks on the sand of Iona
And the blue rocks of Canarvon.
And all the birds of the deep rise up
Over the luxury liners and scream,
"You killed him! You killed him.
In your God damned Brooks Brothers suit,
You son of a bitch.

It is interesting to note that "Possum," Eliot, ruling deity of the poetry establishment, appears among Rexroth's list of murderers of poetry. Both Ginsberg and Rexroth are on record, however, denying any such influence. Ginsberg's poem achieved both acclaim and notoriety unlike any other poem of its time. Like it or not, Rexroth's name would be associated with the Beats for the rest of his life. And public poetry readings would play a major role in making American poetry in the twentieth century a true revolution.

But Kenneth Rexroth would not be caught in a "coffin of circumstance." His house had become a weekly meeting place for existentialist poets, free-love advocates, anarchists, artists and literary hangers-on. He would later say of those years that, if nothing else, he finally had some readers he didn't know on a first name basis. In the early days, these gatherings had been vital and exciting, but by the time Snyder and Whalen had left for Japan, Duncan for Mallorca, and Brother Antoninus for a Dominican retreat, Rexroth was about out of patience with strung out "Beatniks" who arrived with their imitations of *On the Road*. He charged them with being "mere examples of a veneer, a gastro-pharmaceutical change rather than of a profound spiritual awakening." Most of his closest friends in San Francisco were "Beat poets." Was he? "An entomologist," he declared, "is not a bug." He disliked what he saw on the San Francisco horizon as his marriage fell apart and America began building for its war in southeast Asia.

He had married a third time(to Marthe Larsen) and was the father of two girls when his marriage collapsed in 1955. By the late fifties, his personal life was in chaos. He was poverty-stricken and suffered severe attacks of paranoia. He wrote newspaper columns. He withdrew. A gourmet who insisted that today's groceries be purchased today and who always wore a jacket to his well-set table, he lived from hand to mouth, insisting, "In America, being poor is no excuse for not eating well." Devastated by another failed marriage and a string of lovers, and alienated from many of his old friends, he sought refuge in lecture and reading tours. His performances were legendary. He read to jazz, to koto music, alone or with friends invited to join. But his last years in San Francisco were mostly difficult and lonely, and finally, after forty-four years there, he decided to leave.

He moved to Santa Barbara in 1968 and several years later married his longtime assistant, Carol Tinker. He taught two courses at the University of California: a poetry-and-music class designed for a dozen or so students, but which drew over 400 students during the protests against American involvement in Viet Nam; and a weekly "evening-with-Kenneth" modeled on the salon he'd orchestrated in the city. He reveled in the company of young people eager to learn from a scholar out of office. Friends and students gathered at his little house in Montecito with wine and cheese, and Rexroth would install himself in a huge easy chair in a corner of the tiny living room and read in French, Japanese, Greek, Latin, or Spanish, giving spontaneous translations of the poems along with capsule biographies of the poets under discussion. Everything lead into his great web. He was happiest in this element. One could hardly be expected to understand Trakl without understanding German expressionism, traditional taboos pertaining to incest, pre-World War I economic conditions in Europe, the history of German rebellion against the Catholic church, the peculiarly German approach to anarchism in Trakl's milieu, and of course the poet's troubled mind. He believed poetry embodied a great history of ideas and could become a path to enlightenment. His appetite for knowledge was insatiable and he had almost perfect recall.

He was a unique polyglot iconoclast, a pacifist who loved tweaking the noses of bourgeois complacency and pretension, but whose bouts of paranoia sometimes left friends utterly confounded. He believed the embodiment of justice could not be separate from the physical and emotional expression of compassion, and could still declare, "You killed him . . . You son of a bitch!" His poetry reflects an increasing interest in Shingon Buddhism while he loudly objected to what he perceived to be the abuse of power by Buddhist teachers in the U.S.

The Buddhist bodhisattva of compassion, Kuan Shih Yin (in Chinese, "who-listens-to-the-world's-cries"), in Japanese Kannon, figures prominently in his later books. She is the embodiment of Buddhist compassion for the suffering of all sentient beings, a figure of eternal mercy who "pours the morning dew."

Suchness

In the theosophy of light,
The logical universal
Ceases to be anything more
Than the dead body of an angel.
What is substance? Our substance
Is whatever we feed our angel.
The perfect incense for worship
Is camphor, whose flames leave no ashes.

Rexroth brings an essentially Catholic attitude to his sacramental practice, but the equation, the realization is fundamentally Buddhist. In his sacrament he finds Buddhist emptiness, the essentce of the "dead body of an angel." Buddhism has no angels. The flame without ash is the light of coming to comprehend the essential emptiness or thusness at the heart of Zen practice.

Toward the end of his life, his poems achieved a grand simplicity that should not be mistaken for lack of consequence. Incense and sacrament are rituals preparing one for the door that is straight and smaller than the needle's eye. Like his favorite poet, Tu Fu, he was a deeply spiritual and political poet who included rather than excluded the world's religions. Unlike Tu Fu, he was a poet of erotic love without peer in his lifetime, perhaps without peer in the American language, as Eliot Weinberger has written. "Erotic love," Rexroth was fond of saying, "is one of the highest forms of contemplation." Spirituality and erotic love could not be separated in his poetry, except mockingly ironically. This same spirituality produces, in an earlier poem:

The Advantages of Learning

I am a man with no ambitions
And few friends, wholly incapable
Of making a living, growing no
Younger, fugitive from some just doom.
Lonely, ill-clothed, what does it matter?
At midnight I make myself a jug
Of hot white wine and cardamon seeds.
In a torn grey robe and old beret,
I sit in the cold writing poems,
Drawing nudes on the crooked margins,
Copulating with sixteen year old
Nymphomaniacs of my imagination.

Does he mock himself or is his tongue firmly in cheek, tweaking noses? The poem draws heavily from Greek and Latin traditions and even more from the classical Chinese. It achieves tragic proportion through self-mockery, and boldly reveals its poetic tradition. It could almost pass as a version of Catullus or of Li Po. His humor is often a double-edged sword. He delighted in the scandalous, both in his behavior and in his writing, for years telling his audiences, "I write poetry to seduce women and to overthrow the capitalist system. . . . In that order." And yet he was a feminist who did more to encourage young women poets (and women in general) than any writer of his generation. No artist can do more than contribute to a tradition and leave a legacy. Rexroth was our Catullus, our Li Po, shocking his audience with laughter, his tradition one of celebratory eroticism and social protest and his legacy a devotion to learning.

The erotic cannot be separated from the scientific. Rexroth combined the study of science with personal experience and philosophy like no poet before him. He was among the first American poets to recognize the complex utter interdependence of things in the ecology of the imagination as in biological reality. Reading Lyell's nineteenth century study of geology, he composes, "Lyell's Hypothesis Again," (another poem for Marie Kass Rexroth, his second wife) that looks hard at the "ego, bound by personal / Tragedy and the vast /Impersonal vindictiveness / Of the ruined and ruining world,/ . . ." and concludes:

> We have escaped the bitterness
> Of love, and love lost, and love
> Betrayed. And what might have been,
> And what might be, fall equally,
> Away with what is, and leave
> Only these ideograms
> Printed on the immortal
> Hydrocarbons of flesh and stone.

Ultimately, he finds his tenderness in stone and in time. His mystical transcendence is as rooted in modern science as in traditional wisdom-teaching. The later books are the culmination of a lifetime's struggle toward a true spiritual awakening. The erotic and the scientific become one while time is seen in multiple contexts ranging from the momentary to the geologic.

Each of his longer poems, he notes, ends at a point of transcendent experience. The same is often enough true of his shorter poems, especially his erotic poetry. "It's one thing to write a love poem at twenty," he would laugh, "and quite another at seventy."

Confusion of the Senses

> Moonlight fills the laurels
> Like music. The moonlit
> Air does not move. Your white
> Face moves towards my face.

Voluptuous sorrow
Holds us like a cobweb
Like a song, a perfume, the moonlight.
Your hair falls and holds our faces.
Your lips curl into mine.
Your tongue enters my mouth.
A bat flies through the moonlight.
The moonlight fills your eyes
They have neither iris nor pupil
They are only globes of cold fire
Like the deers' eyes that go by us
Through the empty forest.
Your slender body quivers
And smells of seaweed.
We lie together listening
To each other breathing in the moonlight.
Do you hear? We are breathing. We are alive.

We live in an age in which the poetry of mature erotic love is out of fashion. Our poets and critics tend to prefer the cool cerebral play of Stevens to the naked jig of Dr. Williams. Much of our poetry takes no political or emotional risk. Rexroth was fond of quoting Yvor Winters, "Emotion in any situation must be as far as possible eliminated," following it with a pregnant pause and a great guffaw. What he claimed for the poetry of Lawrence may be claimed equally for his own poems, for"behind the machinery is an intense, direct, personal, mystical apprehension of reality" that is informed by his acceptance of responsibility in the cruelest century. For Rexroth, love is the ultimate expression of that responsibility. Like Camus, whom he admired, he engaged philosophy for the sake of clarity of commitment. "Practical philosophy," he often told his students, "has a test: If your mother or father or closest friend suddenly died, would you turn first to your philosophy professor for understanding?" Unlike Camus, he sought a "personal, mystical apprehension of reality" that was fundamentally Buddhist.

To some, Rexroth is a quintessential erotic poet; to others, a great nature poet; to still others, a political, literary or spiritual master; and to still others, the great translator of classical Chinese and Japanese poetry at mid-century. Often, all or most of these aspects congeal within a single poem, just as the whole body of his poetry reveals a universe. In few other poets has sixty years of prolific writing so consistently followed and expanded the themes of the earliest work.

In his note to *The Collected Longer Poems,* he wrote, "They seem to me almost as much one long poem as do *The Cantos* or *Paterson.*" He also says, "Most poets resemble Whitman in one regard—they write only one book and that an interior autobiography." Rexroth's poetry is vast and contains multitudes. The longer poems may indeed be read as a single poem. Or they may be read as they turn up among the shorter poems. And sometimes shorter poems are revealed again within the longer ones, changing their context. Like Pound and Williams, he built with many blocks. If his life is to be found and known through the poetry, it is only in moments of awakening to a transcendent insight, whether in poems informed by years of hiking and camping in the California mountains or by spiritual and philosophical inquiry.

His last years were remarkably productive. In 1967, he visited Japan for the first time and wrote "The Heart's Garden / The Garden's Heart," one of his most accomplished suites of poems. There was a Fulbright Fellowship to Kyoto in 1974, and some significant literary recognition including a Guggenheim Fellowship and the Copernicus Award for his lifetime's achievement. He made several other visits to Japan, including establishing a modest Kenneth Rexroth Award for Young Women Writers in 1975. He used his influence at Seabury Press to publish the first volumes of Czeslaw Milosz and Homero Aridjis, among others, in American English. Remembering Rexroth's generosity, Milosz has written, "For me, however, he was above all a splendid poet and a splendid translator of Chinese and Japanese poetry."

There is a particular sweetness, a depth of love, in the later poems that is probably a result of the poet's "feminization." During his last years he produced, in collaboration with Ling Chung, the remarkable *Collected Poems of Li Ch'ing-chao,* one of China's greatest poets and a woman who also wrote a deeply personal poetry; *The Orchid Boat* (later retitled *Women Poets of China* for its paperback release); and, in collaboration with Ikuko Atsumi, *The Burning Heart* (retitled *Women Poets of Japan* for the paper edition); he edited *Seasons of Sacred Lust,* selected poems of Kazuko Shiraishi; and, in one of the most remarkable of feats, pulled off the invention of "a young woman poet from Japan," Marichiko, whose love poems are explicit.

VII
Making love with you
Is like drinking sea water.
The more I drink
The thirstier I become,

Until nothing can slake my thirst
But to drink the entire sea.

XXV
Your tongue thrums and moves
Into me, and I become
Hollow and blaze with
Whirling light, like the inside
Of a vast expanding pearl.

He calls her a follower of Marichi, "an avatar of the Shakti of Shiva," and, "A great Indian prostitute/ Who was really an incarnate/ Bodhisattva. The girl herself [Marichiko]/ Turned out to be a Communist." His persona was so convincing that a number of Japanese scholars went in search of Marichiko.

Critics and biographers have spent much more ink on Rexroth's personality and his stormy relationships with wives, lovers and friends than on his work. Born in 1905 in Indiana, he was particularly close to his mother until she died, bed-ridden, with the young Kenneth at her side in 1916. Unable to care for a child, his father left him with his grandmother in Toledo who routinely beat him with a cane. Eventually rescued by his father, he ended up in Chicago where he quit school and began his astonishing journeys. Although apparently incapable of monogamy, he nevertheless believed in marriage as the ultimate sacrament. Like many an inconoclastic genius, he was a mass of contradictions, but there is little doubt that at the root of his complex personality lay an orphaned, battered child, a man who over-compensated for deep self-doubts while struggling to embody profound spiritual awakening.

Millions of pearls in the mist
Of the waterfall added
Together to make a rainbow.
Deep in the heart one pearl glows
With ten million rainbows.
. . .
Not by flesh, but by love, man
Comes into the world, lost in
The illimitable ocean
Of which there is no shore.

His last major suites of poems, "The Heart's Garden/The Garden's Heart," quoted above, and "On Flower Wreath Hill," are journey poems in which the search for love and its embodiment and the search for spiritual realization become completely integrated. But the nirvana that can be glimpsed is not the nirvana that can be realized. Nirvana cannot be reached through the desire to reach nirvana. Kannon responds to the suffering of the world with infinite compassion as she pours the morning dew.

> The promise of the vow of
> The Bodhisattva is so
> Powerful the stormy ocean of
> Karma turns to an unruffled mirror.

And yet the poet finds his own heart cannot achieve such calm transparency except in the eternal moment of the poem. "My heart is not a mirror./ I cannot see myself in it." He cannot fully embody the Bodhisattva's vow to remain in the cycle of birth and death until the last sentient being becomes enlightened and enters nirvana. He cannot master the practice of infinite compassion, although he comprehends its possibility. Hell, to some, is seeing an image of unattainable paradise. But Rexroth never believed the bodhisattva vow to be unattainable. He simply could not quite get there before he died. The boy who began life witnessing his mother's agonizing death and then was abandoned by his father and beaten by his grandmother began his last poetic journey, "On Flower Wreath Hill," with a search for the primally feminine in Kyoto:

> An aging pilgrim on a
> Darkening path walks through the
> Fallen and falling leaves, through
> A forest grown over the
> Hilltop tumulus of a
> Long dead princess, as the
> Moonlight grows and the daylight
> Fades and the Western Hills turn
> Dim in the distance and the
> Lights come on, pale green
> In the streets of the hazy city.

A dead princess, whatever else she may be, is unattainable. The poet therefore eventually finds only himself in a world that is simultaneously ancient and contemporary, and where

> The mist
> Dissolves everything else, the
> Living and the dead, except
> This occult mathematics of light.

Ultimately, he realizes, "this / Transcendent architecture / Lost in the forest where no one passes / Is itself the Net of Indra. " And in "the occult mathematics of light" within the poem, Rexroth brings even the "music of numbers into the tragedy of blood." The poem concludes on the note of a "soundless flute" resonating in the void.

The man who survives in these poems is a great man, wise beyond words, a poet polished by great loss and small glory. He has given in his work exactly what he sought in life: a sense of a compassionate moral center from which the possibility of ultimate awakening may be realized.

When he died, on the anniversary of D-Day, 1982, his passing went almost unnoticed by the literary establishment. Newspaper obituaries were brief, noting only the passing of the "father of the Beat Generation." No doubt his vocal disdain for the "eastern literary establishment" and bourgeois taste-making in general kept his work from being more favorably and widely reviewed in the media. If he was sometimes paranoid, arrogant, or self-absorbed, he was much more often funny, generous and compassionate. He played the *enfant terrible* to the end, even as a grand old man. He was the author of fifty-four books and an enormous unpublished anthology of poetry of pre-literate peoples from around the world. Much of his archived work remains uncatalogued two decades after his death.

Rexroth is buried in Santa Barbara on a bluff above the Pacific. All the other graves face the continent. Rexroth alone faces the ocean, the west that leads into the east. His epitaph: "The swan sings / In sleep / On the lake of the mind."

Two Buddhist Poets

Wang Wei and Saigyō

Perhaps no aspect of classical Chinese poetry in translation has touched contemporary American verse more deeply than the "nature poetry" of the T'ang dynasty. From the 300-odd poems of Cold Mountain (Han Shan), poems that often fall into a kind of Buddhist doggerel, to the almost selfless poems of Wang Wei, the western poet has been drawn to the evocative and descriptive powers of the ancient Chinese poet writing alone in his hermitage deep in the mountains.

While the translations by Gary Snyder, Burton Watson, and Red Pine have brought a large audience to Han Shan, Wang Wei has generally fared less well. Several accurate translations have been available in recent years, but none have sparkled like any of the above. That may be in part because Wang Wei is a better poet, a more subtle stylist, and far less ecstatic or declamatory.

In his wise introduction to *Hiding the Universe: Poems by Wang Wei* (Mushinsha Grossman, 1972), Wai-lim Yip compares Wang's "Bird-Singing Stream" with Wallace Stevens's "Of Mere Being," noting that in Wang's poems things tend to "emerge as they are without being contaminated by intellectuality." In Stevens, "A gold-feathered bird/ Sings in the palm, without human meaning,/ Without human feeling, a foreign song." And Stevens "oftens ends up writing about the process of becoming the objects with much analysis between himself and the objects," whereas Wang presents phenomena as it is:

Bird-Singing Stream

Man at leisure. Cassia flowers fall.
Quiet night. Spring mountain is empty.
Moon rises. Startles—a mountain bird.
It sings at times in the spring stream.

Yip's translation conveys something of the density of the original, but only at some expense to the poem's American English dress: it sounds fragmented, and Wang Wei is in no way a poet of shards and fragments—to the contrary, he is a poet of totality. Yip is quite literal, taking no great interpretive liberties with his text. But Wang, among the most contemplative of poets, wrote in a style that might best be described as effortless and selfless, and Yip's English misses that tone. Nonetheless, he does capture much of the classic four-line, five-character-per-line form of the original.

A devout Buddhist, Wang Wei did not "view nature" from an outside perspective; rather, he was himself a part of nature. His treatment of the natural world was neither objective nor analytical. But his poems are loaded with associative and evocative power. The "white clouds" that frequently appear in his poems may be considered real, literal clouds. In other Buddhist poets, "white clouds" often represent "barriers" between the novice Buddhist and "highest perfect enlightenment." In Wang's nature poem, there is only "nature."

In G. W. Robinson's translation, *Poems of Wang Wei* (Penguin, 1973), this poem becomes:

Birds Calling in the Valley

Men at rest, cassia flowers falling
Night still, spring hills empty
The moon rises, rouses birds in the hills
And sometimes they cry in the spring valley.

While the movement of the whole is a bit less fragmented, the on-again, off-again punctuation with the weight of heaped-up phrases at the beginning of the poem make it move with more awkwardness than it should. The "hills" in the third line is redundant. This translation is adequate, but slack.

Pauline Lu, in *The Poetry of Wang Wei* (Indiana University Press, 1980) sounds a lot like Wai-lim Yip:

Bird Call Valley

Man at leisure, cassia flowers fall.
The night still, spring mountain empty.
The moon emerges, startling mountain birds:
At times they call within the spring valley.

Her translation carries a better sense of movement than either of the former, each line turning on a kind of axis as it does in the original, creating a lucid, literal equivalent. But the poem still leaves me disatisfied in its English garb. The language lacks a poet's touch, it doesn't carry what a good ear could contribute. "Man at leisure"? Too indefinite in English. "At times they call" is also too slack to convey the tension of the original.

While each of these versions is in some way "good enough" for study or commentary, none really rises to the occasion like this new version from the collaborative team of Tony Barnstone, Willis Barnstone, and Xu Haixin, from *Laughing Lost in the Mountains: Poems of Wang Wei* (University Press of New England, 1992):

Birds Sing in the Ravine

Few people see the acacia blossoms fall,
night is quiet, the spring mountain empty.
The sudden moon alarms mountain birds.
Long moment of song in the spring ravine.

While the "person at leisure" magically becomes "few people," I don't feel the spirit of the poem has been violated. I would also remove the "is" in line two. Line and syntax work harmoniously. The "sudden" moon lends a little tension, and the "alarm" grants permission as it were for the closing sentence fragment, a fragment that opens out *into* nature like birdsong itself. If this translation fails to note the spaces *between* bird cry and bird cry, it nonetheless compresses the experience of the poem. And the wonderful lilt of song of the closing line! I think Mr. Wang would be pleased.

Wang Wei was the eldest of five brothers raised in a literary family in Shansi province. He was a precocious poet, musician, and landscape painter who passed his advanced examinations at age twenty-two. He served in various official posts, reportedly attempted suicide when he was imprisoned during the An Lu-shan Rebellion, and only a poem written to his friend Pei Di from Bodhi Temple saved him from being charged as a collaborator during the aftermath of the rebellion. He was returned to office, and died while serving in the Department of State while in his early sixties.

But he is revered mostly for his nature poems. Far less exuberant or reckless than Li T'ai-po, and far simpler and less cerebral than the incomparable, passionate Tu Fu, Wang made elegant simplicity his greatest asset. As a devout Buddhist with a notable Taoist influence, he was perhaps a perfect counterpart to Tu Fu's Confucianism and Li Po's Taoism. Whereas Tu Fu's nature poems are a record of exile and a sweeping social conscience, Wang's represent a great spiritual vision.

The introduction to the Barnstone translation draws an interesting comparison between Wang and the modern Spanish poet Antonio Machado:

> Wang an official, Machado a teacher in a rural *instituto,* both poets find their eyes in nature. They were not scribes of the imagination, like Dante, but of their daily and nightly vision. They tended to dream—but not nocturnal dreams associated with sleep and fantasy. Theirs was a reverie of ordinary landscapes, which their minds transposed as they gazed at them with eyes wide open. In nature Wang—and later Machado—found a literal script for his vision.

Not only a reverie of ordinary landscapes, but certainly in Wang's case, a reverence for ordinary landscapes. The translators stress the Taoist influence especially, quoting Chuang Tzu's advocacy of stillness, emptiness, of not-having, and underscoring the point by noting Wang's frequent use of "empty mountain" in poems like "Deer Park" and "Living in the Mountains on an Autumn Night." They also note that the character used for "empty" is *kong,* the Chinese word for the Sanskrit *sunyata,* the Buddhist concept of emptiness that is altogether different from our customary use of the word *empty.* And indeed, his poems are also loaded with empty forests and empty nights, Buddhist-inspired images that ring with clarity and numinous detail. Zen was in many ways a Chinese adaptation of Indian Buddhism, bringing to its fundamental teaching a profoundly Taoist interpretation: "In China," the Chinese say, "everything becomes Chinese."

You Asked about My Life. I Send You, Pei Di, These Lines

A wide icy river floats to far uncertainty.
The autumn rain is eternal in the mist.
You ask me about Deep South Mountain.
My heart knows it is beyond white clouds.

The poet combines definite images with signifying abstraction—icy river connected to uncertainty; "eternal" rain to mist. Are the "white clouds" Buddhist barriers between the poet and Nirvana, or are they literal white clouds passing between the poet and his beloved home in the mountains? Perhaps both. Longing for one's home is a kind of desire, and as a poet and

Buddhist Wang aimed to transcend desire. In this poem, implied desire figures prominently, carrying the emotional center. The transcendent vision remains virtually unspoken, buried in the evocation of the natural world. Rain, mist, and white clouds are standard Buddhist symbolism, but in Wang's hands take on added luuminosity.

The Barnstones quote Burton Watson's classic *Chinese Lyricism* (Columbia University Press, 1971) on a type of Buddhist poetry "in which the philosophical meaning lies [far] below the surface. The imagery functions on both the descriptive and the symbolic levels at once, and it is not often possible to pin down the exact symbolic content of an image." This kind of poetry is not forthrightly didactic—it delivers no sermon and cites no sutra. It represents Buddhist philosophy in a practice so refined as to transcend Buddhist liturgy.

Years ago, I translated Wang's "Return to Wang River:"

In the gorge where bells resound
there are few fishermen or woodsmen.

Before I know it, dusk closes down the mountains.
Alone, I return again to white clouds

and trembling water chestnuts
where the willow catkins easily take flight.

Spring grass colors the eastern landscape.
Snared in a web of grief, I close my wooden door.

In the Barnstone translation, the poem reads:

Bells stir in the mouth of the gorge.
Few fishermen or woodcutters are left.
Far off in the mountains is twilight.
Alone I come back to white clouds.
Weak water chestnut stems can't hold still.
Willow catkins are light and blow about.
To the east is a rice paddy, color of spring grass.
I close the thorn gate, seized by grief.

It is a poem others have tackled with varying degrees of success. Robinson leaves out all punctuation and gets quite wordy: "And I am going alone towards the white clouds home / Water-chestnut flowers so delicate so hardly still . . ." and closing, "Colours of spring on the banks of the marsh to the east / And I am melancholy as I shut my door."

In one of the stranger crimes against the Chinese, David Young has translated this poem in his *Four T'ang Poets* (Field, 1980), turning each line into a triad, even changing the title to "Returning to My Cottage." It's a good example of how *not* to translate a poem. His closure is, well, pathetic: "it's sad / to walk in the house / and shut the door." This is not "elegant simplicity," but what Willis Hawley called "dumbing it down."

I admire the uncluttered completeness of the Barnstone translation, the ease of the poem as a whole. No artificial language, but enough ear at work to let the line—each line—convey its own sense of unity. I do not like "Far off in the mountain is twilight" because of the inversion and its tinny ring, and because it fails to convey the poet's sense of discovery of twilight. The use of "twilight" where I had used "dusk" however is a good stroke, carrying the added weight of implication by plurisignation—is it the poet's own twilight? The choice of "twilight" over "dusk" also demonstrates the translator's need to interpret.

All poetry offers variable possibilities in translation. Often, small subtle matters of interpretation make all the difference. Robinson, while "getting the meaning" all right, completely misses the right tone for Wang Wei in American English; in London, all those piled up prepositional phrases may please the ear, sounding remarkably simple, direct, and uncluttered like the original. In contemporary American English, it sounds mundane, flabby, prosy. Young tries to turn Wang Wei into William Carlos Williams-style imagism, but his structure is at odds with the structure of the original, composed in couplets, as is most classical Chinese verse.

To the Chinese, Wang is *the* great poet of impersonality. His poetry is a record of a lifelong struggle to be free of desire, free even of the desire to be free of desire, a non-struggle to attain non-attainment. Often severely self-critical, he begins "Written in the Mountains in Early Autumn" by saying, "I'm talentless and dare not inflict myself on this bright reign. / Perhaps I'll go to the East River and mend my old fence." Humility before his task is a signature of Wang Wei. Autumn "abruptly falls," and he listens to crickets and cicadas. "Alone in the empty forest, I have an appointment with white clouds." He completely disappears into "nature" without losing *presence*.

At a conference on "the power of animals" years ago, Gary Snyder pointed out that we are often most deeply into our "animal intelligence" when we are alone. The aloneness of a Zen mountain poet like Wang Wei is not the pathetic melancholy Robinson's translation might suggest. Nor is it the portentous "sadness" of Young's version. The poem is *not* about sadness at all, but grief and aloneness—an entirely different emotional complex that must be seen in a Buddhist context. It is the aloneness of completion, the aloneness that is not-alone, the aloneness of transcendental animal consciousness, of mere beingness almost without self-consciousness. He becomes a part of his white clouds, the clouds become a symbol of transcendent grace, the speaker and the listener and the images blending into a single note of eternal resolution.

Wang's poetry arises out of the complex simplicity of his language, but can't be found in a dictionary. Capturing his tone, his grace-note, is the translator's greatest challenge. Eliot Weinberger's delightful essay, *Nineteen Ways of Looking at Wang Wei* (Moyer Bell, 1987), examines nineteen versions of a poem of one quatrain, "Deer Park," with wonderful insight. The final line of the poem, in literal:

Return (again) shine green moss above

Of all the versions under Weinberger's discussion, only Gary Snyder notes that the light is shining through the moss *overhead*—apparently only Snyder among these nineteen translator's recognizes that moss grows in trees. The noted Sinologist James J. Y. Liu even goes so far as to supply "ground" for the moss. In the Barnstone translation it reads:

Deer Park

Nobody in sight on the empty mountain
but human voices are heard far off.
Low sun slips deep in the forest
and lights the green hanging moss.

To make translations work at their best in English, the translator must aspire to the poet's powerful evocation. The language is very simple; the vision is very complex. The slant rhyme of "off" and "moss" is just right. The *l* and *s* sounds in the closing couplet also convey some sense of musicality.

My own translation of this poem may be more literal:

No sign of men on the empty mountain,
only faint echoes from below.

Refracted light enters the forest,
shining through green moss above.

There are certain kinds of parallelism that are common in classical Chinese poetry. Wang Wei directs our attention to what is below, then to what is above. The empty mountain represents samsara, our life on earth; the shining light is transcendent, from above.

In "Autumn Meditation," the moon sails "Heavenly River," the Milky Way, and in four lines reveals a world:

The balcony's ice wind stirs my clothing.
Night. The drum endures. The jade waterclock slows.
The moon sails the Heavenly River, soaking its light.
A magpie breaks from an autumn tree. Many leaves fall.

The human element vanishes in falling leaves. The poet transcends the "world of illusion" by achieving pure consciousness through attentive meditation. The world is as it is: transient. In the hands of most modern poets, the magpie would become personified or the imagery would carry added abstract philosophical argument. Here, the poet and the world are one.

Laughing Lost in the Mountains is the best translation of a substantial number of Wang Wei's poems to appear in English. In addition to breathtaking poems of nature and hermitage, there are many wonderful formal court poems, letter poems, and portraits, all in suitable American English dress. This should become the standard Wang Wei for a generation of readers.

Four hundred years after the birth of Wang Wei, the most famous medieval Buddhist nature poet of Japan was born to a minor branch of the powerful Fujiwara clan in the old capital city of Heian, present day Kyoto. Saigyō (1118-1190) spent twenty-three years in and around court life in Heian-kyo, Peace-and-Tranquility Capital, becoming a captain in the elite guard of the imperial family before taking Buddhist vows and removing himself to a hermitage. His biography is clouded in legend and folklore. Scholars agree that he lived at times near Mt. Koya and Mt. Yoshino, and his poems record many long journeys.

Like Wang Wei—who surely must have provided a model from among
Saigyō's many Chinese sources—Saigyō is an advocate of self-transcendence,
albeit more openly didactic in his approach. This poem, from among Saigyō's
earliest, was first published anonymously in an imperial anthology in 1151:

So, then, it's the one	*yo o sutsuru*
Who has thrown his self away	*hito wa makoto ni*
Who is thought the loser?	*sutsuru ka wa*
But he who cannot lose self	*sutenu hito koso*
Is the one who has really lost.	*sutsuru narikere*

This translation from William R. LaFleur's 1978 *Mirror for the Moon* (New
Directions) shows the young Saigyō immersed in Buddhist philosophy, but
not yet able to transcend the need to pass judgment. He is not yet able to
completely "cast off" (*sutsuru*, used three times in the poem above) the self.

During his fifty years of Buddhist and poetic practice, he became the
archetype for many generations of Zen poets, especially for Bashō, who
studied and quoted Saigyō at great length and whose own journey into the
northern interior recorded in *Oku no hosomichi* (*Narrow Road to the Interior*)
was inspired by two such journeys undertaken by Saigyō some five hundred
years before.

A wandering poet-priest, Saigyō is best known through his major
contribution (94 poems) in the imperial anthology *Shinkokinshū*, and his
collected works, *Sankashu* or *Mountain Home Collection,* preserves fifteen
hundred poems. It represents all he left to the world. He never explained
why he left court life, but he lived during a period Japanese Buddhists had
declared *Mappo*, the End of Law, when true faith declines and the world is
ruled by mere formalism; he may have been driven from his position through
personal intrigues at the court; or perhaps he simply tired of the depressing
collapse of a once-great culture. Political power was being stripped from the
ruling Fujiwara clan by "warrior" clans like the Minamotos and Tairas, whose
wars are recorded in *Tale of the Heike.*

Even as a young officer, Saigyō had closely studied earlier poet-monks
such as the priest Nōin (998–1050), so the tradition of the Buddhist mountain
recluse was not merely a rejection of depressing social circumstances, but a
reasonably knowledgeable conscious choice. In any case, in 1140, the young
poet abruptly left military service to take Buddhist vows.

As a Buddhist mountain poet, he was capable of achieving a luminosity to match that of Wang Wei. In a poem from the *Shinkokinshū* closely echoing a poem by Nōin, Saigyō writes:

Was it a dream	*Tsu no kuni no*
That spring in Naniwa	*naniwa no haru wa*
In the land of Tsu?	*yume nare ya*
Now the wind blows over	*ashi no kareha ni*
The dead leaves of the reeds.	*kare wataru nari*

This translation is from Burton Watson's *Saigyō: Poems of a Mountain Home* (Columbia University Press, 1991.) Nōin's poem is a plea for someone "of real feeling" with whom to share the sights of springtime in Naniwa, an area of present-day Osaka. Saigyō responds with a bleak winter landscape that still contains the seeds of spring if only in remembrance. Remembering spring in the midst of dry winter, Saigyō becomes the "person of real feeling" with whom Nōin—dead a hundred years—may realize his wish, through whom he may be said to be reborn by way of Saigyō's direct echo of his poem.

In its own subtle Buddhist way, this poem runs parallel to "Ode to the West Wind," but with a different philosophical apparatus. The implied sense of temporality in the seasons, as in a poet's life, lends the poem, almost miraculously, an air of timelessness.

Burton Watson may be trusted—almost absolutely—to add *nothing* to the original in making his versions but for the necessary article, conjunction, or preposition. Unlike many who translate classical Japanese *waka* (short poems), he does not "fill out" his lines to an equal number of syllables in English. Poems in Japanese language generally require more syllables than their English-language offspring. Many translators, myself included, often insert a little gloss here, a careful interpretive adjective there, in hopes of approaching something of the syllabic musicality of the original. Watson sticks very closely to the original in meaning. He is one of the great translators in an age of translation. His poems from classical Chinese and Japanese are invariably sturdy and accurate and intelligent and altogether readable. He never plays fast and loose with images, and he never tries to invent new forms to accommodate modish free interpretation. He is and has been for forty years a model of the scholar-translator.

My own translations of Saigyō's poems take a few liberties, but I take them in part to respect the *order* of the imagery in the original as much as possible (dream, *yume*, is in the third line of the Japanese), especially in losing the direct mention of the sound (*nari*). My use of the word "harsh" is purely interpretive. It is the adjective that implies the sound of wind through dry leaves:

> In the land of Tsu,
> That glorious Naniwa spring –
> Only just a dream?
> Over the dead leaves of reeds
> A harsh wind blows.

In addition to holding fast to the original order of perception, I wanted to create in English something that might suggest an echo of the 31-syllable musicality of the original. In the Japanese, one may hear the rhyming *u* sounds of *Tsu, kuni,* and *yume*; the off-rhyme of *naniwa* with *kareha*; the off-rhymes of *nare, kare(ha), kaze,* and *nari*. In searching for a replication, I found *o* sounds and *e* sounds most effective in suggesting slant rhyme, and they also add a certain wind-sound to the poem, playing against the long *u* vowel that ends the first line. I did not feel compelled to try to fill out the customary seven syllables in the last line, thinking any addition would soften the poem too much, especially after the weight of: "harsh wind blows," with its sullen sounds and cadence.

Having *two* decent versions of a poem is helpful. My version was born in part from Watson's. Noting that he altered the order of images, I began to rework the poem; reworking the order of images, I had to make sounds; having to make the sounds of poetry, I listened; listening to Watson's translation, listening to Saigyō, I began to make a parallel poem, a parallel music. It's a good test of translation, and there is something to be learned from each version, and probably still something to be gained from a third version.

Saigyō's contemporaries revered all things Chinese. And from among many Chinese literary ideals, they were particularly drawn to the idea of *sabi* "loneliness" or better, an "aloneness," of a particularly Taoist/Zen kind—a loneliness that does *not* call for pity, but which arises most significantly from encounters with "nature." And the models for this kind of spiritual loneliness were drawn mostly from the T'ang dynasty, Wang Wei among them. Like his contemporaries Sunzei and Teika, and like Master Wang before them, Saigyō often ignored the more flashy or exotic image in favor of seeking the numinous mundane.

Fishermen home from
their day's work:
on a bed of seaweed,
little top shells, clams,
hermit crabs, periwinkles

In his introduction, Burton Watson points out that this poem may be read two ways at once: it may be a peek into a fisherman's basket with a childlike sense of discovery and delight; it may also be said to be a Buddhist reproach to one whose daily business is the taking of sentient life. Consequently, the attentive reader "gets it" both ways at once: delight and sadness, perhaps even a suggestion of *sabi*.

Here are two versions of the same Saigyō poem, the first translation by Burton Watson:

I'll forget the trail	*Yoshinoyama*
I marked out on Mount Yoshinokozo	*no shiori no*
last year,	*michi kaete*
go searching for blossoms	*mada minu kata no*
in directions I've never seen before	*hana o tazunen*

Watson has altered the order of images, moving the trail (*michi*) to the first line, and the blossoms (*hana*) from the last line to the penultimate. He adds nothing to the imagery of the original, and delivers a very readable, accurate translation.

In William R. LaFleur's translation it reads:

Last year, Yoshino,
I walked away bending branches
To point me to blossoms—
Which now are everywhere and I can
Go where I've never been before.

While I'm drawn to the particularity of "bending branches," the poem as a whole suffers from a confused meaning. If Saigyō has walked away "bending branches to point to blossoms—which now are *everywhere*," how can he go where he's "never been before"? *Mirror for the Moon* (New Direc tions, 1978) is a fine book overall, an excellent translation, and useful to read alongside the new Watson translation, but has since been supplanted by the more thorough and more polished *Awesome Nightfall: The Life, Times, and Poetry of Saigyō* (Wisdom Publications, 2003). LaFleur's study of Buddhism and literary arts in medieval Japan, *The Karma of Words* (University of California Press, 1983) is a must read for anyone interested in Japanese poetry, religion, or both.

Both translators remain very close to the original. Watson has a beautiful simplicity that is truer in *English* to the spirit of the original. The following poems are all from Watson's *Poems from a Mountain Home*:

> I used to gaze at the moon,
> my mind wandering endlessly—
> and now again
> I've come on one of
> those old time autumns

Is that "old time autumn" a remembered autumn from the poet's youth, or is it an autumn from a bygone era? Probably both. The same question may be asked about the remembered spring in the poem above. And while I have chosen simple poems by Saigyō for the most part, it should also be noted that his syntax often contains knots or complex shifts of meaning. He is not a strict adherent to a school of "direct simplicity" despite writing a great many poems that might serve as examples of such a lineage.

In addition to his Buddhist mountain poems, Saigyō wrote many beautiful love poems, often in the voice of a woman:

> He never came–
> the wind too tells
> how the night has worn away,
> while mournfully the cries of wild geese
> approach and pass on

As a love poet, he draws on all the strengths of the tradition, often turning the poem on a closing image in otherwise conventional style:

> Her face when we parted,
> a parting
> I can never forget–
> And for keepsake she left it
> printed on the moon

It is good to remember that in Japanese seeing a face printed on the moon is a striking image: where we habitually see "the man in the moon," the Asian poet sees "the moon-rabbit." Saigyō's moon-face is utterly original. But without a light, deft touch on the part of the translator, it turns into something reminiscent of country-western kitsch.

Saigyō is also capable of composing a poem of almost Creeleyesque domestic tension, as when he says,

> "I know
> how you must feel!"
> And with those words
> she grows more hateful
> than if she'd never spoken at all.

Nevertheless, Saigyō is at his greatest in the Buddhist-inspired lyric. Musing on the *Nirvana Sutra*, he read: "All phenomena are fleeting,/ this is the law of birth and death./ When you have wiped out birth and death,/ nirvana is your joy." And he writes a poem that will inspire Bashō and dozens of other Zen-influenced poets over many generations:

> I think of past times
> so swift
> in their vanishing,
> the present soon to follow–
> dew on the morning glory

Here again the personal and the social/historical commingle, the whole poem hinging on its closing image, the "meaning" of the poem contained in its interpretation.

Poems of a Mountain Home contains two hundred of Saigyō's best poems in a capable, gifted translation. Watson and LaFleur have given us remarkable translations of a major poet. The influence of Wang Wei and Saigyō and the whole Buddhist mountain poetry tradition on contemporary American poetry can be seen in the poetry of Gary Snyder and other American Buddhist poets, in the poetry of Kenneth Rexroth, of course, and also in the poetry of James Wright, Robert Bly, and other "descriptive" or imagistic poets in the same way that Ezra Pound's excursions into Li Po's poetry (*Cathay*) influenced Imagism.

Indeed T.S. Eliot, no one's example of the "nature poet," went to school on the *Upanishads* and the *Bagavad Gita* while a student at Harvard, primary Hindi-Buddhist texts that no doubt informed Wang Wei and Saigyō. Eliot certainly also knew the multi-volume translation of Confucian classics by James Legge, especially the *Poetry Classic* (*Shih Ching*) anthology also translated by Arthur Waley and by Ezra Pound.

In an essay for *American Poetry Review* several years ago ("An Answering Music," reprinted in *A Poet's Work*), I traced the extensive influence of classical Chinese poetry on contemporary American poets from Eliot, Pound, and Williams, through Bly, Wright, John Haines, Denise Levertov, Allen Ginsberg, Lucien Stryk, Colette Inez, Carolyn Kizer and others. Here I underscore the extensive influence of Chinese poems of nature and friendship in particular.

All notions of influence and literary standing aside, these translations of Wang Wei and Saigyō enlarge and enhance our understanding of this world, offer some beautiful poems in English, and are a welcome gift for which we should all be grateful.

Bashō's Road

Introduction to *Narrrow Road to the Interior & Other Writings of Bashō*

The moon and sun are eternal travelers. Even the years wander on. A lifetime adrift in a boat or in old age leading a tired horse into the years, every day is a journey, and the journey itself is home.

—Bashō: *Oku no hosomichi*

Bashō rose long before dawn, but even at such an early hour, he knew the day would grow rosy bright. It was spring, 1689. In Ueno and Yanaka, cherry trees were in full blossom, and hundreds of families would soon be strolling under their branches, lovers walking and speaking softly or not at all. But it wasn't cherry blossoms that occupied his mind. He had long dreamed of crossing the Shirakawa Barrier into the mountainous heartlands of northern Honshu, the country called Oku—"the interior"—lying immediately to the north of the city of Sendai. He patched his old cotton trousers and repaired his straw hat. He placed his old thatched-roof hut in another's care and moved several hundred feet down the road to the home of his disciple-patron, Mr. Sampu, making final preparations before embarkation.

On the morning of May 16th, dawn rose through a shimmering mist, Mount Fuji faintly visible on the horizon. It was the beginning of the Genroku period, a time of relative peace under the Tokugawa shogunate. But travel is always dangerous. A devotee as well as a traveling companion, Bashō's friend, Sora, would shave his head and don the robes of a Zen monk, a tactic that often proved helpful at well-guarded checkpoints. Bashō had done so himself on previous journeys. Because of poor health, Bashō carried extra nightwear in his pack along with his cotton robe or *yukata*, a raincoat, calligraphy supplies, and of course *hanamuke*, departure gifts from well-wishers, gifts he found impossible to leave behind.

Bashō himself would leave behind a number of gifts upon his death some five years later, among them a journal composed after this journey, his health again in decline, a journal made up in part of fiction or fancy. But during the spring and summer of 1689, he walked and watched. And from early 1690 into 1694, Bashō wrote and revised his "travel diary," which is not a diary at all. *Oku* means "within" and "farthest" or "dead-end" place; *hosomichi* means "path" or "narrow road." The *no* is prepositional. *Oku no hosomichi:* the narrow road within; the narrow way through the interior. Bashō draws *Oku* from the place of that name located between Miyagino and Matsushima, but it is a name that inspires plurisignation.

Narrow Road to the Interior is much, much more than a poetic travel journal. Its form, *haibun,* combines short prose passages with *haiku.* But the heart and mind of this little book, its *kokoro,* cannot be found simply by defining form. Bashō completely redefined haiku and transformed haibun. These accomplishments grew out of arduous studies in poetry, Buddhism, history, Taoism, Confucianism, Shintoism, and some very important Zen training.

Bashō was a student of Saigyō, a Buddhist monk-poet who lived five hundred years earlier (1118-1190), and who is the most prominent poet of the imperial anthology, *Shin-kokinshū.* Like Saigyō before him, Bashō believed in co-dependent origination, a Buddhist idea holding that all things are fully interdependent, even at point of origin; that no thing is or can be completely self-originating. Bashō said of Saigyō, "He was obedient to and at one with nature and the four seasons." The *Samantabhadra-bodhisattva-sutra* says, "Of one thing it is said, 'This is good,' and of another it is said, 'This is bad,' but there is nothing inherent in either to make them 'good' or 'bad.' The 'self' is empty of independent existence." From Saigyō, the poet learned the importance of "being at one with nature," and the relative unimportance of mere personality. Such an attitude creates the Zen broth in which his poetry is steeped. Dreaming of the full moon as it rises over boats at Shiogama Beach, Bashō is not looking outside himself—rather he is seeking that which is most clearly meaningful within, and locating the "meaning" within the context of juxtaposed images that are interpenetrating and interdependent. The images arise naturally out of the *kokoro*—the heart/mind, as much felt as perceived.

Two hundred years earlier, Komparu Zenchiku wrote, "The Wheel of Emptiness is the highest level of art of the Noh—the performance is *mushin.*" This is the art of artlessness, the act of composition achieved without "sensibility" or style—this directness of emotion expressed without ornament set the standards of the day.

At the time of the compiling of the *Man'yōshū,* the first Imperial anthology, completed in the late eighth century, the Japanese critical vocabulary emphasized two aspects of the poem: *kokoro,* which included sincerity, conviction, or "heart," and also "craft" in a most particular way. *Man'yōshū* poets were admired for their "masculinity," that is, for uncluttered, direct, and often severe expression of emotion. Their sincerity (*makoto*) was a quality to be revered. The poets of the *Man'yōshū* are the foundation upon which all Japanese poetry has been built.

One of the first *karon*, or essays on literary criticism in Japanese, is that of Fujiwara Hamanari (733-799), author of *Kakyō-hyōshiki*, an essay listing seven "diseases of poetry," such as having the first and second lines end on the same syllable, or having the last syllable of the third and last lines differ. There were various dissertations on "poem-diseases," all largely modeled on the original Chinese of Shen Yo (441-513). The idea of studying craft in poetry must have caught on quickly, because by 885 the first *uta-awase*, or poetry-writing contests, were being held and were judged by guidelines drawn from these various essays on prosody.

At the time of the compilation of the *Man'yōshū*, very little poetry was being written in Chinese; Hitomaro and Yakamochi, the great eighth century poets, wrote without many allusions to Confucian or Buddhist classics, their poems drawing inspiration from landscape and experience that are uniquely Japanese. Another court anthology contemporary with the *Man'yōshū*, the *Kaifusō*, represents the introduction of poetry written in Chinese language and styles, despite the few samples in the *Man'yōshū*.

Through the influence of the monk Kūkai, also called Kōbo Daishi (774-835), the study of Chinese became the norm for what amounted to a Buddhist aristocracy. As founder of the Shingon or True Word sect in Japan, Kūkai followed a tradition of secret oral teachings passed on from master to disciple, and had himself spent two years studying in China under Hui Kuo (764-805). The later influence of Sugawara-no-Michizane established Chinese as the language of scholarly poets, so much so that upon his death, Michizane was enshrined as a god of literature and calligraphy. His followers found Japanese forms too restrictive for their multilayered poetry. Every good poet was a teacher of poetry in one way or another, many taking on disciples. Michizane's influence was profound. He advocated both rigorous scholarship and genuine sincerity in composition; his own verses were substantially influenced by the T'ang dynasty poet, Po Chu-i. The form was *shih*, lyric verse composed in five- or seven-character lines written in Chinese; but, unlike most earlier Japanese poets, Michizane's poems were deceptively simple, and like the poetry of Po Chu-i, strengthened by a combination of poignancy and conviction. Poetry written in Chinese was called *kanshi*, and Michizane established it as a major force.

In his *kana* (phonetic syllabary) preface to the *Kokinshū* in the tenth century, Ki no Tsurayuki, author of the famous travelogue, *Tosa Journal*, lists six types of poetry:

1. *soe-uta:* suggestive or indirect expression of feeling
2. *kazoe-uta:* clear, direct expression of feeling
3. *nazurae-uta:* parabolic expression
4. *tatoe-uta:* expression which conceals powerful emotion
5. *tadagoto-uta:* refinement of a traditional expression
6. *iwai-uta:* poem expressing congratulations or praise

Tsurayuki's list owes something to Lu Chi's catalogue of genres in his third century Chinese *Art of Writing* (*Wen Fu*), which is itself indebted to various treatises on the Confucian poetry anthology, *Shih Ching* or *Classic of Poetry.*

Much of the penchant for cataloguing and classifying types of poetry is the result of the Confucian classic, *Ta Hsueh* or *Great Learning*, in which Confucius says, "All wisdom is rooted in learning to call things by the right name," and that when "things are properly identified, they fall into natural categories and understanding [and, consequently, *action*] becomes orderly." Lu Chi, the dedicated student of Confucius, reminds us that the art of letters has "saved governments from certain ruin," and "clarifies laws" of nature and society. He finds within the study of writing itself a way to set his own life in order. Such thinking undoubtedly lies behind Bashō's notion of the Way of Poetry.

Studying Chinese, the Japanese literati picked up Lu Chi's habit of discussing poetry in terms of form and content. And from the 5th century Chinese scholar, Liu Hsieh, they drew the term *amari no kokoro*, a translation of Liu's original *yu wei* or "aftertaste." As a critical term, it would be used and reshaped, and used again; it is still a part of literary evaluation in the late twentieth century. Narihira says of a poem in the *Kokinshū*, "*Kokoro amarite—kotoba tarazu,*" or "Plenty of heart; not enough words." Kuronushi says, "*Kokoro okashikute, sama iyashi,*" or "Interesting *kokoro*, but a rather common form." The poet strives for the quality called *amari no kokoro*, meaning that the heart/soul of the poem must reach far beyond the words themselves, leaving an indelible aftertaste.

For Bashō, this most often meant a resonance found in nature. When he invokes the call of a cuckoo, its very name, *hototogisu* (pronounced with a virtually silent closing vowel), invokes its lonely cry. Things are as they are. Insight permits him to perceive a natural poignancy in the beauty of temporal things—*mono no aware*—and cultivate its expression into great art. *Aware* originally meant simply emotion initiated by engagement of the senses. In its own way, this phrase is Japan's equivalent of William Carlos Williams's dictum, "No ideas but in things."

In *The World of the Shining Prince,* Ivan Morris's study of *The Tale of Genji,* Morris says of *aware,* "In its widest sense it was an interjection or adjective referring to the emotional quality inherent in objects, people, nature, and art, and by extension it applied to a person's internal response to emotional aspects of the external world. . . . in Murasaki's time [ca. 1000 C.E.] *aware* still retained its early catholic range, its most characteristic use in *The Tale of Genji* is to suggest the pathos inherent in the beauty of the outer world, a beauty that is inexorably fated to disappear together with the observer. Buddhist doctrines about the evanescence of all living things naturally influenced this particular content of the word, but the stress in *aware* was always on direct emotional experience rather than on religious understanding. *Aware* never entirely lost its simple interjectional sense of 'Ah!'"

As a more purely critical term in later centuries, *aware* identified a particular quality of elegant sadness, a poignant awareness of temporality, a quality found in abundance, for instance, in the poetry of Issa and in this century in the novels of Kawabata Yasunari. Middle-aged and in declining health, Bashō found plenty of resonance in temporal life, much of it clarified through his deep study of the classics.

Tsurayuki, whose own diary provided a model for Bashō's travelogues 700 years later, ruminated on the art of letters during his sojourn through Tosa province in the south of Shikoku Island in 936. In his preface to the *Kokinshū,* he lists several sources for inspiration in poetry, all melancholy in one way or another: "Looking at falling blossoms on a spring morning; sighing over snows and waves which reflect the passing years; remembering a fall from fortune into loneliness." Tsurayuki's proclivity for melancholy perhaps explains the general tone of the *Kokinshū.* But this, too, is *mono-no-aware.*

At the time of the *Man'yōshū,* Zen was being brought to Japan via a steady stream of scholars returning from China. Along with Zen equations and conversations, the scholars also brought with them Chinese poetics, including a surprising Confucian faith in the power of the right word rightly used. The attitude is paradoxical: the Zen poet believes the real experience of poetry lies somewhere beyond the words themselves, but, like a good Confucian, believes simultaneously that only the perfect word perfectly placed has the power to reveal the authentic experience of the poem.

Ki no Tsurayuki's co-compiler of the *Kokinshū,* Mibu no Tadamine (868-965), introduced another new term to the Japanese critical canon by praising a quality in certain poems which he called *yugen,* a word borrowed from Chinese Buddhist writing to identify "depth of meaning," a character made by combining the character for "dim" or "dark" with the character identifying a deep, reddish black color. Tadamine used *yugen* to identify "aesthetic feeling *not explicitly expressed."* He wanted a term with which to identify subtleties and implications. Over the course of the next hundred or so years, *yugen* would also be adopted by Zennists to define "ghostly qualities," as in ink paintings. But the term's origin lies within seventh century Chinese Buddhist literary terminology. As an aesthetic concept, it was esteemed throughout the medieval period. An excellent study of Buddhism and literary arts in medieval Japan, William R. LaFleur's *The Karma of Words* devotes an entire chapter to *yugen.*

The compilation of the *Kokinshū* also institutionalized the *makura kotoba* or "pillow word" in Japanese poetics. It is a fixed epithet, often like Homer's "wine-dark sea," but frequently allowing for double entendre or multiple evocation. Although such devices appear infrequently in the *Man'yōshū,* by the time of the *Kokinshū,* most readers were aware that "clouds and rain" might mean sexual congress as well as weather patterns. The *makura kotoba* often permitted a poet to disguise emotions; it was both "polite" and metaphoric.

Along with the "pillow word," the apprentice poet also learned how to make use of the *kake kotoba* or "pivot word" that would later become central to the composition of haiku. It is a play on different meanings of a word that links two phrases. It is often nearly impossible to translate except when it creates an intentional pause. The pivot word creates deliberate ambiguity, often implying polysignation. The pillow word and the pivot word have been reassessed and discussed and re-examined time and again throughout the history of Japanese poetry.

As this critical vocabulary developed, poets devised new ways to discuss the *kajitsu* or formal aspects of a poem. The *ka* is the "beautiful surface of the poem," and the *jitsu* is the "substantial core." Studying the "beautiful surface" of the poem along with its interior structure, Fujiwara no Kinto (966-1041) composed his *Nine Steps of Waka* (*waka* is a generic term for classical poems of five lines measured in syllabic lines of 5-7-5-7-7) to establish standards based almost solely upon critical fashion. Certain rhymes were taboo at a poem's closure; certain vowel sounds should be repeated at particular intervals. Rather than being a general and moral and emotional discourse such as Lu Chi's, or those of Tsurayuki and Tadamine, Kinto's aesthetic relied exclusively on reasoned study of the architecture of the poem. His critical vocabulary is restricted to that of the poem's structure. His anthology, *Shuishū*, has never enjoyed either the popularity or the controversy of the *Kokinshū* and *Shinkokinshū*.

Zen demolishes much of this kind of literary criticism by pointing out that, seen from the core, the surface is very deep; inasmuch as cause leads to effect, effect in turn produces cause. A poem's "depth" cannot be created by packing the poem with allusions and implications—hermetics alone. Still, *surface* and *core* may be useful terms for establishing a necessary dialectic; they provide frames of reference. Such discussions of depths and surfaces certainly contributed to Bashō's critical vocabulary and to his notion of the Way of Elegance in poetry.

As this critical vocabulary came into use, it was balanced by a vocabulary of the emotions. A contemporary of Saigyō, Fujiwara Teika (1162-1241), attacked structural criticism as hopelessly inadequate. "Every poem," he said, "must have *kokoro*. A poem without *kokoro* is not—cannot be—a true poem; it is only an intellectual exercise." Thus, by combining a vocabulary for the apparatus of poetry with a vocabulary for the emotional states of poetry, Teika believed, a poem could be examined and properly appreciated. His insistence upon the true poem's *kokoro* returns the experience of the poem to human dimensions.

Another term in use at the time, *kokai,* expressed a feeling of regret after reading a poem, a consequence of the poet having failed to think sufficiently deeply prior to its composition. It was a criticism not often applied to Bashō, nor to other poets working in the Zen tradition, but one with which every haiku poet since has struggled. Bashō sought a natural spontaneity, a poetry that would indulge no regrets of any kind. Zen discipline is built in part around the idea of truth articulated in spontaneous response. A "correct" response to a Zen kōan, for instance, need not be obviously rational or logical. Bashō sought a poetry that was a natural outgrowth of being Bashō, of living in this world, of making the journey itself one's home.

The fourteenth century Zen monk Ikkyū Sōjun wrote, *"Ame furaba fure, kaze fukaba fuke."* If it rains, let it rain; if the wind blows, let it blow. Bashō spent many years struggling to "learn how to listen as things speak for themselves." No regrets. He refused to be anthropocentric. The theory of co-dependent origination infuses seer and seen, making them not two things, but one. Seeing the more than two hundred beautiful pine-covered islands off the coast of Matsushima, he wrote:

Matsushima ya

ah Matsushima ya

Matsushima ya

This is the sort of poem that can be done once, and once only. But it is quintessentially Bashō, both playful and inspired, yet with a hint of *mono no aware,* a trace of the pathos of beautiful mortality. A literal translation: "Pine Islands, ah! / Oh, Pine Islands, ah! / Pine Islands, ah!"

Simple as it is, the poem implies codependent origination, physical landscape, and a breathless—almost speechless—reverence. Just as Bashō learned utterly direct simplicity from Ikkyū, he learned from Ikkyū's friend, Rikyū, that each tea ceremony is the only tea ceremony. Therefore, each poem is the only poem. Each moment is the only moment in which one can be fully aware. Standing on the shore, he saw hundreds of tiny islands carved by tides, wind-twisted pines rising at sharp angles. *Matsu* means pine; *shima* is island. *Ya* indicates subject, but also works simultaneously as an exclamation. It functions as a *kireji* or "cutting word." The township on the mainland is itself called Matsushima. Bashō entered Matsushima by boat in June, 1689, and was so taken by its beauty that he declared it to have been made by Oyamazumi, god of the mountains.

Bashō walked and dreamed along the beach at Ojima beneath the moon of Matsu-shima. From his pack, he withdrew a poem written by a friend and former teacher, Sodō, an acknowledged haiku master. The poem described Matsushima and was written in Chinese. Another, a poem in Japanese about Matsugaura-shima composed by an Edo doctor, Hara Anteki. The poems, Bashō said, were his companions during a long sleepless night.

Two days later, he visited an elegant temple, Zuiganji, founded thirty-two generations earlier by Makabe no Heishiro upon his return from a decade of studies in China. Bashō wondered whether it might be "the gates of Buddha-land." But he was no flowerchild wandering in Lotus Land. His journey is a pilgrimage, it is a journey into the interior of the self as much as a travelogue, a vision quest that concludes in *insight.* But there *is* no conclusion. The journey itself is home. The means is the end, just as it is the beginning. Each step is the first step, each step the last.

Bashō visited temples only in part because he was himself a Zennist. Temples often provided rooms for wayfarers, and the food, if simple, was good. The conversation was of a kind the literate pilgrim especially enjoys. Bashō, among the most literate poets of his time, seems to be everywhere in the presence of history. *Oku no hosomichi* overflows with place-names, famous scenes, literary Chinese and Buddhist allusions, literary echoes called *honkadori*—borrowed or quoted lines and paraphrases. But he didn't stay at many temples during his most famous journey; he rarely stayed at inns; he was generally and generously entertained by local haikai poets and put up by wealthy families. His health failing and each year passing more quickly, he enjoyed his modest celebrity and its benefits.

His literary and spiritual lineage included Kamo no Chōmei (1154-1216), *Shin-kokinshū* poet, author of the *Mumyōshō,* a kind of manual of writing, and of the *Hōjōki,* an account of Chōmei's years in a "ten foot square hut" following a series of calamities in Kyoto. Like Chōmei, Bashō, despite being deeply versed in Chinese and Japanese literature, philosophy, and history, enjoyed talking with working people everywhere. Besides being one of Bashō's models for travel writing, Chōmei was a model for the practice of compassion.

After "abandoning the world," Chōmei moved to the mountains on the outskirts of Kyoto. But his was not to be the usual life of the Zen ascetic. He made very regular trips to town, if for no other reason than to listen to the people he met there. Reading the *Hōjōki,* it is easy to forget that Chōmei served as a kind of journalist, a deeply compassionate witness to the incredible suffering of people during his lifetime. His world was shaken to the core when winds spread a great fire through Kyoto, leveling a third of the capital city in 1177. In 1181, a famine began that lasted two years. These and other calamities informed Chōmei's understanding of the First Noble Truth, that "being is agonizing," and inspired his profound sense of compassion. Just as a disciple of Sakyamuni Buddha, Vimalakirti, provided a model for Chōmei's retreat, Bashō found in Chōmei a model for compassionate engagement with others. Chōmei had written, "Trivial things spoken along the way enliven the faith of my awakened heart."

Chōmei's interest in people in general was a trait Bashō shared. He also could not separate his life from his art. Bashō also felt a deep connection to history. He speaks as though all eternity were only yesterday, each memory vivid, the historical figures themselves almost contemporaneous; he speaks confidentially, expecting his reader to be versed in details so that his own brief travelogue may serve to call up enormous resonances, ghosts at every turn. But Bashō doesn't pack his lines with references. His subjects and his knowledge flow freely, casually, through his writing.

Chōmei bore witness to countless thousands of deaths after the great fire swept Kyōto. "They die in the morning and are born in the evening like bubbles on water." Bashō walks across the plain where a great battle once raged. Only empty fields remain. The landscape reminds him of a poem by Tu Fu (712-770) in which the T'ang poet surveyed a similar scene and wrote,

> The whole country devastated,
> only mountains and rivers remain.
> In springtime, at the ruined castle,
> the grass is always green.

For Bashō, the grass blowing in the breeze seems especially poignant, so much so that his eyes fill with tears. If Tu Fu, both as a poet and as a man, is a fit model—to be emulated, not imitated, Bashō insists—he is reminded of how little we have learned from all our interminable warfare and bloodshed. The wind blows. The grasses bend. Bashō moistens his brush months later and writes, remembering,

Natsugusa ya	Summer grasses—
tsuwamono domo ga	all that remains of great soldiers'
yume no ato	imperial dreams.

His echo of Tu Fu underscores the profound irony. For Bashō, the journey into the interior of the way of poetry had been long and arduous. His simple "summer grasses" haiku carried within it the sort of resonance he sought throughout his life. The grasses with their plethora of associations, the ghosts of Hidehira, Yoritomo, and Yoshitsune, an allusion drawn from a famous Noh drama, —Bashō framed his verse with rich and complex historical, literary, and philosophical associations. The poem implies that the grasses are the *only* consequence of warriors' dreams, that the grasses are all that remains of the immeasurable desires of all passing generations.

The haiku itself is spare, clean, swift as a boning knife. The melopoeia combines *a, o,* and *u* sounds: *tsu, gu* in line 1; *tsu* and *yu* in lines 2 and 3; the *tsu* sound is very quick. The *a* sound punctuates the whole poem: *na, sa, ya* among the five syllables of line 1; *wa* and *ga* among the seven syllables of line two, the four remaining being *mono* and *domo;* and a semi-concluding *a* before *to.* Among the seventeen syllables are six *a* syllables, six *o* syllables, and four *u* syllables.

The Western reader, accustomed to being conscious of reading translation and having fallen into the unrewarding habit of reading poetry silently, often misses Bashō's ear by neglecting the *Romaji* or "Romanized" Japanese printed with the poems. Onomatopoeia, rhyme, and slant rhyme are Bashō's favorite tools, and he uses them like no one else in Japanese literature. He wrote from within the body; his poems are full of breath and sound as well as images and allusions.

What Bashō read, he read deeply and attentively. As a poet, he had blossomed slowly, ever-changing, constantly learning. The poetry of his twenties and thirties is competent and generally undistinguished. It is the learned poetry of received ideas composed by a good mind. It lacks breadth and depth of vision.

As his interest in Chinese poetry continued to grow, he studied Tu Fu assiduously during his twenties and thirties, and he read Li Po for his rich imagination and inventive styles of writing. Foremost among his studies, he claimed to have "always traveled with a copy of *Chuang Tzu.*" He seems to have struggled with Zen discipline and Chinese poetry and philosophy all during his thirties, and the result was a poetry at first clearly derivative, but later becoming ever more his own as he grew into his studies. Upon entering his forties, Bashō's verse began to change. He learned to be comfortable with his teachers and with his own scholarship. His Zen practice had steadied his vision. Fewer aspirations stood in his way.

Born in 1644 in Ueno, Iga Province, approximately 30 miles southeast of Kyōto, the son of Matsuo Yozaemon, a low-ranking samurai, Bashō had at least one elder brother and four sisters. As a young man, he served in the household of a high-ranking local samurai, Todo Shinshichiro, becoming a companion to his son, Yoshitada, whose "haiku name" was Sengin. Bashō often joined his master in composing the linked verses called *haikai no renku,* but was still known by his samurai name, Matsuo Munefusa, despite having taken his first haiku name, Sobo. Bashō also had a common-law wife at this time, Jutei, who later became a nun. And although there is little verifiable information on these years, he seems to have experimented a good deal. He would later say upon reflection, "I at one time coveted an official post," and "There was a time when I became fascinated with the ways of homosexual love."

Whether because of a complicated love-life or whether as a result of the death of his friend and master, Bashō apparently simply wandered off sometime around the beginning of 1667, leaving behind his samurai name and position. It was not unique for a man like Bashō to leave samurai society. Many who did so became monks. Most others entered the merchant class. Bashō, uniquely, did neither. Some early biographers claim he went to Kyōto to study philosophy, poetry, and calligraphy. In any event, he re-emerged in 1672 as editor and commentator for a volume of haikai, *The*

Seashell Game (Kai Oi). With contributions from about thirty poets, *The Seashell Game* shows Bashō to be witty, deeply knowledgeable, and rather light-hearted. It was well-enough received to encourage him to move to Edo (present-day Tokyo).

While it is not clear whether he initially made his living in Edo working as a haiku poet and teacher, Bashō does tell us that those first years in the growing city were not easy ones. He would later recall that he was torn between the desire to become a great poet and the desire to simply give up verse altogether. But his verse was, in many ways, his life. He continued to study and write, and to attract students, a number of whom were, like himself, drop-outs from samurai or *bushidō* society who also rejected the vulgar values of the class below the samurai, the *chonin* or urban merchant class. Bashō believed literature provided an alternative set of values which he called *fuga no michi*, "The Way of Elegance." He claimed that his life was stitched together "by the single thread of art" which permitted him to follow "no religious law" and no popular customs.

He admired the Zen mind; but the "Buddhism" attached to Zen was, to him, almost superfluous. During his years in Edo, he studied Zen under the priest Butchō (1642-1715), apparently even to the point of considering the monastic life, but whether to escape from decadent culture or as a philosophical passion remains unclear. Despite his ability to attract students, he seems to have spent much of his time in a state of perpetual despondency, loneliness everywhere crowding in on him. No doubt this state of mind was compounded as a result of chronically poor health, but Bashō was also engaging true *sabishi*, a spiritual "loneliness" that served haikai culture in much the same way *mu* or "nothingness" served Zen.

In the summer of 1676, Bashō visited his homeland for the first time since moving to Edo. Returning in late summer, he brought with him a nephew, Tōin, who was sixteen and who would remain in Bashō's care the remainder of his short life. Desperately in need of money to care for his nephew, the poet worked from 1677 to 1681 for a district waterworks company, while establishing a name in haiku contests and collaborating with other poets.

In the winter of 1680, his students built him a small hut on the east bank of the Sumida River, where he could establish a permanent home. In the spring, someone planted a plaintain (or *bashō*) tree in the yard, giving the hut, "Bashō-an," its name, and the poet his final new *nom de plume*. He wrote, "After nine springs and autumns of living in poverty in the city, I have now moved to the Fukagawa district. Perhaps because I am poor, I remember the T'ang dynasty poet who observed, "Chang-an (the Chinese capital) has always been a place for those seeking fame and fortune. But it's a tough place for the empty-handed wanderer.'"

The original Bashō-an burned to the ground when a fire swept through the neighborhood in the winter of 1682. Friends and disciples built a new one during the winter of 1683. His disciples were also beginning to earn names of their own. Bashō wrote of one, Kikaku, that his poems contained the "spiritual broth" of Tu Fu. But his followers were also time-consuming. And there were suddenly second generation disciples, literally hundreds of "Bashō group" poets springing up. More and more projects were offered for his possible participation. He longed for quietude. And he immersed himself in studying the Taoist masterpiece *Chuang Tzu,* and in his Zen studies under Butchō. Several of his poems from this period draw directly from Chuang Tzu's allegories, perhaps most obviously:

> In this season's rain
> the crane's long legs
> have suddenly been shortened

> Samidare ni
> tsuru no ashi
> mijikaku nareri

But for the "seasonal word," the poem is almost a quotation, and unusual for its syllabic structure of 5-5-7. He would later write to a disciple, "Even if you have three or four extra syllables, or even five or seven, you needn't worry as long as it *sounds* right. But if even one syllable is stale in your mouth, give it all of your attention."

The first full-length anthology of "Bashō School" haiku (*Minashiguri—* or *Withered Chestnuts*) was published in the summer of 1683 with an Afterword by Bashō in which he spells out the "four principal flavors" of the poems as the lyricism of Tu Fu and Li Po, the Zen of Han Shan, and the romantic love of Po Chu-i. He continues to find models and inspiration drawn from the T'ang dynasty poets.

During 1684 and early 1685, Bashō traveled to Kyōto, Nara, and his old home in Ueno, and composed *Travelogue of Weather-Beaten Bones* (*Nozarashi Kikō*), the first of his travel journals and one notable for its undertone of pathos. His mother had died in Ueno the previous year, but Bashō had been too poor to be able to make the journey to her funeral.

He spent only a few days in Ueno, but his meeting with his brothers inspired one of his most famous poems:

If I took it in hand,
it would melt in my hot tears—
heavy autumn frost

Te ni toraba
kien namida so atsuki
aki no shimo

The trip was a long eight months, arduous and extremely dangerous. The forty-year-old poet had spent thirty years in Iga and a decade in Edo before beginning the wanderer's life for which he became so famous. This first travelogue reads almost as though it were translated from Chinese, allusions and parallels drawn from Ch'an (Zen) literature in nearly every line. Bashō was struggling to achieve a resonance between the fleeting moment and the eternal, between the instant of awareness and the vast emptiness of Zen.

In 1687, he traveled with his friend, Sora, and a Zen monk to Kashima Shrine, fifty miles east of Edo, where, among other things, Bashō visited his Zen master, Butchō, who had retired there. His record of this trip, *Kashima Travelogue,* is very brief, and the poems included are almost all by Bashō's disciples.

During his years of Zen training, he had spoken of striving to achieve the "religious flavor" of the poetry of Han Shan (*Kanzan* in Japanese, Cold Mountain in English); he had wanted to "clothe in Japanese language" the poetry of Po Chu-i. But in *Kashima Travelogue,* he chose a far simpler syntax, writing almost exclusively in *kana,* the Japanese phonetic syllabary, rather than in *kanji,* Chinese written characters. He was simplifying and clarifying his methods without sacrificing depth.

In late 1687, Bashō made another journey, visiting Ise, Nagoya, Iga, Yoshino, and Nara, traveling with a disciple and drinking companion, Etsujin. The writing from this journey would not be published until 1709, more than ten years after the poet's death. Scholars date completion of the *Knapsack Notebook* (*Oi no kobumi*) at about 1691, the same time the poet was writing *Oku no hosomichi.* Bashō attributes to his friend a great fondness for sake drinking and a splendid talent for singing ancient poetry to the accompaniment of the Japanese lute, or *biwa,* and records a number of parties held in their honor. Their travels through Ise, Yoshino, Suma and Akashi resulted in some luminous haiku and some striking commentary on the Way of Poetry. He says in the *Knapsack* manucript, "Nobody has succeeded in making any improvement in travel diaries since Ki no Tsurayuki, Chōmei, and the nun Abutsu . . . the rest have merely imitated."

Clearly, he was searching for a style that could reinvigorate an ancient form. He must have felt that he had gained a powerful knowledge which only a simple style could accommodate. He also said in *The Knapsack Notebook,* "Saigyō's waka, Sōgi's renga,/ Sesshu's sumi, Rikyū's tea,—the spirit which moves them is one spirit." But he was not filled with confidence, either, noting that all his attempts to reivigorate the travelogue and to "become the equal" of Japan's greatest poets may amount to no more than "mere drunken chatter, the incoherent babbling of a dreamer." Nevertheless, he felt driven to take these risks, both physical and literary.

His next journal, *Sarashina Travelogue,* is the result of a short moon-viewing trip Bashō had wanted to make to watch the moon rise through the trees over Mount Obasute. In a particularly poignant moment, offered a toast, he and his his companions were given cups by the innkeeper, cups that caught his attention. Although cheap and gaudy, because of the locale, he found them to be "more precious than the blue jeweled cups of the wealthy."

After flirting with dense Chinese diction, Bashō was turning toward *wabi,* an elegant simplicity tinged with *sabi,* an undertone of "aloneness." *Sabi* comes from the more pure "loneliness" of *sabishi.* It was an idea that fit perfectly with his notion of *fuga no michi,* the Way of Elegance, together with his rejection of bourgeois values. Elegant simplicity. His idea of *sabi* has about it elements of *yugen, mono no aware,* and plenty of *kokoro.* His poetry, so indebted to Japanese and Chinese classics, could be simplified; he could find a poetry that would instill in the reader a sense of *sabi.* Perhaps he had followed classical Chinese rhetorical conventions a bit too closely. He wanted to make images that positively radiated with reality.

Whether he had arrived at his mature style by that early spring morning in 1689, he was eager to begin his journey north to Sendai and on to Hiraizumi, where the Fujiwara clan had flourished and perished. He would then push west, cross the mountains, turn south down the west coast of Honshu along the Sea of Japan, then turn east again toward Ise, the vast majority of the trip to be made on foot. He left behind the idiosyncrasies and frivolities of the Teitoku and Danrin schools of haikai. He left perhaps as many as sixty advanced students of the Bashō School who, in turn, were acquiring students of their own.

When his disciple, Kikaku, over-praised a Bashō image of a cold fish on a fishmonger's shelf, saying he had attained "true mystery and depth," Bashō replied that what he most valued was the poem's "ordinariness." He had come almost full circle from the densely allusive Chinese style into a truly elegant simplicity that was in no way frivolous. He had elevated haiku from word-play into powerful lyric poetry, from a game played by educated poetasters into a genuinely spiritual dimension. "Abide by rules," Bashō taught, "then throw them out!—only *then* may you achieve true freedom." His freedom expressed itself by redefining haiku as a complete form capable of handling complex data, emotional depth and spiritual seriousness while still retaining some element of playfulness. R. H. Blyth wrote, "Zen is poetry; poetry is Zen." In the case of Bashō, the practice of Zen and the practice of poetry produce a seamless union.

Confucius says, "Only the one who attains perfect sincerity under heaven may discover one's 'true nature.' One who accomplishes this participates fully in the transformation of heaven and earth, and being fully human, becomes with them a third thing." Knowing this, Bashō tells his students, "Do not simply follow in the footsteps of the ancients; seek what they sought." To avoid simply filling the ancient footsteps of his predecessors, he studies them assiduously, attentively. And when he has had his fill of ancient poets and students and the infinite dialectic that is literature and art, when his heart is filled with wanderlust, he chooses a traveling companion, fills a small pack with essentials—and, of course, a few *hanamuke*—and walks off into the mid-May dawn, into the geography of the soul that makes the journey itself a home.

Afterward

Bashō arrived in his hometown of Ueno in November, 1689, exhausted by his travels and weakened by failing health. But after a couple of months, he once again took to the road accompanied by a friend, Rotsū, this time to see the famous Shinto festival at Kasuga Shrine in Nara in early January of 1690. By early February, he was in Kyoto to visit his friend Kyorai, and from there went to the village of Zeze, on the shore of Lake Biwa, where he was welcomed by a throng of students on New Year Day (February 9 on the lunar calendar). Bashō left Rotsū there a few days later and returned alone to Ueno, where he spent the next three months being feted and attending haiku gatherings.

It was during this stay in Ueno that he first began to advocate the poetic principle of *karumi,* "lightness," urging his followers to "seek beauty in plain, simple, artless language" by observing ordinary things very closely. Karumi, together with existential Zen loneliness (*sabi*) and elegantly understated, unpretentious natural beauty (*shibumi*), characterize his final work. His life had been profoundly shaped by *wabi,* a principle as much moral as aesthetic, and which suggests a spiritual prosperity achieved through material poverty together with a deep appreciation of things old, worn, modest, and simple. These last years, he wrote at the height of his powers, a lifetime of devoted study bringing him full circle, back to the most simple, least consciously artful, poetry imaginable.

Around the first of May, he returned to Zeze, where his students had refurbished a tiny mountain cottage, naming it *Genjū-an,* the "Phantom Hut," in his honor. From his hillside behind Ishiyama Temple, he enjoyed a panoramic view of Lake Biwa and the Seta River. Except for a ten day visit with Kyorai in Kyoto, he rarely left his retreat over the next four months. Near the end of his stay, he wrote a short prose meditation, *Genjū-an no ki,* in which he concludes, "In the end, without skill or talent, I've given myself over entirely to poetry. Po Chu-i labored at it until he nearly burst. Tu Fu starved rather than abandon it. Neither my intelligence nor my writing is comparable to such men. Nevertheless, in the end, we *all* live in phantom huts."

Near the end of August, 1690, he moved a little further up the shore to another cottage, located on the grounds of another Buddhist temple, perhaps because his health was once again failing and this one brought him closer to his students who might need to care for him. He stayed there until late October, when he returned once again to Ueno.

As his health improved, he made several trips to Kyoto and participated in a number of haiku gatherings. In the late spring of 1691, he moved into a cottage in Kyoto that Kyorai had prepared for him, and there, during the month of May, he composed that last of his haibun, *Saga nikki (Saga Diary).* But he was rarely alone there, and often in the company of Kyorai and another colleague, Bonchō, who were busy editing the haiku anthology *Sarumino* (*The Monkey's Raincoat*), and were constantly seeking his advice. He spent a month at Bonchō's house.

On July 20, 1691, he moved into a new cottage on the grounds of Gichū Temple, near the Genjū Hut where he'd been the previous year. His new cottage, *Mumyō-an,* "Nameless Hut," quickly became his favorite. He was especially fond of looking out on the mountains and fields of the Iga Basin:

Under the harvest moon,
fog rolling down from foothills,
mist and clouds in the fields

Meigetsu ni
fumoto no kiri ya
ta no kumori

His poem plays with a pillow word or fixed epithet, "clouds and rain," often used to allude to sexual union in classical Japanese and Chinese poetry. It's a faint but profound allusion to the eroticism of the fields and the food they produce. Typical of late Bashō, he begins and ends in simple objective description, behind which lies a wealth of evocation.

On his deathbed three years later, dictating his will, he asked to be buried at Mumyō-an. He remained there until late November, when he finally felt strong enough to make the return trip to Edo. He had been gone two and a half years.

When he arrived in Edo a month later in the company of his traveling companions, he moved into a house in the Nihonbashi district, having given up his cottage in Fukagawa at the beginning of his journey north. In a prose introduction to haiku written upon his return, he says, "Having no real place of my own, I have traveled for six or seven years and suffered from many ailments. Memories of old friends and disciples and their warm hospitality drew me back to Edo." But all was not tranquil. Bashō fell out with several former disciples who had succumbed to ambition. He scolded one in the opening haiku of a linked verse:

It should have remained green.
So why has it changed color,
this red pepper?

Aokute mo
aru beki mono wo
tōgarashi

He wrote to a friend in Zeze in the spring of 1692, complaining, "Everywhere in this city I see people writing poetry to try to win prizes or notoriety. You can imagine what they write. Anything I might say to them would no doubt end in harsh words, so I pretend not to hear or see them." He skipped his customary spring cherry blossom viewing, saying bitterly, "All the famous cherry blossom sites are overrun with noisy, ambitious seekers after fame." Once again, he considered abandoning the world of poetry, writing, "I tried to give up the Way of Elegance (*fūga no michi*) and stop writing poems, but something always stirred my heart and mind—such is its magic."

In May, 1692, friends and disciples under the direction of Sora and Bashō's former patron, Sampū, completed construction of the third Bashō-an at the mouth of the Sumida River, and the poet moved in. He participated in a few select haiku gatherings over the following months, and welcomed several friends from distant places where he had journeyed. By the end of the year, he was busy with students and social responsibilities once again, complaining that he could find no peace.

By this time, the poet's nephew, Tōin, was dying of tuberculosis, and Bashō provided a home for him, borrowing money to pay for his care. He was also caring for a woman named Jutei and her three children, although their relationship is unclear. She may have been Bashō's mistress years earlier, before becoming a nun. It seems clear that Bashō was not the father of her children, leading some scholars to speculate that she was the wife of Tōin. In any case, the poet borrowed again to care for her and her children. Tōin died at Bashō-an in the spring of 1693. Jutei moved into Bashō-an in early 1694, shortly after the poet returned to Ueno, and she died there in midsummer.

Bashō fell into a deep depression following Tōin's death. He complained of "too much useless chatter" among his visitors, but was forced to participate in haiku gatherings in order to pay bills. He sweltered and again suffered terrible headaches and fever all summer until August, when he closed and bolted his gate, refusing to see anyone. He remained a hermit for the following two months before gradually reemerging for literary gatherings as his health improved and his depression began to lift.

By early 1694, Bashō was overcome by wanderlust again. On the one hand, he longed to journey southwest to visit Shikoku and Kyushu on a major adventure like his northern trip; on the other hand, as he observed in a letter, he felt he was nearing the end. He planned to depart in April, but his plans were postponed week by week because he suffered once again from chills and fever and migraine headaches.

Finally, on June 3, the weakened poet was placed on a litter by Jutei's son, Jirōbei, and Sora, and they departed, leaving Bashō-an to the dying nun and her two daughters. Jirōbei and Bashō arrived in Nagoya nearly two weeks later, their journey made ever more difficult by traveling during the rainy season. After a night of celebration and two days recovering their strength, they moved on to Ueno. Bashō was pleased to be celebrated in his hometown, but was far too weak to participate in any festivities. His chills, fever, and headache persisted.

After a couple of weeks, the poet feeling a little stronger, they visited the Ōtsu area again, then moved on to Kyoto, where Bashō spent most of a month visiting with his students and writing linked verse, always advocating on behalf of *karumi*. He believed that poetry should arise naturally from close observation, revealing itself in the careful use of ordinary language. Still weakened, he was nevertheless in good spirits despite being constantly pressured to meet social responsibilities.

Upon learning of the death of his mother, Jirōbei returned to Edo. Bashō returned to his cherished Nameless Hut on the southern shore of Lake Biwa. It was likely at the Mumyō Hut that he made his last revisions of *Narrow Road to the Interior,* the manuscript of which he had carried through his many journeys, editing, revising and polishing as he went. Near the end of August, he visited Kyoto again before moving into a new cottage built by his students behind his elder brother's house in Ueno. He moved in just in time to host a harvest moon viewing party.

Several weeks later, Jirōbei returned from Edo. The two were joined by Bashō's nephew and a couple of students, and the party of four set out for Osaka at the urging of more Bashō followers there. They made a brief stay in Nara to enjoy a chrysanthemum festival along the way. Despite being overcome by persistent fever, chills, and headaches once again on the very evening of their arrival in Osaka, the poet felt obliged to attend festivities in his honor. He was exhausted.

Weakened by his recurring fever, he struggled for a week just to maintain himself, and his condition improved somewhat by the second week of November. But by the middle of the month, his exhausted body was ravaged by diarrhea. He became severely dehydrated. He grew increasingly emaciated. He stopped eating altogether, and dictated his will. He gathered all his strength to write a brief note to his brother, then asked students to write him a final verse, warning them against expecting advice "on even as much as one word." He also asked them to burn incense. "Your teacher is gone," he told them.

Bashō's longtime friend Kyorai asked about the master's *jisei* (death poem), and was told, "Tell anyone who asks that all of my everyday poems are my *jisei.*"

Sick on my journey,
only my dreams will wander
these desolate moors

Tabi ni yande
yume wa kareno wo
kakemeguru

Kyorai wanted to know whether "Tabi ni yande" should be considered the master's death poem. Bashō replied, "It was written in my sickness, but it is not my *jisei*. Still, it can't be said that it's *not* my death poem either." He had summoned a student and dictated the poem well after midnight just a few days earlier, promising, "This will be my last obsession."

But once again he succumbed to the magic of *fūga no michi*, writing a last poem:

A white chrysanthemum—
and to meet the viewer's eye,
not a mote of dust

Shiragiku no
me ni tatete miru
chiri mo nashi

The second line is lifted entirely from a famous poem by Saigyō. He tried several poems using "chiri mo nashi," and it remains uncertain whether this was his final version. That dust mote, present or not, moves back beyond Saigyō to recall the teachings of the earliest Ch'an masters. The dust mote on the mirror is the foundation of a famous kōan. At the end, Bashō remained as he began: a follower, not an imitator, of the great tradition of Japanese and Chinese Zen poetry. The whole tradition is brought to bear in the utterly clear simple language of his poem: elegant simplicity.

Bashō was visited by his oldest follower and friend, Kikaku, but was too weak to say much of anything. He slept for hours. The following day, he awoke to flies buzzing around his screen, and laughed, "Those flies *like* having a sick man around." They proved to be his last words. In the afternoon, he slept again, breathing his last at 4 p.m.

The next day, his body was carried back to Mumyō-an at Gichū-ji, where he was buried.

His fundamental teaching remained his conviction that in composing a poem, "There are two ways: one is entirely natural, in which the poem is born from within itself; the other way is to make it through the mastery of technique." His notion of the poem being "born within itself," should under no circumstances be confused with its being self-originating. A fundamental tenet of Buddhism runs exactly to the contrary: nothing is self-originating. Bashō's poems were in fact a natural product of his close observation of the natural *relationships* of people and things, our presence in "nature." He prized sincerity and clarity and instructed, "Follow nature, return to nature, be nature." He had learned to meet each day with fresh eyes. "Yesterday's self is already worn out!"

Another of his last poems might serve equally well as his *jisei:*

All along this road
not a single soul—only
autumn evening

Kono michi ya
yaku hito nashi ni
aki no kure

The "road" or path of this poem is as much aesthetic and metaphysical as literal. Bashō's *kadō,* or Way of Poetry, is singular. The "autumn" of the poem is as much the autumn of his life as it is a season. His is the aloneness of everyday *kenshō,* daily enlightenment, and of all who live and practice the arts of Zen, the arts of the Tao, following the Way of Poetry.

In the Company of Issa

Introduction to *Spring of My Life & Selected Haiku* by Kobayashi Issa

Kobayashi Yatarō, revered throughout the world as Issa, which means One Cup of Tea (or even One Bubble in a Cup of Tea), was born in 1763 on a farm in Kashiwabara village in central Japan, now Nagano Prefecture. The surrounding mountains of his beloved Shinano countryside are eternally associated with his name, just as the mountainous north country made famous by Bashō's Narrow Road to the Interior is often referred to as "Bashō country."

But it is Issa's unfortunate life much more than the landscape that has made him such an endearing figure. He spent most of his life obsessed with a sense of loss, exiled from his home by a stepmother so repugnant as to seem almost lifted from a fairy tale. His poverty during adulthood was so profound that he often had no home at all, sleeping at the homes of friends or students and calling himself Issa the Beggar.

And yet his poems reveal an abiding love for suffering humanity, even for animals, insects, and plants, a devoutly Buddhist spiritual compassion.

> Fly, butterfly!
> I feel the dust of this world
> weighting my body!

Issa's poems about animals and insects are learned by every schoolchild in Japan, and almost everyone can recite a few of his poems on occasion. Writing poetry was a fundamental part of his spiritual practice, and he wrote with dedication, producing more than twenty thousand haiku, hundreds of tanka, and several works of haibun, a combination of poetic prose and haiku.

> Under shady trees,
> sharing space with a butterfly—
> this, too, is karma

Issa never dwelled long on karma, although he must have felt that he'd sown some ugly seeds in some previous incarnation. Shortly after his second birthday, his mother died. He was sent to be raised by his grandmother, who provided for his study with a local haiku poet, Shimpo, to begin his education. When Issa was seven, his father remarried. Near his tenth birthday, his stepmother gave birth to a son. No one will ever know exactly what transpired thereafter, but years later Issa wrote that his clothes were "perpetually soaked with urine from the baby" and that he was beaten "a hundred times a day." Whenever the baby cried, Issa was blamed and beaten. He claimed to have spent nights weeping at Myōsen Temple. Finding refuge there undoubtedly had a profound effect on the boy.

He was sent to work in the fields, and his studies with Shimpo ended. When Issa was thirteen, his beloved grandmother died. His father, thinking to ease familial antagonism and suffering, sent the young poet to apprentice himself to a literary man in Edo (now Tokyo) who offered lodging in exchange for copy work. However, Issa never made use of the letter of introduction. He disappeared into busy city life, and no record of these years exists. He may have worked as a clerk at a Buddhist temple.

So much money made
by clever temple priests
using peonies

Years later, Issa would write that he often lived hungry, cold, and homeless in Edo.

By the late 1780s, Issa's name began to appear in association with a group of haiku poets studying under Chikua, who followed in the "Bashō tradition," cultivating a plain, direct style steeped in the broth of Zen. A hundred years earlier, Bashō had single-handedly elevated haiku from a form of intellectual poetic exercise to high art. He advocated the Way of Poetry (kadō) as an alternative to the values of the emerging merchant class, also following a Way of Elegance (fuga no michi), claiming that his life was "stitched together by a single thread of art." Bashō felt bound by "neither religious law nor popular custom," but sought through haiku and haibun to "follow in the footsteps of the masters" of classical Chinese poetry and Zen. It is said that Bashō always carried a copy of the Taoist text Chuang Tzu and that this pre-Zen spiritual classic flavors his poetry with mono no aware, a sense of beauty intensified by recognition of temporality, and *sabi,* a kind of spiritual loneliness. Chuang Tzu's lively sense of humor is also reflected in many of Bashō's verses.

The qualities of *mono no aware* and *sabi* are everywhere evident in Issa's poetry; *sabi* is derived from *sabishi,* "loneliness," a word he used again and again. His early haiku often reveal the profound influence of Bashō despite sometimes slipping into self-pity. Issa, like Bashō, went to school on the poetry of the great poet-monk Saigyō, who brought the distinct flavor of Zen to Japanese "nature poetry" in the twelfth century. Issa's own unique voice emerged fully only after years of daily practice and a profound assimilation of Buddhist ethics and poetry classics.

In early 1792, at age twenty-nine, he vowed to follow the Way of Poetry. He gave up the name Yatarō, and "began the new year anew" as Issa, living the life of a solitary sojourner for ten years as he explored Japan from its southern tip and eastern islands to the western Sea of Japan. Taking Bashō's Narrow Road to the Interior as a model, he traveled not for recreation or to find a tourist's view of his world, but to find himself. Issa the Beggar was born in the conviction that poetry can be a path to enlightenment. He believed that one part of that path is shikan, a meditative state in which perception is utterly free of discrimination between mind and matter, self and object; where the only permanence is impermanence and change, whether subtle or violent, remains the essence of being.

> Just being alive!
> —miraculous to be in
> cherry blossom shadows!

The cherry blossom in classical Japanese poetry represents much more than the beauty of the blossoms themselves. Because of the brevity of its life, a cherry blossom is a supreme figure of mono no aware, its beauty intensified because of its temporality. All great Japanese poems about cherry blossoms express a tinge of sadness, usually indirectly. "Just being alive!" may celebrate the beauty of the day, of the moment, but the blossoms suggest that life is brief and that we, too, shall soon disappear.

> Loneliness already
> planted with each seed in
> morning glory beds

"*Haya sabishi* (the loneliness is already there)," Issa says. There is loneliness in the first act, in the seed itself. Death and life are present in a cherry seed or morning glory seed and within the wandering poet. An old Zen proverb suggests "Live as though you were already dead!" The seed of death and the seed of life are one.

In the haiku tradition, the poem springs from attentive observation of ordinary life. Issa was a master at revealing the unsayable dimensions of the mundane, his poems always somehow conveying more than what the words alone suggest.

> Simply for all this,
> as if there were nothing else,
> heavy wet spring frost

In the hands of a lesser poet, this poem would drown in pseudo-profundity. Issa's gift is representative simplicity: "Simply for all this." There is no placement of detailed landscape. Issa enters the world of frost. It is almost rice-planting time, a task Bashō called "the beginning of culture." The spring calls forth ancient traditions and labors and all their consequences. It represents an end to winter, and by the lunar calendar, a beginning of a new year. Issa's restraint allows for complex evocation while acknowledging that utter simplicity underlies it all.

Issa was not the least bit reluctant to engage his imagination to manipulate circumstances to benefit his work. In "The Spring of My Life (Oraga haru)," he presented what would become one of his most famous haiku as having been composed upon the death of his daughter:

> This world of dew
> is only the world of dew—
> and yet . . . oh and yet . . .

> Tsuyu no yo wa
> tsuyu no yo nagara
> sarinagara

There is an enormous sigh in the repeated "nagara (pause) sarinagara" that many translators have ignored. "And yet . . . oh and yet . . ." Leaving out that "sarinagar" destroys the poem.

Nobuyuki Yuasa points out in his 1960 translation of *Oraga haru* that this poem actually was composed earlier, upon the death of Issa's firstborn son. Whether Issa found no voice in direct response to his daughter's death or whether he simply thought the previous poem said it best doesn't really matter. Issa attributed the poem in a way that best suited the work in progress. In this, too, he followed Bashō's example.

Subject to the severe mood swings and almost constant undertone of melancholy that are a signature of abused children, Issa found both a spiritual path and a source of emotional stability in following the Way of Haiku. *The Spring of My Life,* his most famous work, represents a single year chosen almost at random, but is inspired and shaped by all of a fully lived life. This magnum opus is not just a notebook and an anthology, but also a testament and a sanctuary. Perhaps the most literal translation of the title would be simply "My New Spring," but while *haru* indeed means spring, in Japanese vernacular it refers to the New Year. On the lunar calendar, the first day of spring and the New Year often coincide.

Like Bashō, Issa did not settle immediately on the pen name by which he is known today. Earlier names included "Kobayashi Ikyo" and "Nirokuan Kikumei." Although he showed great promise at an early age, he was not satisfied settling for mere popularity, and in 1792, he adopted the nom-de-plume Haikai-ji Nyudo Issa-bo, Temple-of-Haiku Lay Brother Issa.

With spring's arrival,
Yatarō becomes reborn
as Issabo

Haru tatsuya
Yatarō aratame
Issabo

He explained to a friend that his choice was inspired by a single bubble in a cup of tea rather than the tea itself, as the name would ordinarily suggest. He was not particularly fond of the tea ceremony as such, but felt that, like the bubble, our lives are brief and transparent. That poetry in general and haiku in particular indeed became his temple, and he a lay monk in its service, is beyond doubt. He took his vows seriously, and from that day on he lived a life of commitment.

Issa spent the following five or six years wandering throughout southern Japan, making "poetry friends" along the way. It was only after his return to

Edo in 1778 that publication of his journals began to make him famous. Although less formally composed than The Spring of My Life, they reveal his deep study of Chinese poetry, anthologize many haiku and tanka by Japanese poets, and offer a view of Issa as a working poet who eagerly revised his poems, often leaving as many as six or seven "finished" versions of the same haiku.

In 1801, Issa's father was overcome with typhoid fever. Issa returned to Kashiwabara in time to nurse his father for a month before he finally succumbed. Issa's stepmother and stepbrother challenged his father's will, successfully depriving Issa of his inheritance for thirteen years. The poet wrote a poetic journal about his father's death, much of it marred by relentless, albeit understandable, sentimentality and self-pity.

For more than a decade, Issa lived in poverty, traveling back and forth between his native village and Edo, locked in a legal battle with his stepmother. These years weighed heavily on him. As he approached the age of fifty, he must have felt the family's internecine quarrels would never end. In 1810, he wrote:

O moonlit blossoms—
I've squandered forty-nine years
walking beneath you

Finally, in 1813, negotiations with his family were completed and Issa returned to Kashiwabara. He married a young woman, and in 1816, she gave birth to a son who survived only a month. It was for this child that Issa wrote the "world of dew" poem. A daughter was born in 1818, only to died of smallpox a year later. It is this daughter, Sato, who is memorialized in The Spring of My Life, composed the following year.

Issa's life was plagued by sorrow. His second son, born in 1820, died several months after his birth. In 1822, a third son was born, but Issa's wife died painfully of illnesses related to arthritis shortly after his birth, and the boy died a few months later, in 1823, while in the care of an irresponsible nurse. During these years Issa also suffered failing health that resulted in periodic paralysis. In 1810, having temporarily lost his ability to speak, he had written:

Such irritation!
Even wandering wild geese
can manage to speak

The poet recovered time and again from what may have been a series of small strokes, and married again in 1824, probably too soon, for this marriage dissolved in a matter of months. He had chosen for his new wife a woman from an esteemed local samurai family, and she apparently viewed his house and his ramshackle life with contempt, returning to her father's home after no more than a few weeks of marriage. Issa was overcome by some form of paralysis again while visiting Zenkō Temple and remained for a time in the care of a physician.

Seemingly undaunted, in 1826, at the age of sixty-four, he married for a third time. But the following year, his house caught fire and burned to the ground. Refusing offers to stay with students or friends, Issa and his pregnant wife moved into a tiny storehouse with neither windows nor stove, where they lived for several months. By all appearances, he seemed well on his way to overcoming this latest disaster when he died suddenly on November 19, 1827. His death prevented him from seeing the birth of his only surviving child, a daughter.

Two poems are attributed as Issa's last. One was found under his deathbed pillow:

> Gratitude for gifts,
> even snow on my bedspread
> a gift from the Pure Land

The other "death poem" may indeed be his last, especially if he deliberately placed the above, written earlier, as a final statement to be read following his death, which seems likely. The second poem:

> From birthing's washbowl
> to the washbowl of the dead—
> blathering nonsense!

Like so many of Issa's poems, this one invites several readings. Is the "blathering nonsense" the noisy busyness of suffering humanity and the world of desire, or has the poet come to a concluding caustic comment on his own life of letters? Is the poem an admonishment or a joke, a summation or a guffaw? Perhaps Issa had in mind the teaching of the Samantabhadra Bodhisattva Sutra that "the self is empty of independent existence," and all the "blathering nonsense" is the ambient noise of needless desire. Behind Issa's seemingly effortless simplicity, time and again, we find a complex universe.

If his life was shaped by intense feelings of exile and rejection, and punctuated by deep personal loss, it was shaped equally by remarkable courage and fearless conviction. In his day, as now, a monklike vow to live in the service of poetry was rare. Issa's faith in poetry as a path to enlightenment required living in accordance with what he had learned from noble old masters like Tu Fu, Po Chu-i, Saigyō, and Bashō. Issa paid no obeisance to rank, and roamed the streets of Edo in shabby robes, almost as famous for his behavior as for his verse. Once, summoned by a local daimyo, he was questioned about his art. Issa looked squarely into the eyes of the most dangerous man in the province and replied that he could not reduce his art to the level of dilettantes. Yet to most people he was a gentle eccentric. Children came to revere him as the poet-representative of small birds, bugs, and flowers.

Issa's poems reveal a deep engagement with the teachings of Zen, as well as with the Way of Haiku advocated by Bash¯o, and it is probably for these strengths of character, including his unabashed honesty, that he was admired by almost everyone regardless of social rank.

Japan has a long history of revering its poets—posthumously for the most part. There are many "Issa sites" and "haiku stones" with his poems engraved for posterity; his old homestead in Kashiwabara has been preserved. And, thanks to his only surviving child, his lineage continues.

In translating Issa's poems, I held in my ear the sound of the original, the assonance and consonance, rhyme and slant rhyme that provides the foundation of the music of the original. Haiku grew out of the 5–7–5–7–7 syllabic structure of waka (later including tanka), which means simply "Japanese poem." Sounded out in the original, the "song" of haiku often includes a pregnant pause created by use of a "cutting word" (*kake kotoba*). Haiku was the first Japanese poetry (except that in the folk song tradition) to be written in the vernacular rather than in the highly refined language of the court. With its roots in the lyric tradition, it is meant to be heard.

Much of what passes for haiku, or the translation of haiku in American English, is not really either. Issa's poems have often been reduced to fragmentary English bearing little resemblance to the music, meaning or syntax of the original. I sometimes made use of interpolation to fill out the music of these translations (American English tends to use fewer syllables than Japanese). But I made no Procrustean bed of syllabic structure. Sometimes a variation of a syllable or two suffices, especially when a long or heavy syllable is involved or when there is a sustained pause. My primary concern is to say what the poet says without rearranging the original order of perception.

Until I began translating Issa, I was not comfortable with his occasional sentimentality, despite its deep roots in Japanese culture. But living with him, as I now do, I return again and again to his great companionability, sharing a little of my own sentimentality—mostly privately, but also in a poem now and then— with an old friend. This, despite sharing in his conviction that the self is mostly an illusion.

Richard Wright's Haiku

Haiku: This Other World by Richard Wright

During the last eighteen months of his life, struggling with failing health while living in exile in Paris, Richard Wright devoted himself almost exclusively to writing haiku. His emotional life was agonizing. In 1959, he lost two of his closest friends, and his mother died. He was hounded by the U.S. government and was homesick. Inspired by R. H. Blyth's classic four-volume study of haiku, Wright found spiritual resilience, joy, humor and pathos writing in a strict poetic form. He carried his notebooks with him wherever he went, eventually compiling 4000 haiku, from which he selected 817 to be preserved in book form.

> I am paying rent
> For the lice in my room
> And the moonlight too

In these poems, Wright often walks the thin line dividing Zen-inspired haiku from its more comic cousin, *senryu*. Anyone well-versed in the poetry of Bashō, Issa, and other major haiku poets will find remarkable paraphrases and associations seen with the freshest of eyes throughout this remarkable book.

Bashō wrote: "All along this road / not a single soul—only / autumn evening." Wright's re-visioning of the poem:

> I see nobody
> Upon the muddy roadway
> In autumn moonlight.

The old Japanese Zen haiku master would love Wright's work here. Bashō himself drew equally heavily from the writings of Chuang Tzu, Tu Fu, Po Chu-i and many other classical Chinese poets, and Wright's poem brings the experience delightfully into modern English, including the self-referencing.

As close as it is to Bashō's original, simply by adding the first person and the moonlight, Wright strikes a worthy and original chord.

Bashō wrote: "Awakened at midnight / by the sound of the rice jar / cracking from the ice." Wright draws inspiration from the poem perhaps when he awakens late one night and writes:

The sound of a rat
Gnawing in the winter wall
Of a rented room.

In one of the most famous poems in *Narrow Road to the Interior,* Bashō writes, "Eaten alive by / lice and fleas—now the horse / beside my pillow pees." Wright's horse-pee experience:

The horse's hot piss
Scalds a fragile nest of ants
In a sea a foam.

In his *Sarashina Travelogue,* Bashō writes, "Now I see her face,/ the old woman, abandoned, / the moon her only companion." Wright turns to memory:

I last saw her face
Under a dripping willow
In a windy rain.

It is clear throughout *This Other World* that Wright took to his studies seriously. While these examples may appear to be mere derivations, such a reading would be a major mistake—after all, *all* poetry is in some ways derivative. Wright schooled himself in sensibility as well as in musical measure and composition. There are literally hundreds of poems of utter originality.

As the popcorn man
Is closing up his wagon,
Snow begins to fall.

Bashō argued on behalf of elegant simplicity, on behalf of poems drawn from mundane reality, but with everything clarified. Wright's "popcorn man" fits Bashō's criteria like a hand in a glove. Even the implied simile is mundane. And yet the poem is as crisp as the environment it presents.

It might seem odd at a glance: the great African-American novelist who invented the inarticulate, fearful, irate Bigger Thomas finds himself in declining health, living in exile, mourning the deaths of those closest to him, hounded by McCarthyites and the CIA, and he picks up a volume of Japanese poetry in translation, and his life is utterly transformed. Poetry is magical. In turning to haiku, he sought to engage and extend a remarkably fertile and supple literary tradition. He wanted, he said, to bring "the Black experience" to haiku. And he wanted to stay as tightly within the traditions of haiku as possible. For eighteen months, he wrote and revised and evaluated constantly.

> In the still orchard
> A petal falls to the grass;
> A bird stops singing.

At his best, he is as good as any haiku poet this country has ever produced. He has amazing instincts and effortless control as he reveals whole relationships—most often between people and nature.

> A freezing night wind
> Wafts the scent of frying fish
> From the waterfront.

In haiku, what is left unsaid is every bit as important as what is stated. Wright had the courage to let us see his sources as well as the accomplished writer's resistance to self-absorption. Nevertheless, he is self-revealing:

> As my anger ebbs,
> The spring stars grow bright again
> And the wind returns.

The Way of Poetry (*kadō* in Japanese, the Tao of Poetry, the way or path of poetry) is a path toward enlightenment. It is not a destination, but a way, a path. Wright began to see in Zen "nothingness" the superficiality of momentary emotions. Bashō instructs, "Follow nature, return to nature, be nature. Yesterday's self is already worn out!" There can be no doubt that for Richard Wright, the haiku-mind brought him into a far deeper engagement with the world around him, assuaging his mourning and his bitterness toward his homeland that had treated him with such cruelty.

From the dark still pines,
Not a breath of autumn wind
To ripple the lake.

It is inconceivable that World Publishing Company rejected Wright's manuscript. And it is astonishing to think that it has taken nearly forty years to make his remarkable poetry available. Richard Wright is indisputably one of the giants of American letters, and he has a rightful place among our best poets. *Haiku: This Other World* belongs in everyone's library beside *Native Son* and *Black Boy.*

Salt and Honey

On Denise Levertov

When I was a boy memorizing my first poems, Robert Frost's "The Road not Taken," gave me more problems than almost any other short poem. I never could get the closing couplet right:

> I shall be telling this with a sigh
> Somewhere ages and ages hence:
> Two roads diverged in a wood, and I—
> I took the one less traveled by,
> And that has made all the difference.

It seems that whenever I'd recite the poem, I'd leave out that *by* which makes no real sense and which is there only to fill out the syllabic count and to rhyme. Frost the literary technician traveled roads that might be best described as expressways or thoroughfares, his ear was a conventionally educated ear. He knew his material and his knew his craft. As far as it went. Frost preferred his domesticated snowy woods to the uninhabitable rainy forests of the northwest or to the sun-scorched plains. He preferred Latin iambics to those of the Romantics, and fixed or closed forms to those of his contemporaries, Eliot, Pound, and Williams. He knew his own limitations perhaps as well as any poet of this century, and he pushed against those same limitations perhaps as gently as any.

As an adolescent, I used to take this poem and condense it, sometimes writing a version as brief as two quatrains, but each ending with a version of the poet's closing couplet without that *by.*

Frost's poem touches something in the hearts of each of us—a nostalgia perhaps for a time in which decisions could be made in tranquil deliberation, like the poet as he stops for a moment to consider a fork in the road, and sees, looking into the blank distance, a future beginning. We Americans are uniform in our passionate defense of individuality. Growing up on Frost, we adopted him as our national literary-curmudgeonly Grandaddy, a flag of white hair waving above a sadly lined face at the inauguration of Camelot. Post-war babies were in their teens and television brought it into their homes so that they were somehow participants in the unfolding drama. Frost spoke our language. A great many of my childhood poems were revisions of Frost. But I never learned to remember "traveled *by.*"

These memories of my early struggle with Frost's road were prompted by reading the first poem in Denise Levertov's new book, *A Door in the Hive.*

To Rilke

Once, in dream,
 the boat
pushed off from the shore.
You at the prow were the man—
all voice, though silent—who bound
rowers and voyagers to the needful journey,
the veiled distance, imperative mystery.

All the crouched effort,
creak of oarlocks, odor of sweat,
sound of waters
running against us
was transcended: your gaze
held as we crossed. Its dragonfly blue
restored to us
a shimmering destination.

I had not yet read of your Nile journey,
the enabling voice
drawing that boat upstream in your parable.
Strange that I knew
your silence was just such a song.

Levertov's poem, like Frost's, presents an archetypal metaphor, but with several profound differences. First, she is journeying in a dream; second, she places herself, both psyche and physical body, completely under the control of another. Where Frost turns alone in a gesture of near invulnerability, Levertov remains particularly vulnerable, her conscious mind given over to the dream, her vision and her body being guided her Virgil. The experience is transcendent. Finally, like Frost, she has the capacity to enter the future deeply enough to be able to look back into the present. But her insight is not informed by a prescient need to prepare a public utterance. Where Frost foresees himself speaking knowingly, Levertov embraces the silence of completed wisdom, closing her poem in a song of *listening*.

In Levertov's melopoeia, there are no tricks, no Procrustian beds, no learnéd devices. Her language is sincere, pragmatic, and condensed without being compacted; it flows in natural cadences, opening with a five-syllable couplet followed by a seven-syllable couplet followed by a twelve-syllable couplet. The second stanza is, syllabically, less formal, but listen to the echo of "crouched effort" in "creak of oarlock;" listen to the echo of "against us" in "transcended" and again in "destination." Her music is subtle, sophisticated, opening to its own revelation as it develops. Anyone who has sung Frosts's "Whose woods / these are / I think I know" to the tune of "Hernando's Hideaway" has learned something about the nature of closed form, of predetermined form. In Levertov's poems, the form is the music revealing itself, the rubbing of syllable against syllable, syllable against silence, her ear alert to syllabic resonance rather than predictable end-rhyme. The whole poem unfolds as naturally as sprout from seed. And what a seed!

The "imperative mystery" and the journey within are the very *stuff* of Levertov's poetry and have been from the beginning. Thirty-five years ago, she wrote a poem, "People at Night," which was "derived from Rilke" and in which she spoke of "going up to some apartment, yours/ or yours, finding/ someone sitting in the dark:/ who is it, really? . . ." The "anybody" she finds is "No one." With Rilke serving as both guide and muse, she has explored the mystery, perfecting her vision.

Levertov journeys into the interior dark in her most social-political poetry as when she returned from the Bach Mai Hospital in Viet Nam declaring her intention to "bring the war home." But also in poems like "The Mutes" and "A Wedding Ring," she embraces harrowing experiences of another—although less life-threatening—kind, only to emerge with a profoundly compassionate optimism.

The third poem in *A Door in the Hive* again presents the poet as "A Traveler" along a Way:

> If it's chariots or sandals,
> I'll take sandals.
> I like the high prow of the chariot,
> the daredevil speed, the wind

a quick tune you can't
quite catch
 but I want to go
a long way
and I want to follow
paths where wheels deadlock.
And I don't want always
to be among gear and horses,
blood, foam, dust. I'd like
to wean myself from their strange allure.
I'll chance
the pilgrim sandals.

This is another telling of the Road Less Traveled. The "high prow of the chariot" and "daredevil speed" are the "strange allure" of physical—whether personal or national—power. "Pilgrim sandals" lead into a world where such power becomes meaningless, where the pilgrimage follows narrow footpaths of those searching for the authentic sacramental rites of the soul's own transit. In the earlier poem, she addressed Rilke, "You at the prow were the man—" where she now presents only a general masculine image, "I like the high prow of the chariot,/ the daredevil speed," declining gracefully the latter's seductive excitement in favor of the more feminine sense of interior abundance, of traveling slowly as though in gestation, wanting to be "weaned" from masculine power.

Neither of Levertov's "road taken" poems is as chatty, as self-consciously *made* as Frost's famous poem. There are no awkward inversions, no formal high-stepping to a pre-determined beat, no sighing for one's self.

In a wonderfully common-sense essay in *Chicago Review* in 1979, later gathered with other prose work in *Light Up the Cave* (New Directions, 1981), Levertov writes "On the Function of the Line":

"What is the nature of the alogical pauses the linebreak records? If readers will think of their own speech, or their silent inner monologue, when describing thoughts, feelings, perceptions, scenes or events, they will, I think, recognize that they frequently hesitate—albeit very briefly—as if with an unspoken question,—a "what?" or a "who?" or a "how?"—before nouns, adjectives, verbs, adverbs, none of which require to be preceded by a comma or other regular punctuation in the course of syntactic logic. To incorporate these pauses in the rhythmic structure of the poem can do several things: for example, it allows the reader to share more intimately the experience that is being articulated; and by introducing an alogical counter-rhythm into the logical rhythm of syntax it causes, as they interact, an effect closer to song than statement, closer to dance than to walking. Thus the emotional experience of empathy or identification plus the sonic complexity of the language structure synthesize in an *intense aesthetic order that is different from that which is received from a poetry in which metric forms are combined with logical syntax alone.*" [My italics.]

Metrical forms, Levertov observes, also *may* permit such alogical pauses. The use of line-breaks bears directly upon the *melos* of the poem, she says, affecting the poem's *pitch pattern* among other things. And she quotes X. J. Kennedy on the definition of the run-on line: "It does not end in punctuation and therefore is read with only a *slight pause* after it." In other words, the line is a musical structure, not merely the tick-tocking of a metronome. The line carries pitch, breath and pulse, sonic stress, cadence, and rhyme. "On the Function of the Line" ought to be taught in every public school and every college poetry class in the country.

Ben Jonson, dangerously obese, poverty-stricken, imprisoned and released, vents his frustration with the confining nature of rhyme by composing "A Fit of Rhyme Against Rhyme," ("Rhyme, the rack of finest wits,/ That expresseth but by fits,/ True conceit,/ Spoiling sense of their treasure,/ Cozening judgment with a measure,/ But false weight./ . . .") but in a rare example of blank verse has his Lord Lovel say in *The New Inn*,

The things true valour is exercised about
Are poverty, restraint, captivity,
Banishment, loss of children, long disease:
The least is death. Here valour is beheld,
Properly seen; about these it is present:
Not trivial things which but require our confidence.

It is astonishing, reading volume after volume of recent North American poetry, just how little of it relates any sense of social or political responsibility. There is, to be sure, plenty of propagandistic poetry; there is the smug, hip rage of the "politically correct" who speak only to one another; but so much of our recent poetry reflects the general malaise of Yuppie complacency and expediency in the perpetual search for immediate self-gratification, whether in material goodies or in pseudo-self-realization.

Levertov returns us to that greater, more noble tradition with "El Salvador: Requiem and Invocation" in *A Door in the Hive*. A libretto commissioned by the Back Bay Chorale and the Pro Arte Chamber Orchestra for composer Newell Hendricks, it opens with a cacophony of violent words and sounds, then moves from pre-Columbian times through an extremely compacted history utilizing, among other devices, adaptations of Mayan prayers. Arriving in contemporary times, she quotes directly from speeches by the martyred Archbishop Oscar Romero and from letters by the murdered nuns, Sisters Dorothy, Maura, and Ita. Perhaps most powerful is her use of a list of "the week's murdered" made up largely of names of but one extended family, mostly children. This list, and a later one listing the names of murdered priests and nuns, is composed of actual names. Here, "valour is beheld; / Properly seen." The poem closes on a coda, a prayer drawn from the prayers of Archbishop Romero.

There are a great many beautiful lyrical poems in *A Door in the Hive,* and great variety. But it is her gentle, insistent spiritual hunger that most unifies her vision quest. Her sense of spiritual as well as personal accountability has informed her poetry from the beginning. In "Complicity," she says to a hummingbird, having compared it to "a child whose hiding-place/ has not been discovered,"

> I saw
> a leaf: I shall not betray you.

and a moment of charm, of poignancy, takes on a much larger emotional complex. "Betrayal" carries a train-load of implication. And how can the hiding child not call up an image from Nazi Germany, especially when we remember that the poet was a young nurse in England during the war? Many of Levertov's poems invite a psycho-analytical interpretation. They engage the reader, making of him or her a participant in the poem itself.

I used to read "The Mutes" to my students in various prisons, many of them batterers themselves struggling with their own phobias and smashed self-esteem. Out of this universal experience, they would come to glimpse another side of their rude behavior and begin to understand how they might transform themselves. Poetry is—or ought to be—that important.

In recent years, we have endured a veritable avalanche of Rilke Industries—multiple translations, scholarly examinations, literary exegesis, biographies, you-name-it—with the inevitable result: more and more bad imitative poems, often picking up Rilke's worst habits at the expense of his best. Levertov has written derivative poems in the very best sense of that often-abused word; she has wrestled with Rilke's vision, adapted it, learned from it; Rilke has indeed been a Virgil to her Dante, leading her deeper into the mystery which so resonates in all of her poetry. There have, of course, been a great many other major influences on her work, figures as diverse as Cesare Pavese and Robert Duncan and Anton Chekhov. Indeed, she remains one of our most "literary" poets in a time when the literary is completely out of fashion: most of our poets most often sound like they read nothing at all, almost as though they would apologize for erudition, embarrassed by it.

In "The Life of Art," Levertov begins,

> The borderland—that's where, if one knew how,
> one would establish residence. That watershed,
> that spine, that looking-glass . . . I mean the edge
> between impasto surface, burnt sienna, thick,
> striate, gleaming—swathes and windrows
> of carnal paint—
> or, canvas barely stained,
> where warp and weft peer through,
>
> and fictive truth: a room, a vase, an open door
> giving upon the clouds.//

She begins by defining a circumstance wherein one may find what John Haines has called "a place of sense," that is, a place where one feels at home, a part, connected to watershed, that spine and mirror which sustains us all. Then, she narrows the focus to her own canvas as she paints. But it may be a vase, it may be the opening door in a poem by Rilke or clouds by Matisse.

> A step back, and you have
> the likeness, its own world. Step to the wall again,
> and you're so near the paint you could lick it,
> you breathe its ghostly turpentine.
>   But there's an interface,
> immeasurable, elusive—an equilibrium
> just attainable, sometimes, when the attention's rightly poised, . . .

The poet's attention, rightly poised, becomes numinous just at such an intersection, at the bordering of two or more worlds, each casting light upon the other so that they are one thing, —poets, worlds, sounds. The melopoeia draws us in. The *a-* sounds of *A, have, back, again, paint, interface, immeasurable* and *attainable* set up a resonance. The lines are spoken in almost casual speech. Has anyone ever used "interface" as voluptuously, as sensually? "The Life of Art" is both philosophy and metaphysics, a poem that brings the reader into the borderlands where a "looking-glass" slowly spins.

Levertov has described herself at the beginning as "a British Romantic with almost Victorian background," and Kenneth Rexroth introduced her poetry to its U.S. audience in *New British Poets: An Anthology* forty years ago, saying that her tendency toward "pulsating rhythms, romantic melancholy and undefined nostalgia" were her "outstanding virtues." Hindsight points not to pulsating rhythms, but to subtle modulations and a plenitude of variation; not to romantic melancholy, but to a spiritual depth of understanding and an even greater spiritual hunger; not to an undefined nostalgia, but to a sweeping social engagement. In short, she realizes Jonson's ideal. Many of her poems reveal epiphany located within common, mundane things without stooping to the trivial. In the elegies for her mother in *Life in the Forest*, she offers several of the most memorable poems of recent years. She would appear to owe more to Wordsworth's meditations than to Shelley's flights of fancy, more to the hard thinking of the English poets of the 17th century than to the narratives of Browning. Nor has she ever indulged in the pretty-little-picture poems so often found in *The New Yorker*.

Reading Levertov—as I have: all my adult life—I find myself turning not to single poems which have moved and inspired me so much as to whole books, or sometimes a suite of poems within a book, hungry for the sounds she makes and for the deep quietude that follows an hour's reading. And there has been a simultaneous presence of history, the poet's engagement with "poverty, restraint, captivity, banishment," and the work of "bringing home the war." The ambitions are lofty. But they are ambitions, not pretensions. Levertov is a thinker, a pilgrim, not a cheerleader. Now, when I once again open *The Sorrow Dance*, I return to the murderous summer of 1968, and to a small camp along the Novarro River where I lived in an old panel truck. I had left my first wife and daughter—my daughter my only blood relative—to return to school. I was active in civil rights and anti-war campaigns. So I retreated to the real world and spent days walking the river, watching hawks, reading *The Sorrow Dance*.

The Mutes

Those groans men use
passing a woman on the street
or on the steps of the subway

to tell her she is female
and their flesh knows it,

are they a sort of tune,
an ugly enough song, sung
by a bird with s slit tongue

but meant for music?

Or are they the muffled roaring
of deafmutes trapped in a building that is
slowly filling with smoke?

Perhaps both.

Such men most often
look at is groan were all they could do,
yet a woman, in spite of herself,

knows it's a tribute:
if she were lacking all grace
they'd pass her in silence:

so it's not to say she's
a warm hole. It's a word

in grief-language, nothing to do with
primitive, not an ur-language;
language stricken, sickened, cast down

in decrepitude. She wants to
throw the tribute away, dis-
gusted, and can't,

it goes on buzzing in her ear, it changes the pace of her walk,
the torn posters in echoing corridors

spell it out, it
quakes and gnashes as the train comes in.
Her pulse sullenly

had picked up speed,
but the cars slow down and
jar to a stop while her understanding

keeps on translating:
'Life after life after life goes by

without poetry,
without seemliness,
without love.'

Levertov's "The Mutes" has had perhaps greater import on my life than any other contemporary poem. Its *melos,* its *logos,* its sacred compassionate teaching has brought me to discuss it in essays and classes over two decades. And this is what Rilke is *really* about: that poem changed my life. And the poems gathered in "Life at War" were a poultice for the human soul:

The disasters numb within us
caught in the chest, rolling
in the brain like pebbles. . . .

and she quotes Rilke and dares to imagine mercy and joy and peace. And in a "Second Didactic Poem" she says,

In our gathering, in our containing, in our
working, active within ourselves,
slowly the pale
dew-beads of light
lapped up from flowers
can thicken,
darken to gold:

honey of the human.

Maybe the hippies in San Francisco during "The Summer of Love" were lapping up the various honeys of the human, but most of the people I knew were concerned primarily with rivers of blood flowing in Asia and in the still-segregated streets of the U.S. of A.

Nearly a quarter century has passed, and every two or three years, another book of poems by Denise Levertov. I cannot open *The Sorrow Dance* without returning to remembrances of Martin Luther King, David Harris, Eugene McCarthy, and Michael Harrington. And yet with all its grief and darkness, that book, like so many of hers, does indeed include the honeys of hope and joy. History is far more than an accounting of military maneuvers, imperialism, and bloodshed. Denise Levertov's poetry offers a sweeping personal and public vision of our times. Now, reading "Ikon: The Harrowing of Hell," I am drawn into a world where

> there must take place that struggle
> no human presumes to picture:
> living, dying, descending to rescue the just
> from shadow, were lesser travails
> than this: to break
> through earth and stone of the faithless world
> back to the cold sepulchre, tearstained
> stifling shroud; to break from *them*
> back into breath and heartbeat, and walk
> the world again, . . .

Another borderworld. One where the political, the spiritual, and the practical intersect. The road taken is a narrow path through the nearly impenetrable underworld, which is a netherworld. And leads once again to transformation:

> His mortal flesh was lit from within, now,
> and aching for home. He must return,
> first, in Divine patience, and know
> hunger again, and give
> to humble friends the joy
> of giving him food—fish and a honeycomb.

An archetypal parable, it also is a "traveling" metaphor made as it were of salt and honey, bittersweet and sublime. If one insists upon a religious interpretation, it is good to remember that *religion* comes from *re-ligio, to re-*

bind. The poem is a journey through Hell in order to find a glimpse of Paradise. A poultice for the wounded soul. The journey itself is a healing. And at the end, there is a feast of human kindness.

Denise Levertov's early books are now being collected into larger volumes. The first volume, *Collected Earlier Poems 1940-1960* underscores the fact of a half century of remarkable poetry. The second, *Poems 1960-1967*, concludes with the poems of *The Sorrow Dance*. Her work has been steady, an accretion rather than an avalanche. She has not gone after the "Big Poem"—which usually is the literary equivalent of the Big Mac anyhow—but has remained a listener, attentive to the poem *as it reveals itself*, whether formally as in a libretto, or in more open structure, whether longer poems, poems-in-sequence, or as small lyrics.

In one of her greatest poems, "The Malice of Innocence" from the 1972 volume, *Footprints*, she says,

> . . . Death and pain dominate this world, for though
> many are cured, they still leave weak,
>
> still tremulous, still knowing mortality
> has whispered to them; have seen in the folding
> of white bedspreads according to rule
>
> the starched pleats of a shroud.
> It's against that frozen
> counterpane, and the knowledge too
> how black an old mouth gaping at death can look
>
> that the night routine has in itself—
> without illusions—glamor, perhaps. It had
>
> a rhythm, a choreographic decorum: . . .

remembering her life as a nurse during the war, tiptoeing from bed to bed, "counting by flashlight how many pairs/ of open eyes were turned to us," scrubbing lockers, passing out trays of unappetizing food, all the while loving "the knowing what to do" and the orderliness of the night work. But her own remembering propels her into the "death rooms" remembering "just as a soldier or one of the guards/ from Dachau might" and sees suddenly that her love of order delivers her the duty of "writing// details of agony carefully into the Night Report."

She has an uncanny ability to connect with all human experience, and to remain, nonetheless, emotionally uncluttered. It is no accident that this leading anti-war poet of our time connects with the psyche of soldiers at Dachau—the love of order is, in part at least, a love of the power to impose one's sense of order. The basic universal impulse of poetry is naming, thereby identifying, and, consequently, ordering experience. In perfecting the poem, the melopoeia, phanopoeia, and logopoeia join seamlessly to present a mythopoeia.

One walks many a road, well-trod and otherwise, in three-plus decades. I have found sustenance and inspiration in the sixteen volumes of poems Denise Levertov has given, and I turn to them now and again as the old friends they are. I am happy I chose the road and the company I did. I'm almost never inclined to change her lines. I once questioned an inversion in a line from her translations of Jean Joubert, *Black Iris*, and was told, "It's my mid-Atlantic accent; I've only been here forty years and don't quite speak American."

There are find no ornamental flourishes, no dead words, no faked emotion, no public posture. Book by book, I have read her poems for their subtle music, for their deep compassionate intelligence, for their imagination, for their author's dignity and integrity and grace; and, most of all, for the indomitable and humble spirit that hungers there. I have savored them like salt, like honey.

Listening In

Hayden Carruth's *The Sleeping Beauty*

"The great contribution of the twentieth century to art is the idea of spontaneous improvisation within a determined style, a style comprising equally or inseparably both conventional and personal elements. What does this mean? It means a great deal more than the breakup of traditional prosody or rules of composition, as announced in 1910 by Ezra Pound and Pablo Picasso. It means the final abandonment of the neo-classical idea of structure as a function of form, which the romantics and post-romantics of the nineteenth century had never given up. Instead structure has become a function of feeling." So saith Hayden Carruth in a marvelous essay on Pee Wee Russell and Willie Yeats collected with other poems and essays in *Sitting In: Selected Writings on Jazz, Blues, and Related Topics* (University of Iowa Press, 1986).

"Form," Robert Creeley observes, "is never more than an extension of content." Which Denise Levertov clarifies, "Form is the *revelation* of content." Carruth's idea of structure as a function of feeling (especially in jazz and poetry) enlarges and clarifies something that has been at the center of critical philosophical debate for most of twentieth century.

Picasso's cubism grew out of his study of African art as surely as the blues grew out of African music transplanted in the New World. And the idea of spontaneous improvisation within a determined style or form is at least as old as the *Shih Ching,* the *Poetry Classic* Confucius compiled 2500 years ago. Perhaps the greatest literary contribution of the Sung dynasty a thousand years ago is the elevation of *tzu,* a verse-form wherein the poet composes new lyrics for a pre-existing tune. The form reached its pinnacle in the poetry of Li Ch'ing-chao. But the *structure* of the poem was an externally fixed form based upon musical measure—new lyrics composed for pre-existing tunes. Carruth is seeking a structure from within—spontaneous and self-articulating.

"Genius, " William Blake said, opening English poetry to a whole universe found in a grain of sand, "is not lawless." Ezra Pound insisted that the line in poetry be composed "by the musical phrase and not by the metronome." Hayden Carruth, that perennial jazz *aficionado* and compulsive "woodshedder" with his clarinet, understands Pound's dictum probably as well as anyone presently writing poetry in the U. S. of A.

"Improvisation, " Carruth says elsewhere in the same book, "is the privilege of the master, the bane of the apprentice. It is the exercise of sensibility in acquired knowledge. When it becomes too often repeated, either in the work of the master or later in that of his followers, it loses spontaneity, because nothing of freshness is happening, and then it is over. Done. . . . Improvisation then is composition, but composition impelled by knowledgeable spirit. . ."

And what is the spirit of a master? And how does the poem arise from one's deepest and most sincere practice? A composition impelled by knowledgeable spirit? It might take the form of poetry by Robert Duncan, or by Denise Levertov, the former still read only by a handful of poets, the latter rather grudgingly granted status as a major poet by a fickle, ignorant public. That we prefer the simple and immediately recognizable in all things can be seen perfectly clearly in the rise of the national fast food chain, in best seller lists, in the idiocy of American television and movie-star politicians, in atrocious pop music fads, and in our poetry anthologies.

The "knowledgeable spirit" arises out of long-standing practice of "wood-shedding" what Duncan called "the scales of the marvelous," or by seeking what Carruth has called "wisdom that is the ghost of wisdom, otherwise called humility before one's task." One primary major task of the poet is to bring the whole of one's life into the presence of disciplined improvisation within a measure, whether that measure be fixed from within or without, or whether that measure is spontaneously variable, as in the case of William Carlos Williams's "variable foot," which brought Charles Olson to observe that "a foot is for kicking."

"To break the back of the iamb, that was the first heave." —E.P.

Well . . . It sagged, it bent . . . but it didn't break. And it won't break as long as we choose to place greater stress upon one syllable than upon another with any degree of regularity or identifiable pattern: the iamb is the foundation of English and American English spoken or sung music. Chaucer's natural speech patterns were probably very close to iambic pentameter, as were Shakespeare's. And it is precisely the flexibility of our tongue that makes it one of the finest poetic languages in the world, capable of compression and expansion, capable of working within externally fixed measures like the metronome (based upon the heartbeat?) and more "organic" measures such as the breath or ear alert to vowel-weights and the durations of syllables rather than their stresses. As poets, we are invited to learn the Greek resonating vowel-scale, the syllabus of elementary linguistics, the regulated syllabic lines which were the foundation upon which our literary ancestors constructed our English heritage, the open motion of "rowing poetry" (as Robert Graves identified it) as opposed to "hammer-and-anvil measures" (which were the source, according to Graves, of that same iambic ancestry). What could be more "hammer-and-anvil" than Rap music?

In brief, our melopoeia is among the most sophisticated, flexible, and most resonant in the world. But, like our most important gift to the arts of the world, North American jazz, its supreme beauty is far more widely understood elsewhere in the world than by the general public (even the literary public) at home.

Graves's research into prosody divides poetry into these two basic measures. But we might also divide poetry into two other categories: 1) the lyric or *sincere* mode; and 2) the bardic or narrative mode. In the latter (as for instance in Chaucer), the tale may or may not be formed primarily by the exercise of exterior structure; but in the former, a flexibility is mandatory since feeling or emotion is paramount because the poet is searching out the *structure of articulate feeling*. The flexibility of the classical Greek line accommodated, inspired, a grandly lyrical form—simultaneously with the development of "rowing" narrative. Or as Carruth, a sincere poet, says, "Structure is a *function* of feeling."

In 1982, Carruth published a masterpiece, *The Sleeping Beauty*, an epic of one-hundred-twenty-four choruses built upon a fifteen-line movement grounded in pentameter and interior and end rhyme and slant rhyme. It is a form he first began exploring in a suite of 13 poems, "The Asylum," in his first book, *The Crow and the Heart* (MacMillan, 1959). A quarter-century of wood-shedding has transformed this variation on the sonnet into a measure entirely his own. More flexible because of its composition in irregular syllabics, the form is neither as emotionally or melodically confined as the sonnet, the more predetermined form.

The poem itself is a long meditation on the exploitation of Woman and the natural world through stubbornly naive romanticism, including the poet's own, since the poem is itself a kind of romance. The "sleeping beauty" of the title is Rose Marie Dorn, the poet's wife, whose dreams insistently involve men with names beginning with the letter H: Homer, Hesiod, Hannibal, Hegel, Hitler, and, not incidentally, the historical/philosophical horrors of Hermaphroditism, the Halocaust, and the Hydrogen bomb. Inter-woven among her dreams, there is a narrative structure, as much philosophical as literal, often articulated in anecdotal passages narrated by a north-eastern back country prophet named Amos. The devices are many and sophisticated.

Opening the poem, beginning "out of nothing," (and with a "nothing" carried over from an epigraph from Goethe— "Vanitas! Vanitatum Vanitas!") Carruth sets his scene and invokes his muse:

> The word is silent . . .
> Oh, begin
> In all and nothing then, the vision from a name,
> This Rose Marie Dorn,
> Woman alive exactly when the Red Army came
> To that crook of the Oder where she was born,
> Woman who fled and fled in her human duty
> And bore her name, meaning Rose in the Thorn,
> Her name, the mythologos, the Sleeping Beauty.(#3)

But this is no neo-Byronic declaration of eternally adolescent love-worship. Carruth's most obvious ancestor is Pound, and it is in the mode of the *Cantos* that the poet seeks to join his narrative with his lyric. "Let the song," he says in the fifth chorus, "Sing, from that inward stress, this world so surely/ Created in her sleep, this beauty in its centuries of wrong."

As the beauty sleeps, the reader awakens to Hesiod, who was "willing to do what nobody else would do," and to the idealized man, the Hero, fashioned out of dreamtime— "And your dream made him. / He was yours and he was wise."—and the real joys and tragedies of love:

> "For fifteen years he never knew I never
> Came. The jerk. I faked, but anyone could have told.
> At last, 'Maybe it could be better,'
> I said. 'Why don't we go
> To one of those counselors?' and we did. Then after
> A spell we stopped. That was in '65. It's later
> Now. It's goddamn '75, and two years ago
> He 'came out,' as he called it, he went gay,
> And I'm—so soon, would you believe it?—I'm in menopause,
> And I don't feel so good,

And no matter what, the diet, the exercise,
I don't age nicely. Too much droop—
Chin, breast, belly, ass. He said I should forget.
And I said what the hell's the use. I sit on this stoop
In the same old chair where grandmother used to set."(#42)

It is as much this dexterity with complicated abstract images of relationship as his melopoeia that distinguishes the poetry of Hayden Carruth, and has for more than thirty years. This sorting through our own masculine and feminine aspects requires most of a lifetime of knowledgeable spirit, and, try as we might, we cannot forget what we have learned. Our tragedies are comic; our comedies all tragic:

His name was Husband, his title Herr,
noblest denomination, since he came from God
In the olden tongue.

. . .

He was Herr Husband,
Householder, Handyman to all your joys,
And if he stumbled or looked askance
You had only to think your clever sexual thought
That brought him to his parfit gentillesse again,
Your knightly teacher whom none but you had taught. (#63)

The echoes and puns and allusions—Sylvia Plath to Chaucer—are no accident, but are a part of the whole resonance, the intellectual melopoeia of the poem, the "dance of the intellect" which inspires a need to speak. The poet's methods owe something to Pound's so-called "ideogrammic method," to the Latin poets, Catullus and Lucretius, and probably to the Provencal poettry-singers whose Arabic roots brought "Romance" to European literature.

Robert Duncan, in his essay, "Ideas of the Meaning of Form," quotes the closure of Williams's masterpiece, "The Asphodel, That Greeny Flower," and says, "The end of masterpieces . . . the beginning of testimony. Having their mastery obedient to the play of forms that makes a path between what is in the language and what is in their lives. In this light that has something to do with all flowering things together, a free association of living things then—for my longing moves beyond governments to a co-operation; that may have seeds of being in free verse or free thought, or in that other free association where Freud led me to re-member (sic) their lives, admitting into the light of the acknowledged and then of meaning what had been sins and guilts, heresies, shames and wounds;/that may have to do with following the sentence along a line of feeling until the law becomes melody. . . ."

Omnia, quae sunt, lumina sunt.

Or as Pound says in Canto 76: "nothing matters but the quality/ of the affection—/ in the end—that has carved the trace in the mind/ dove sta memoria . . ." Pound's own resonance is established by his quote from Guido Cavalcanti's "Donna Mi Prega," which recalls the hieratic triad Pound offers in his famous (and now largely unread) essay on Cavalcanti:

"memoryintelligence will"

Pound being equally concerned with quality of affection which creates— *carves*— quality of memory.

Identifying *qualitative* measures in "affection" is a very dangerous social undertaking, as any feminist must know. In a society built upon the exploitation of the Social Lie, it is truly revolutionary, threatening the very foundation of social structure. Carruth's poem is in every sense a feminist poem. After making love with a woman in his cabin—refraining from objectifing her through graphic titillation—lying in an eternal moment, He says:

His being and hers were indistinguishable,
So intermingled that he could not tell
Which was man, which woman. Is that
What Plato meant by the reunited
Soul? Or his own sex-whelmed mind defecting?
Neither hypothesis
Appeals to him. He knows his feminine aspect,
Always his, deeply and dearly his.
He wonders: necessarily so are we all
And why is it hidden? Without this synthesis
How could we be, alone or together, whole?(#76)

He is filled with self-doubts and mistrusts even his own mind which may be "defecting,"—a fascinating choice of word— telling him that his qualities of affection may be delusionary, a self-beguilment. But he also recognizes that only a complete synthesis of masculine and feminine within each of us can ever make us "whole" again. Two verses later, he thinks of classical women, "Helen, Julia, Amarintha," and others:

Julia had no wart? Or
Cynthia no straggling yellow tooth?
Then they were mere conceptions, youth
Feminized, sexual but eternal, held
In the long access of rhyme
That you, dear dreamer, are inventing, romance unwilled
And unrelenting.
 And yet that time,
He thinks, was actual: they lived, unknown women,
Flawed and misnamed, their soft rank bodies prime
For idealization. Convention is also human.(#78)

And later, in another verse, "No love without hurt? No lovesong without
distortion?/ . . . We must love humanly, no debasement. We must sing/ Our
passion, as ineluctable as breath,/ Without distortion, yet still this wondrous
thing." Even in his rejection of most—not all, but most—of the conventions
of the romantic tradition, Carruth composes a Romance in the act of
composing himself.

Aristotle divided poetry into lyric, elegiac, epic, and dramatic; his
categories were clearly conceived, and his organization is, at an elementary
level, effective. But, much to the chagrin of our unifarcity departments of
Literature, all such classification remains ultimately false.

The drama, the epic, in Sophocles and Euripedes unfolds—is spoken—
in lyric lines. Even the concerns of poetry themselves defy classification as
they seek out truths as ancient as human knowledge. Near the end of
Philoktetes, Sophocles has Neoptolemos tell Philoktetes, "And those who
choose to clutch their miseries/ and not release them deserve no pity./ You
have become a savage through your anger;/ you refuse good advice and hate
him who offers it . . ."

Ugolino tells Dante in the depths of Hell, "Io no piangeva; si dentro
impietrai," or "Because I did not speak, I turned to stone inside." Hesiod
believed, "Angels deliver light; the Muse delivers form."

Obeying the need to make music, the poem reveals itself in the act of
being made. Carruth explores improvisation within a form in order to
confront the demons of history that have traditionally punished woman
for being woman, thereby separating (arbitrarily and irrationally) the
masculine from the feminine within each of us, and, by dividing, rendering
each impotent. The "meaning" of his long poem is inseparable from the
sounds of the poem.

All criticism, Eugenio Montale observes, is after the fact of the poem itself. The poet speaks from a deep need to *make music*. The one who has not courage to speak and the will and courage to wrestle with his or her own angel/muse is condemned to a silence that turns one to stone inside, that delivers one into the bowels of Hell. Valéry says, "An epic poem is a poem that can be told. When one *tells* it, one has a bilingual text." The poetry, of course, is *in the telling*. In verse 120, Carruth says,

> The border is what creates illegal aliens,
> Dividing what one knows from what one knows,
> This called an "imaginary line,"
> Not even drawn on the snow,
> With a huge officious multilingual sign,/ . . .
> Action and knowledge are one, free, far in the depths of consciousness.

It is not the poet's intention to cross borders, but to demolish them. And by the 124th chorus, he tells his awakening Beauty,

> The sun
> Will rise on the snowy firs and set on the sleeping
> Lavender mountain as always, and no one
> Will possess or command or defile you where you belong,
> Here in the authentic world.
> The work is done.
> My name is Hayden and I have made this song.

Beginning his song with a loose pentameter, and having played in and with its tenets and variations for one hundred and twenty-four choruses, all but one restricted to fifteen lines, he closes his poem on a pentameter. It is a song that includes resonant quotes and echoes from history, mythology and philosophy, literature, music (especially jazz), The Arts in general—but not as though they were different things. They are not other than the dance of the intellect, the life of the imagination. Nor are they more or less important than the "nine little birds" of chorus 27. They are resonances which are what music is, their sounds heard clearly only by those who have learned to listen, by the knowledgeable spirit.

The Sleeping Beauty is perhaps Hayden Carruth's grandest achievement. It is astonishingly inclusive, making use of his enormous narrative skills as revealed in *Brothers, I Loved You All;* formal without being metronomically heavy-handed, predictable, awkward or self-conscious; lyrical in its execution and epic in its proportion; sweeping in its broad affections and horrors. Squarely in the American romantic-mythopoeic tradition, *The Sleeping Beauty* is a sustained visionary icon of our culture. It returns to us a spirit now too often missing in our poetry, one that dares the sustained experience, a spirit which encourages as many literary lions as housecats.

There was a time when we still believed in classics—not only the ancient classics, but the modern and the contemporary as well—no matter that the list was and is constantly changing. *The Sleeping Beauty* is a classic. And because it is a contemporary classic written in the purr and roar of a lion, it has been read almost exclusively by Carruth's fellow poets.

It is time for a little lyrical genius to trickle down into the economy of our communal souls.

O the thought of what America would be like if the classics had a wide circulation!

Listening to Olga Broumas

Eros seizes and shakes my very soul
like the wind on the mountain
shaking ancient oaks —Sappho

Silent on the subject of vengeance,
I cling to innocence —Sappho

I have no hope, nor absence of hope.
I have the sweeping. I bow. —Olga Broumas

With our almost uniquely American obsession with the new, we often forget the age-old wisdom of the *Talmud,* "There is nothing new under the sun." What we perceive to be new is always a product of what preceded because, as Zen tradition proclaims, "Nothing is entirely self-originating." In *The Great Learning,* Confucius reminds us, "Things have roots and branches; affairs have scopes and beginnings. To know what precedes and what follows is nearly as good as having a head and feet." This is true in physics and biology and equally true about art and philosophy.

If the traditions upon which a poet draws are shallow and sentimental and self-serving, the poetry he or she adds to such a tradition will be equally so. Most often, what we perceive to be new and powerful in a poem is the result of some kind of cross-pollination that produces a fresh energy, a fresh perspective.

"Nothing's worth seeing," Bashō said, "that is not seen with fresh eyes." And nothing's worth hearing that is not heard with fresh ears. Olga Broumas's tradition is emphatically Sapphic. The new is born deep within the ancient.

Poor Sappho. In our time, her name is far more familiar than her poetry or what little we know of her life. Born to a patrician family in Mytilene on the island of Lesbos about 630 B.C.E., she must have been a popular political activist, for she was exiled, according the Parian Chronicle, between 604 and

596, and returned to Lesbos only after a general amnesty was granted to all political prisoners and exiles in 581.

Her father's name suggests that her grandfather must have earned distinction fighting along the Scamander River in the early stages of the battle of Troy. Her poetry suggests she was on intimate terms with the most prominent and influential families of her age. Whatever the reason for her exile, it must have been serious. Cicero mentions a statue in the marketplace at Syracuse, suggesting she may have spent her exile in Sicily. In any case, she lived in exile for years and doubtless learned much from the new culture.

She appears to have become, certainly following her return to Lesbos, and perhaps even before her exile, something of a cult leader, establishing a salon of Lesbian women writers and musicans who were said to perform ancient rites. Had someone proclaimed Sappho a divinity, thereby offending the patriarchy? We learn nothing of such intrigues from her poetry. Her name is often used in conjunction with the most overtly political writing, and yet one would be hard-pressed to find a overtly political statements in the extant lines of Sappho. Her politics is personal and devotional. As close as she comes to engaging in direct political speech is at the end of her famous prayer to Aphrodite, that "wile-weaving daughter of Zeus," whom she invites to "be my ally," using the Greek *sum machos,* which suggests preparation to do battle. Exactly what battle is left undefined.

Sappho's social criticism is is given by inference, confined to her personal observation, whether criticizing her brother's involvement with a well-known prostitute or simply stating her aesthetic and philosophical preference for the vision of a woman's "lovely step" over the grand spectacle of the "whole Lydian army on the march." It is probably her attitude, her philosophy about the way of poetry itself, that is most influential to this day. Whether her "preparation for battle" was meant to be taken literally or figuratively is anyone's guess, but clearly her allusions to historical and political events are evidence of a highly educated and deeply engaged mind.

Her gift to Greek poetry was an intensely personal devotional lyric. Her wedding songs were celebrated, and her rhythmic structure created a world far beyond her own. Sappho's contribution to poetic form, the Mixo-Lydian mode, a diatonic scale in a key corresponding to our G minor, became the foundation for the "heavenly music" of the early Catholic church. Her Aeolic Greek dialect adapted smoothly to the rhythms of the Lydian *pektis,* a stringed instrument plucked with the fingers. Thus her *lyricism*—the Greek root words mean "words of the lyre"—would extend her influence far beyond the usual boundaries of classical poetry.

Of nine volumes of her poetry collected during the Alexandrian period, only a single complete poem is known to exist. The rest are fragments quoted by scholars. Nevertheless, these shards of ancient poetry reveal a poet deeply concerned with the role of poetry and the poet in aristocratic society, a society moreover that did not drawn exact lines between homosexuality and heterosexuality as we do today. Relations between women in a patriarchal culture were social and political, ally-forming, and as would be expected, intimate in a variety of ways.

Sappho celebrates loving women in every sense.

If cultural cross-pollination and ally-building were essential elements of Sappho's art, they lie equally at the heart of Olga Broumas's poetry over the past thirty years. Broumas, moreover, has embodied the tradition and the practice of Sappho more than any other poet in our time. Born in Syros, Greece, in 1949, she published her first poems there in 1967. Her first book of poems in English, *Beginning with O,* was selected by Stanley Kunitz for the *Yale Younger Poets Award* in 1977. In the years since, she has published seven volumes of distinguished original poetry ranging from the fragmentary to the prosaic, from the imagistic to the narrative, including booklength collaborations, and devoted a number of years to the translation of poetry and prose by Odysseas Elytis, Greek recipient of the Nobel Prize for Literature in 1979.

"Poetic metaphor," Elytis wrote in his selected essays, *Open Papers,* "instantaneously transcending terrible distances, renders the spiritual physiognomy of objects at their birth." Poetry is a means by which we may come to understand our own spiritual dimension. And others. Through the poem, through embodying the poem, we may "transcend terrible distances" such as time, space or language.

I give my hand to justice
Transparent fountain source at the peak
My sky is deep and unaltered
What I love is always being born
What I love is beginning always

When a great artist gives over his or her life to the very process of art, to the demonic magical practice of that art, and when that commitment is articulated as an act of devotion, a world is transformed. Just as Elytis found his poetic vision and practice in part through translating the poetry of Rimbaud, Lorca, Mayakovsky, Ungaretti, and Brecht, Broumas's practice has been deepened and immeasurably enriched by her many years of devotion to bringing Elytis's lyric voice into American English.

"Contrary to those who strive an entire life to 'fix' their literary likeness," Elytis wrote, "I'm intent every hour and each moment on destroying mine; my face turned to prototype alone, whose nature is to be endlessly created, ready to begin again precisely on account of the oneness of life and art." Such a consideration of "oneness of life and art" no doubt finds its prototype in Sappho herself and in her tradition of being fully at the service of one's art and muse. Broumas, Elytis, and Sappho each search in a distinct, conscious manner for a poetry of deep moral awareness, passionate openness, and each develops a distinct personal mythology. In "The Choir," Broumas writes,

> I walk and I rest while the eyes of my dead
> look through my own, inaudible
> hosannas greet
> the panorama charged serene
> *and almost ultraviolet with so much witness.*

Charged with the "hosannas of witness," Broumas has become a great poet of affirmation, which has little to do with either optimism or pessimism, and everything to do with a Zen-like serenity found in the acceptance of *thusness,* which itself must include perpetual awareness of birth-and-death, the cycle of *samsara,* as the source of human agony.

A significant part of Broumas's practice of poetry is her vision of the role of the poet in society. She became a licensed bodywork therapist in 1982, and has brought the study and practice of meditation and general healing arts to the practice of poetry while continuing to teach at Brandeis University. As much as any poet writing today, it may be said emphatically that she writes with the whole mind and and body, accomplishing complete integration of disciplined breath and ear and silent pause, so that the syllable, the line, becomes truly embodied by its music.

The range of her voice includes the communal, the whispered intimacy of the lover, the cries of agony and joy, the mantra-like brief syllable, and the incantatory. She is, above all else, a poet of the erotic.

> "I like it when my friend has lovers, their happy moans,
> *unrestrained, fill the house with the glee of her prowess."*

But it would be foolish to reduce Broumas's celebrated eroticism to her celebrations of sexuality only. Sometimes too much is made of a poem simply because of its topic, and if someone has been shocked when Broumas celebrates a clitoris, it has sometimes been the case that "Sapphic" becomes a convenient cubbyhole for the slightly embarrassed reader. The body *is* electric, and Broumas, singing it, has been unembarrassed in her love of the body from the start. The masseuse understands that embarrassment about the body stands between one's own healing hands and cognitive compassion. In this, she has been a Whitman singing the body electric for our time.

The eroticism is her very language, in its conveyance—it is in the way she releases each syllable from within her mouth, from the deep breath and the quick, the way she's attentive to each drawn and released breath in the act of embodying syllables, moving through and within each line. The eroticism is in her attentive eye and ear and earthy unabashed honesty and in her authentic affection. This is far more important that the "subjects" of her poems.

But yes, the subjects are sometimes startling. In "After *The Little Mariner*," she describes a dream following completion of her translation of Elytis's difficult, brilliant epic poem. She lies in bed "paralyzed / transparent" before "the crossroader / the atmospheric horseman," and:

> I could see
> a ribbon of song begin
> from the lungs of his penis
> inside my body like a swallow
> of ice-cold milk in August
> gleaming and slow like mercury
> upstream and through my lips
> and then my soul
> fell into or my body rose.

The act of translating lyric poetry is an act of love, a deeply erotic discipline that often approaches erotic servitude or submission. Her relationship with Elytis was profound, and deeply, intimately erotic without being overtly sexual in the usual sense. Like her friend and teacher, she is a poet of light and sea and landscapes both interior and exterior, and like Elytis, she has re-visioned ancient mythologies in order to create a clarity approaching transparency.

Both translation and collaboration require freedom from the irrational demands of ego. In such difficult genres, she has been inventive and selfless.

Questioned about her collaborative work with Jane Miller or with T. Begley, one quickly learns that none is certain much of the time about exactly who wrote exactly what.

It is clear that Broumas's work as a therapist and as teacher have taught her patience and deepened her compassion, qualities everywhere evident in her poetry from the very beginning. She practices and refines serenity, and poetry in such a practice is a primary tool in opening mind and heart. Her very contemporary American poetry reveals glimpses of a Greek world beyond this one, and beyond that an ancient Greek world, and beyond that a Zen world, and beyond that a mythological world eternally at its beginning.

No longer "exactly Greek," she says, "The Greek language evolves so quickly!" And "not exactly American," she has, like Sappho, made a marriage of two worlds and more, her body of work constantly evolving, her face turned to prototype alone, to realizing a world that is just beginning to be born.

Listening to W. S. Merwin

Born in Union City, New Jersey in 1927, W.S. Merwin's life in poetry has been an Odyssean journey through New York City, southern France, London, Mexico, and finally Hawaii. His poetry has embodied a constantly evolving style and vision rooted in the moral necessity of bearing witness, of testifying to the times, whether the voice of the poem is that of seer or fool, knowing or unknowing, public or intimate. The son of "a strict, unemotional Presbyterian minister," Merwin claims to have been more interested in riding horses at the Princeton University stable than in his classwork there, except that he began writing poetry under the tutelage of the poet and critic R. P. Blackmur and the poet John Berryman. The latter told the young poet to "get down on your knees and pray to the muse every day," adding that he meant it literally, and that what "permitted everything and transmuted it / in poetry was passion."

From the beginning, Merwin has been a poet of doubt, a poet whose vision is realized through a state of unknowingness. In an early *ars poetica,* "On the Subject of Poetry," he writes in part,

> I do not understand the world, Father.
> By the millpond at the end of the garden
> There is a man who slouches listening
> To the wheel revolving in the stream, only
> There is no wheel there to revolve.

The strange man who sits in the garden listening to the wheel that is not there, "always before he listens / He prepares himself by listening." The speaker is made uncomfortable, but insists that it is the world he does not understand. In another early poem, Merwin observes that poetry's "mumbled inadequacy reminds us always / In this world how little can be communicated." In his insistence upon acknowledging the "inadequacy" of poetry and thus language itself, he follows in a tradition that would include such ancient Chinese sages as Lao Tzu and Chuang Tzu and such modern philosophers and the existentialists, abd indeed one finds elements of existential doubts throughout Merwin's body of work.

The young poet went into the world and became a tutor for Princess de Braganza of Portugal, a tutor for the son of Robert Graves on the island of Majorca, and translator of French and Spanish literature for the BBC. In 1954, he bought a farmhouse in southern France, writing, "I realized that I did not know how to grow a single thing that I ate every day, and I decided to go back there and try to learn to grow food in the garden—something which all my peasant neighbors knew how to do."

Nearly fifty years later, W. S. Merwin lives in Hawaii, where he works to preserve Hawaiian culture, flora, and fauna, and tends a garden that is famous in literary circles. He still spends a part of each year in southern France. His bibliography is staggering, and includes such diverse translations as Dante's *Paradiso*, Spanish ballads and romances, *The Song of Roland,* and *Poem of the Cid,* the Zen poetry of Muso Soseki and brief poems and epigrams drawn from all over East Asia, the poetry of Pablo Neruda, Antonio Porchia, Roberto Juarroz, Jaime Sabines, and Jean Follain. Not to mention translations of poetry from Swedish, Russian, Urdu, Greek, Mayan, Incan, Sanskrit, and more. On a recent visit to the Pacific Northwest to make this recording, he was most eager to visit a major local botanical garden. Confucius wrote of the ancient Chinese *Poetry Classic* says that poetry functions in part by teaching us the proper names of plants and animals and relationships, whereby "we can watch with affection the ways things grow."

It is helpful to understand that Merwin's study and practice in the garden, including planetary ecology, is not separate from his practice of poetry. Poetry and language are not self-originating. Nothing is. "My words," he has written, "are the garment of what I shall never be / like the tucked sleeve of a one-armed boy." What is unsaid is as important, perhaps more important, that what is said. Part of what remains unstated is that which is simply unsayable, while another part is left in deliberate ambiguity or silence. Surely, a part of his doubts about language and communication spring from his experience as a translator. One who has no knowledge of a second language has a very tentative grasp on a first one. Merwin's translations, a valuable gift, book by book, are a part of what he himself becomes, the garden in which he blossoms, the garden in which the poet comes to fruition, not the other way around. He speaks of "the visitation that is going to be a poem," and we can understand that rich, well-prepared soil creates a better point of visitation for the seed. The traditions and major languages of poetry are its very soil.

Like a number of his contemporaries, including Robert Creeley and Denise Levertov, he has insisted upon the inseparability of form and content. His sense of composition insists upon foremost attention to the line. "I think the line is a matter of absolutely essential importance. If the line is not that important, why is one writing verse in the first place? One of the meanings of verse after all is 'a line.'"

His earliest poetry demonstrates the young poet's mastery of traditional English prosody, but quickly begins to explore more open forms that accomodate a vast array of poetic influences, the voices of his poems ranging from the oracular to the epigrammatic, the mythological ("The Mountain") to the meditative ("Low Fields and Light"). While he is not often overtly autobiographical, "Grandfather in the Old Men's Home" and "Grandmother Watching at Her Window" are revealing. Speaking in her voice in the latter, Merwin writes:

> I brought the children up clean
> With my needle, taught them that stealing
> Is the worst sin; knew if I loved them
> They would be taken away, and did my best
> But must have loved them anyway
> For they slipped through my fingers like stitches.

Absence and silence and a sense of loss are almost constant presences in Merwin's poetry, and some have accused him of a kind of pessimism. His own response comes in an interview in which he is asked about his relarionship with Whitman, when he says he "tried over the years to come to terms with Whitman," but doesn't think he ever really succeeded because "Whitman's positivism and the American optimism disturb me." He clarifies, "That bothers me, but in particular it's his rhetorical insistence on an optimistic stance, which can be quite wonderful as a statement of momentary emotion, but as a world view and as a program for confronting existence it bothered me when I was eighteen and bothers me now. . . . I keep thinking about the buffalo, about the Indians, and about the species that are being rendered extinct. Whitman's momentary, rather sentimental view just wipes these things out as though they were of no importance. There's a cultural and what you might call societal chauvinism involved." He points to "the great phony myth of the 'winning of the West'—it was the *destruction* of the West." In "The Animals," he finds himself tracking "over empty ground / Animals I never saw," for whom he will have to invent names.

Ultimately, this is not a poetry of supreme pessimism or optimism, but a voice of responsibility, one realizing fully that there can be little hope for this panet while human populations continue to expand and the direct consequence being poisoned air, soil, and water, and little hope for a people who deny their own history. He has written poems on William Bartram, Powell and many other historical figures, and has struggled to come to grips with the chasm between American history as it is generally represented in schools and media, and the astonishing and irrefutable facts of genocide and ecocide.

Merwin credits R. P. Blackmur with "insisting the artist—and by extension the life—can have no formula for survival," and for giving the young poet "a tenacious esteem not for the human alone but for the inchoate in humanity, as it struggles inexplicably to complete itself through language." In "Provision," he writes, "I will take with me the emptiness of my hands / What you do not have you find everywhere."

He may have been an indifferent student at Princeton, but he has clearly spent a lifetime devoted to learning, and his subsequent practice of poetry has been uniformly passionate and compassionate, sometimes bravely insisting upon moral courage, as when, upon receipt of a Pulitzer Prize in 1971, he publicly addressed "a shame which many Americans feel, day after day," over the war in Vietnam. Moral courage and political nerve are not necessarily the stuff of great poetry, often enough quite the contrary, but in Merwin's work, they arise—as that old Chinese gardener-poet sage Su Tung-p'o said they should—as naturally as mushrooms in manure.

When asked about the "topical" in his verse, Merwin observed, "It has to do with a consistent feeling about poetry, which is that no deliberate program for writing a poem works. A poem begins to be a poem when a sequence of words starts giving off what you might describe as a kind of electric charge, when it begins to have a life of its own that I sense the way . . ." In this, he reflects in a way the ideas of Ezra Pound whom Merwin met when he was eighteen. What most impressed him about the inventor of American modernist verse, Merwin has said, was the elder poet's "insistence on being a poet, not on following other people's paths."

W. S. Merwin's path through five decades of poetry has been unique, a singular path breaking new ground at every step while conserving the best literary traditions. A perfectly good case could be made for declaring him the most influential American poet of the last half century. The work is the embodiment of an extraordinary practice, profound and congenial, alternately disturbing and assuring, and constantly provocative. Underlying and informing it all is that rarest of qualities, real wisdom.

A Little Homage to Robin Blaser

As a street kid hanging around the fringes of the "beat scene" during the San Francisco Renaissance of the late 1950s, I loved listening to Kenneth Rexroth hold forth on poetry and politics. He often said that the seeds of the beat scene were sewn a decade earlier with the poets of the "Berkeley Renaissance." And he often remarked that the development of the "serial poem" was the primary gift of that community of poets, as evidenced particularly in the poetry of Robert Duncan and Jack Spicer. But while Duncan and Spicer are generally recognized for their significant role in the development of "West Coast poetry" over the years, the third member of the Berkeley triad, Robin Blaser, is probably best known as editor of the *Collected Books of Jack Spicer* rather than for his own accomplished poetry over the past forty years.

Following his appearance in Donald Allen's influential *The New American Poetry* in 1960, Blaser moved to Vancouver, British Columbia, in the mid-sixties to teach at Simon Fraser University and all but disappeared from the American scene. A chapbook, *Cups,* was published by Four Seasons in 1968, and Ferry Press in London published his *Image-Nations 1-12* in 1974. Cobblestone Press of Vancouver, B.C. published more "Image-nations" in 1975, but Blaser's poetry remained largely unavailable south of the border until publication of *Pell Mell* (Coach House Press) in 1988. All during these years, he has continued work on his great serial poem, *The Holy Forest,* each of the aforementioned suites contributing to the larger whole, as recently published by Coach House Press.

His association with Duncan and Spicer and the obvious influence of Charles Olson (and Pound, H.D. and Williams, et al) might lead one to assume that his poetry is "difficult"—how we tremble in the face of Difficulty, as though it bore the sour breath of Geryon. (And how few of our younger poets go to school on the high moderns nowadays.) *The Holy Forest* is not a difficult book despite its nearly 400 pages. It is not. It *is* noble. It is honest. It is modest in its immense learning.

Blaser has always been possessed of a philosophical turn of mind, and these poems arise out of his inquisitive nature, study and daily practice, attentiveness to the ironies and humors and wonders that deliver a state of presence. Here is an early poem, written in Boston in the late 1950s, before he began his major opus:

Herons
I saw cold thunder in the grass,
the wet black trees of my humanity, my skin,

How much love lost hanging there
out of honesty.
I catch those men who chose
to hang in the wind
out of honesty.
It is the body lies with its skin—

Robed in my words I say the snake
changes its skin out of honesty.

And they
hanged there with some symmetry
died young
like herons proud in their landscape.
Now it is age crept in, nobody younger knows
the quick-darting breath is
our portion of honesty.

The young poet's concerns were all there: humanity's skin, vulnerability, and the "quick-darting breath" that delivers "our portion of honesty." How much love lost, he asks. His poems have remarkable variety, from the epigrammatic and imagistic to the longer eight to ten page lyrical poems that I find particularly moving, especially "Image-Nation 24" and his homage, "Robert Duncan," both too long to be reprinted and too beautifully complex to be briefly paraphrased or quoted out of context.

In his introduction to Spicer's poetry, Blaser writes, "Where the poesis reopens the real and follows its contents, the presuming discourse imposes form and closes it, leaving us at the mercy of our own limit. . . . One needs only to notice how much of it is a common experience and also something regained, rather than an invention." He mentions Pound and Williams and Olson and declares, "I am taking the occasion of Jack's book to speak of the battle for the real in poetry in which all contemporary poetry in America is engaged. It began with Pound and continues."

In plain fact, the "battle of the real" has been amplified by an increasingly noisy and dishonest mass media in Canada and in the U.S.A. And one may find a bland all-to common "poetry of common experience" almost everywhere. Pound's struggle to regain "the sublime" through common language became the struggle of Spicer and Blaser, Duncan and Rexroth, the search for our portion of honesty through a poesis that *reveals* the movement of mind—the dance of the intellect among the ten thousand things, as the ancient Chinese said— rather than merely issuing from it.

For all his seriousness, Blaser's poems are filled with modest wonders, what he has called "the random and the given of the hunt, the game, the tour." In an early section called "The Moth Poem," dedicated to H.D., there is "The Literalist," a poem that would, but for its syntactical structure and the last line, be right at home in an Imagist anthology:

The Literalist
the wind does not move on
to another place

bends into,
as in a mirror,
the
breaking

the moth in the piano
will play on
frightened wings brush
the wired interior
of that machine

I said, 'master'

It is the stance of the poet that brings me up short, the poet adopting the stance of the apprentice before the frustrated wingbeats of the moth.

I am reminded of a famous, often-anthologized poem by William Stafford, "Traveling through the Dark," in which the poet finds a wounded deer beside the road and ends up pushing it over the bank after heaving a thoughtful sigh "for us all." It's a poem I've never liked. Blaser's poem deals with a trapped moth. We don't know whether he releases it. The poem has no "outcome" or formal closure except that the poet's final stance *is* a closure in the same way that the opening of a door is also closure. Blaser's poem *opens* his experience, Stafford's *uses* his. Blaser is humbled by his encounter. Stafford thinks hard "for us all."

The poems "closes" with the opening of Blaser's clear, attentive mind. Gary Snyder has written, "A clear attentive mind / has no meaning. / Yet we are here." Blaser's "here" is an opening, and transcendence of self.

In an essay on "The Inner Poem" written in the Sixties, Hayden Carruth quotes a Jack Spicer letter commenting on a poem, "Piazza Piece," by John Crowe Ransom: "The way to read this poem (and most of his) is not to let the deceptive skill hypnotize you into not hearing the poem." Was the letter Carruth quotes written to Blaser? I haven't found it and don't know. But the comments are as true today as they were twenty, thirty, or forty years ago. Carruth remarks, "For Spicer, as for most older readers, Ransom's skill is not a distraction but a hypnosis; yet the effect may be the same."

Too much display of craftsmanship can ruin the new house.

Most of the poetry of "new formalism" is bad not because it is composed in fixed form, but because it fails to attain the virtuosity that produces hypnotic *music.* Just as much of what flows from those who follow "open" forms lacks music and precision.

The Line, Pound advised, should be composed by the musical phrase, not by the metronome. Ransom, Carruth, Spicer, Duncan, Blaser: each understands, having assayed the idea, having learned the traditions; each begins, variously, by being attentive to an inner music. Carruth again: "We lose ourselves in the wonder of it to such an extent that we lose the poem. Because the poem is not the writing, neither the particular prosody nor the sonneteering tradition; it lies within, existing there as a song and a cry, fulfilling its own language exactly. The poem is the entire and practically unlimited spectrum of the unanalyzable but recognizable structures of feeling and thought, of thoughtful feeling."

"Structures of thoughtful feeling." The poem requires *embodiment.* The poem is an embodiment of revelation. Blaser locates within "the random and the given" a "portion of honesty" measured by thoughtful breath and line. But the openness of his structure should not be confused with randomness or formlessness. Nor should his considerable learning veil the essential shared experience of his poetry.

So many years so quickly gone. Rexroth died more than twenty years ago, his poetry virtually vanished from the common canon. Olson and Duncan are gone and are probably better known by reference than by their actual poetry and essays. Carruth and Blaser are now among our elders.

Whither, "West Coast" poetry? Alive and thriving in the poetry of Gary Snyder, Phillip Levine, Adrienne Rich, Carolyn Kizer, Dorianne Laux, Gary Soto, Jane Miller, Jane Hirshfield, Michael Hannon, Henry Carlile, Sharon Doubiago, and dozens of others whose individual work has been variously shaped, directly or indirectly, by the Berkeley Renaissance.

The struggle for the real in poetry continues eternally. But it is made more joyous, more vivid, because Blaser has given his gift, articulating an essential life of the imagination . . . like Ovid, searching for honey in the middle of the stream.

Index